LAG legal aid I

GW01460168

Vicky Ling has worked in the not-for-profit advice sector for over 25 years. She was one of the first managers recruited by the then Legal Aid Board to implement its quality assurance standard and is now an independent consultant specialising in legal aid practice. She has worked with over 200 firms of solicitors and not-for-profit agencies to help them improve practice management and meet LSC requirements. Vicky was a founder member of the Civil Justice Council and is currently serving a second term. She is a Member of the Chartered Quality Institute.

Simon Pugh is a solicitor and head of legal services at Shelter. He has extensive experience of legal aid practice, management and contract compliance in both the private practice and not-for-profit sectors and across civil, criminal and family law. He has written and trained widely on legal aid practice and management, is a supervision assessor for the Law Society Immigration Accreditation Scheme and a member of the editorial board of *Cordery on Solicitors*.

Steve Hynes is director of the Legal Action Group (LAG). Previously he was the director of the Law Centres Federation, the national organisation for law centres, and worked as Co-ordinator of Rochdale Law Centre where he also undertook case work in employment and discrimination law. Steve has written extensively and appeared in the broadcast media commenting on legal aid and access to justice issues. He is co-author, with Jon Robins, of *The Justice Gap* (2009, LAG).

Julia Sherriff is an assistant solicitor in the crime department at Edwards Duthie solicitors in London. She is a fully accredited police station representative. Julia is committed to publicly funded legal services and is a member of Young Legal Aid Lawyers. Julia was also awarded the Legal Services Commission's prize for the best student at the College of Law on the public legal services route in 2008.

The purpose of the Legal Action Group is to promote equal access to justice for all members of society who are socially, economically or otherwise disadvantaged. To this end, it seeks to improve law and practice, the administration of justice and legal services.

LAG legal aid handbook 2011/12

Edited by Vicky Ling and Simon Pugh

LAG Legal Action Group
2011

This edition published in Great Britain 2011
by LAG Education and Service Trust Limited
242 Pentonville Road, London N1 9UN
www.lag.org.uk

© Vicky Ling and Simon Pugh 2011

Chapters 19 and 20 by Steve Hynes © Legal Action Group 2011

While every effort has been made to ensure that the details in this text
are correct, readers must be aware that the law changes and that the
accuracy of the material cannot be guaranteed and the author and the
publisher accept no responsibility for any losses or damage sustained.

The rights of the authors to be identified as authors of this work have
been asserted by them in accordance with the Copyright, Designs and
Patents Act 1988.

All rights reserved. No part of this publication may be reproduced, stored
in a retrieval system or transmitted in any form or by any means, without
permission from the publisher.

British Library Cataloguing in Publication Data
a CIP catalogue record for this book is available from the British Library.

Crown copyright material is produced with the permission of the
Controller of HMSO and the Queen's Printer for Scotland.

This book has been produced using Forest Stewardship
Council®(FSC®) certified paper. The wood used to produce FSC
certified products with a 'Mix' label comes from FSC certified
well-managed forests, controlled sources and/or recycled
material.

FSC
MIX
Paper
FSC® C020438

ISBN 978 1 903307 84 7

Typeset by Regent Typesetting, London
Printed in Great Britain by Hobbs the Printers, Totton, Hampshire

This book is dedicated to the memory of Andrew Wilson,
a fine lawyer who believed passionately in justice for all, fought
tenaciously for his clients, and inspired all who worked with him.

Preface

'*The laws of our country exist for the benefit of the poor as well as the rich; that equality before the law is a pretence if some citizens can assert and protect their rights and others cannot; that the rule of law, to be meaningful, must ensure that justice is available to all, irrespective of means.*'
Lord Bingham, Barnett Lecture June 1998

We believe that legal aid is fundamental to the operation of a democratic society. However, legal aid lawyers do not have an easy life. At times, they are vilified for representing clients who are unpopular with much of society. Legal aid fees are considerably lower than private client fees, and despite the Legal Services Commission's efforts to 'reform' it, the scheme becomes ever more complex and bureaucratic. The pace of reform has not slowed since *Making Legal Aid Work* was published in 2009; since then, the Unified Contract has been replaced with the Standard Contract, there has been a hugely controversial process of re-tendering for all contracts, and not least there has been a change of government. On the day the new contracts started, the Ministry of Justice published proposals to reform legal aid, abolish the LSC, cut £350 million from the budget and remove whole areas from scope. See chapter 19.

The Legal Services Commission's Manual has been slimmed down to three volumes. Even so, it does not describe the all the legal aid payment schemes, as it is supplemented by other guidance, manuals, regulations, case law, correspondence and items buried on the LSC's website. We all yearn for the days when the scheme could be described adequately in the official Legal Aid Handbook, last printed in 1998; sadly, that time is gone for ever.

What we have tried to do in this book is to provide a practical guide to all the various elements that make up legal aid in one volume. Part A of the book, 'Legal aid advice and litigation' is aimed at lawyers and caseworkers and takes you through the rules and regulations that govern the criminal, civil and family schemes. We have included case studies to illustrate particular issues which we know people can find confusing or challenging. We also refer you to primary sources where you may need more detailed information.

Part B of the book, 'Legal aid advocacy' is aimed at anyone who has a right of audience to appear in court or who the court is willing to hear, including lay representatives, solicitor advocates and counsel. We hope that counsel in particular will find it helpful to have all the advocacy schemes set out in one place.

Part C of the book 'Managing legal aid work' is aimed at partners, directors, managers and administrators. It covers getting and keeping contracts.

We would like to express our thanks to Esther Pilger, Steve Hynes and Nim Moorthy from Legal Action Group, who persuaded us to revise *Making Legal Aid Work* and turn it into the *LAG legal aid handbook 2011/12*. We must also acknowledge the contribution made by our long-suffering partners who have supported us as ever as we wrote this book.

We should also like to thank all those who commented on *Making Legal Aid Work* and provided ideas for this update, in particular colleagues at Shelter, Rod Campbell-Taylor, Andrew Keogh, and Jan Luba.

We should particularly like to thank Julia Sherriff for revising the crime chapters and contributing the new crime advocacy chapter at short notice.

Thanks also to colleagues at the Legal Services Commission, particularly Anthony Cox, Eleanor Drucker and Jane Worsey.

However, any errors or omissions are our responsibility.

We should welcome comments on *LAG legal aid handbook 2011/12* because we want to make it as relevant and useful to legal aid practitioners as we can.

The law and legal aid scheme is as stated at 1 February 2010. We have incorporated the changes to the civil scheme as at 15 November 2010 and the family scheme as at 9 May 2011.

Vicky Ling
Simon Pugh

April 2011

Contents

Table of cases

References in the right-hand column are to paragraph numbers.

Table of statutes

References in the right-hand column are to paragraph numbers.

Table of statutory instruments

References in the right-hand column are to paragraph numbers.

Abbreviations

ABH	Actual Bodily Harm
ASU	Asylum Screening Unit
BACS	Bankers' Automated Clearing Service
BVT	Best Value Tendering
CBAM	Criminal Bills Assessment Manual
CCRC	Criminal Cases Review Commission
CCU	Complex Crime Unit
CDS	Criminal Defence Service
CFA	Conditional Fee Agreement
CLAC	Community Legal Advice Centre
CLAN	Community Legal Advice Network
CLR	Controlled Legal Representation
CLS	Community Legal Service
CLSP	Community Legal Service Partnerships
CMRC	Contract Management Review Criteria
CMRF	Consolidated Matter Report Form
CMRH	Case Management Review Hearing
DSA	Duty Solicitor Arrangements
DSCC	Defence Solicitor Call Centre
DWP	Department of Work and Pensions
ECHR	European Convention for the Protection of Human Rights and Fundamental Freedoms
ESA	Employment and Support Allowance
FAQs	Frequently Asked Questions
FILEX	Fellow of the Institute of Legal Executives
GF	Graduated Fee
GFS	Graduated Fee Scheme
HMCS	Her Majesty's Court Service
HMRC	Her Majesty's Revenue and Customs
HR	Hourly rates
IAAS	Immigration and Asylum Accreditation Scheme
IALS	Institute of Advanced Legal Studies
IFA	Independent Funding Adjudicator
KPI	Key Performance Indicator
LSC	Legal Services Commission
MHRT	Mental Health Review Tribunal
MOU	Memorandum of Understanding

MPAs	Multi-party Actions
NAM	New Asylum Model
NASS	National Asylum Support Service
NfP	Not for Profit
OFS	Open Financial Statement
PACE	Police and Criminal Evidence Act 1988
POA	Payment on Account
POP	Point of Principle of General Importance
QM	Quality Mark
QMB	Quality Mark for the Bar
RDCO	Recovery of Defence Costs Order
RSS	Really Simple Syndication
SAAC	Self-Assessment Audit Checklist
SCU	Special Cases Unit
SMP	Standard Monthly Payment
SQM	Specialist Quality Mark
SWL	Social Welfare Law
UASC	Unaccompanied Asylum Seeking Children
UFN	Unique File Number
VHCC	Very High Cost Case

Glossary

Account Manager	Former job title – see Relationship Manager below.
Advice and Assistance	Funding for advice short of representation in criminal cases, granted by the supplier under contract with the LSC.
CMRF	Consolidated Matter Report Form, the monthly Civil Contract claim submitted to the LSC online.
Community Legal Service	(CLS) is a network of LSC funded organisations and advice providers that deliver and promote civil legal aid services.
Contract Compliance Audit	An audit assessing whether, based on a sample of files, an organisation is complying with the requirements of civil or criminal contracts.
Controlled Legal Representation	Representation before the First-tier or Upper Tribunals in immigration or mental health cases, granted by the supplier under contract with the LSC.
Controlled Work	Legal Help, Help at Court and Controlled Legal Representation – funding granted by the supplier.
Corrective Action	Action agreed with an LSC auditor to rectify a breach of a QM or contract requirement.
Criminal Defence Service	Criminal advice and representation funded by the LSC, through private practice and the Public Defender Service.
Devolved Power	A power (eg to grant a Representation Certificate) that may be exercised on the LSC's behalf by the supplier in certain defined circumstances.
Financial Stewardship audit	Type of audit conducted by a Relationship Manager on a provider's premises, focusing on financial issues.
Franchise Representative	See Liaison Manager.

Funding Code	The criteria by which the LSC decide whether to grant all levels of civil funding.
Help at Court	An adjunct to Legal Help, which allows representation at particular hearings in certain cases.
Individual Case Contract	A separate contract between the LSC and a supplier on a particular case, usually because of high costs.
Inter partes costs	Costs between the parties when cases are settled between them or set by Court Order or assessment. The rates are higher than Legal Aid rates.
Legal Aid	Legal advice and representation funded by the central government through the LSC and the Courts.
Legal Help	Advice short of representation, granted by the supplier under contract with the LSC.
Liaison Manager	A member of the organisation's staff designated as the person responsible for quality and contract compliance and the main point of contact for the LSC. This role was previously known as the Quality Representative or Franchise Representative.
Licensed Work	Civil representation certificates – funding granted by the LSC or under devolved powers by providers.
Matter Start	Also known as a 'new matter start' or NMS, a Matter start is a case started under Legal Help, or Controlled Legal Representation where there has been no previous Legal Help.
McKenzie Adviser	A person who is present at a hearing to advise and assist, but not represent, a party.
Prior Authority	A certificate that the LSC considers a disbursement to be reasonable, and therefore that the costs will be paid at the end of the case. May also allow a payment on account.
Peer review	An assessment of the quality of legal work carried out by independent lawyers working under contract with the LSC.
Pro bono	Free legal advice and/or representation.
Procurement area	Geographical area for competitive bidding, usually based on a top tier local authority area.
Provider	Term used by the LSC to describe any type of organisation with which it has a contract to deliver services.

Provider Assurance	New department of the LSC, which carries out data analysis and audits to support Relationship Managers.
Public Defender Service	Solicitors employed by the LSC to do criminal work, in competition with private practice. Four offices in England and Wales.
Quality Concern	A failure to meet a requirement of a Quality Mark. Critical Concerns are more serious than General Concerns. The organisation will be required to put corrective action in place, or in particularly serious cases, will be at risk of contract termination.
Quality Mark	An accreditation scheme regulating conduct and quality of legal services. There are various levels of QM, awarded to different types of service provider. Compliance may be audited by the LSC or authorised third party.
Quality Representative	See Liaison Manager.
Regional Director	Head of an LSC Regional Office, responsible for all funding, policy and partnership issues in the region. This role has been phased out as part of LSC restructuring.
Regional Office	Historically, an office of the LSC dealing with all funding and local policy matters within its region. In future, regional offices will act as processing centres as part of the LSC's restructuring programme.
Relationship Manager	An official of the LSC with responsibility for the entire commercial relationship with a provider. They will be based as close to the provider's lead office as feasible.
Representation Certificate	Funding for representation in civil and family cases, granted by the LSC or in emergencies by the supplier.
Representation Order	Funding for representation in criminal cases, granted by the courts.
Schedule payment limit	The total amount payable to an organisation under a contract schedule.
Special Cases Unit	Department of the LSC, dealing with individual case contracts in high cost civil cases.
Specialist Quality Mark	The highest level Quality Mark, held by solicitors and NfPs which are eligible for funding by the LSC.

Standard monthly payment	The monthly payment to an organisation under contract – usually one twelfth of the schedule payment limit (subject to variation during the year).
Statutory Charge	A charge held by the LSC over property recovered or preserved in funded civil proceedings, intended to allow the LSC to recover the costs of funding the case.
Tolerance work	A case taken on by an organisation in a category in which it does not have a QM or contract.
Transaction Criteria	An audit tool, consisting of checklists used to assess whether a file contains required information. Now superseded by peer review.
Very High Cost Cases Panel	A panel of organisations accredited by the LSC to conduct VHCC crime cases. Only accredited organisations may do these cases.

Legal aid advice and litigation

CHAPTER 1

Read this before you start!

Introduction

1.1   This chapter's title is probably a counsel of perfection, and will be an unfulfilled aspiration for most caseworkers! However, the point we are trying to make is that there are lots of rules and guidance about doing publicly funded work; you need to be aware of what they are, and consult them where necessary.

If you don't, you may have applications or bills rejected by the Legal Services Commission (LSC) for technical errors, or refused because you have not explained your client's case in an appropriate way, or you may have claims for payment disallowed. All these things are important because they may cause your client unnecessary delay, waste your time, and could even threaten the financial viability of your organisation. If you are not sure what to do, look it up and discuss the issue with your supervisor.

The LSC Manual

1.2   The LSC's contracts require all contracted providers to subscribe to the Legal Services Commission Manual.[1] It ought to contain all current documentation; but in recent times it has struggled to keep pace with legal aid developments. In 2010, publication of the Manual transferred from TSO to Thomson Reuters and it was announced that the structure of the Manual would be radically different. Updates would still be issued at six-monthly intervals, however it would become hard bound rather than loose-leaf and there would be three volumes rather than four:

> Volume 1 – Crime
> Volume 2 – Civil
> Volume 3 – The Funding Code

In this book, we refer to the substantive material contained within the Manual and wherever possible, we tell you where you can download a document from the LSC's website. We know the search facility could be improved, so we have given website addresses to help you locate what you need, although these are subject to change.

---

1   Standard Contract 2010, para 7.10.

The LSC website

1.3 Legal aid seems to be subject to continual change and everyone involved with legal aid funding needs to keep up with the latest developments. The LSC is sending out less and less information on paper, and relying on you far more to check what's on its website. You wouldn't want to miss an opportunity to tender, or find that you were using out-of-date forms, for example. So what's the best way of keeping up to date?

You can sign up to the LSC's email newsletter, which will provide you with updates, announcements and changes. The updates give you a brief summary of the issue, and a link to further information. They make keeping up much easier. You can subscribe through the LSC's website navigating from tab to tab as follows: www.legalservices.gov.uk > About us > Our publications > Subscribe to publications. The general, civil and criminal news pages also contain RSS feeds which you can subscribe to in a news reader.

However, if you are really interested in keeping up to date, you cannot beat checking the website, and even particular pages, on a weekly basis, as the LSC does not always alert people to changes. The LSC has announced that its website will transfer to the Ministry of Justice and Directgov websites in 2011.

Civil and family – key documentation

The Standard Contract or the Unified Contract

1.4 The Standard Contract replaced the Unified Contract from 15 November 2010 for civil categories of law. Family law continued under the Unified Contract 2007, as did housing where delivered with family law (but not where delivered as part of the social welfare law bundle).

As with all LSC contracts, they contain many detailed provisions concerning the way you work with clients, as well as setting out the formal relationship between your organisation and the LSC. You can download the applicable contract from the LSC's website at: www.legalservices.gov.uk > Community Legal Service (CLS) > Civil contracts.

Part A of this book sets out where you can find the main provisions in relation to casework; see part C 'Managing legal aid work' for more information on the contractual relationship with the LSC.

The Standard Contract Specification

1.5   The section of the contract that caseworkers will need to be familiar
with is the Standard Civil Contract Specification. It can be downloaded from the webpage noted above. It is split into general rules
and category-specific rules; where the two conflict, the category-
specific rules take precedence.[2] The Specification rules are discussed
in detail in chapters 2–8 of this book.

The Specification contains an introduction to the main workings
of the various funding schemes. Section 1 contains general provisions; for example, it explains how to apply the Funding Code and
regulations, what is in your contract schedule and rules concerning
additional matter starts. Section 2 gives information about service
standards, where work can or must be done, working in consortia,
supervisor standards, and crucially, key performance indicators
(KPIs). These become mandatory under the Standard Contract and
may be taken into account in future tendering exercises. Section 3
explains the scope of controlled work and rules applying to it. Section 4 explains how controlled work is paid for. Sections 5 and 6 discuss the scope and main rules applying to licensed work, payment
arrangements and the statutory charge (although rates of payment
are shown in the Payment Annex).

The remaining sections 7–10 are category-specific:

Section 7 – Family – not in force at the time of writing. Family
practitioners should refer to section 10 of the Unified Contract
Specification.
Section 8 – Immigration
Section 9 – Mental health
Paras 10.1–10.8 – Debt
Paras 10.9–10.14 – Employment
Paras 10.15–10.70 – Housing (including court duty schemes)
– not in force for those organizations with housing and fam-
ily contracts. Housing practitioners in organizations with a
Family contract should refer to section 15 of the Unified Con-
tract Specification.
Paras 10.71–10.82 – Welfare benefits
Paras 10.83–10.99 – Consumer and general contract
Paras 10.100–10.101 – Personal injury
Paras 10.102–10.105 – Clinical negligence
Paras 10.106–10.110 – Education

2   Standard Contract Specification, para 1.12.

Paras 10.111–10.121 – Actions against the police etc
Paras 10.122–10.127 – Community care
Paras 10.128–10.132 – Public law

The Payment Annex contains the fixed fees and underlying hourly rates relevant to civil and family work, including advocacy and mediation.

Frequently asked questions

1.6 The LSC has provided some answers to frequently asked questions in respect of family, immigration and mental health schemes on its website at: www.legalservices.gov.uk > Community Legal Service (CLS) > Pay rates and schemes. They can be downloaded from the document box on the right-hand side. They are useful because they deal with a number of queries that arise in day-to-day practice, and may well provide the answer to the particular question you have.

The LSC aims to update the frequently asked questions in relation to the new family fee schemes at regular intervals, to answer those raised as people start to use the schemes. These will be on the family pages of the website.

Eligibility guidance

1.7 Civil and family eligibility guidance is found in volume 2 of the LSC Manual (for controlled work) or volume 3 (certificated work). You can download it from the LSC's website at www.legalservices.gov. uk > Community Legal Service (CLS) > Civil legal aid eligibility. See chapter 2 of this book for more information about eligibility.

The Funding Code

1.8 The Funding Code is the set of rules that govern whether an individual's case can be funded under legal aid. It is a key reference document, whether you are granting legal aid yourself, as controlled work, or under devolved powers, or whether you are submitting an application for the LSC to decide. It is in volume 3 of the LSC Manual. You can download the Funding Code from the LSC's website at www. legalservices.gov.uk > Community Legal Service (CLS) > Civil legal aid eligibility > What cases do we fund?

The Funding Code includes criteria (which define the services the LSC will fund, from basic legal advice to representation in court proceedings), procedures (which set out how the LSC makes decisions about funding civil legal aid), and decision-making guidance.

Costs assessment guidance

1.9   Many caseworkers focus so hard on achieving the best possible job for their clients that they lose sight of the financial side of the case. This is not sustainable, so it is important to be aware of the rules that govern what you can and cannot claim for.

The LSC has two versions of the costs assessment guidance to cover the Unified and Standard Contracts. The guidance covers both controlled and licensed work. It can be downloaded from www. legalservices.gov.uk > Community Legal Service (CLS) > Guidance on fees and funding. See chapters 10 and 11 of this book for more information about getting paid.

Fee exemption and remission

1.10   The fee exemption and remission scheme is administered by Her Majesty's Court Service (HMCS) and is not part of legal aid funding. Court fees are a recoverable disbursement under a full legal aid representation certificate, but not under Legal Help. Legally aided clients are not automatically exempt from fees, but may apply for exemption or remission on grounds of means. For more information, see HMCS leaflet EX160A 'Court fees – Do you have to pay them?' It can be downloaded from www.hmcourts-service.gov.uk.

Criminal defence – key documentation

The 2010 Standard Crime Contract

1.11   The 2010 Standard Crime Contract replaced the Unified Contract (Crime) on 14 July 2010. It is in volume 1 of the LSC Manual. The contract can be downloaded from www.legalservices.gov.uk > Criminal Defence Service (CDS) > Crime contracts > Standard Contract 2010.

Part A of this book sets out where you can find the main provisions in relation to casework; see part C 'Managing legal aid work' for more information on the contractual relationship with the LSC.

The Crime Specification 2010

1.12   The section of the contract that caseworkers will need to be familiar with is the Crime Specification. It can also be downloaded from the webpage noted above.

Part A covers general rules, among other things: definitions, service standards, qualifying criteria, financial eligibility tests (although this is not the main source document, see below), limits on claims, application rules and forms, unique file numbers, devolved powers, errors, misrepresentation, where you can perform contract work, continuity of service, very high cost cases, change of solicitor/counsel, payment provisions, time standards, matter or case ends, solicitors with higher court advocacy rights, the Independent Funding Adjudicator and duty solicitor requirements. It also provides information about claims assessment and review procedures (although this is not the main source document, see below).

Part B gives specific rules on classes and units of work through the investigations, proceedings and appeals and reviews stages of a case. It also provides rules relating to prison law and associated CLS work. For more information about the way these schemes work, see chapter 9 of this book.

An annex contains the fees.

Eligibility guidance

1.13   Advice in the police station is not means tested.

Representation in the magistrates' court is means tested. Eligibility guidance is in the Criminal Legal Aid Manual (on the LSC website the document is dated April 2010, however, when you open it, you will find the pages marked January 2010). You can download the guidance from www.legalservices.gov.uk > Criminal Defence Service (CDS) > Criminal legal aid eligibility. There is also a calculator which you can use to establish whether or not your client will have to pay a contribution, which can be useful for clients with more complex means. Clients who are not eligible for legal aid in the magistrates' court and pay for their defence privately can apply to reclaim their costs from Central Funds if they are subsequently acquitted.

Representation in the Crown Court became means tested from January 2010. There is training and guidance material on the LSC's website at: www.legalservices.gov.uk > Criminal Defence Service (CDS) > Criminal legal aid eligibility > Crown Court means testing > Training and guidance materials. If clients are found not guilty, their contributions will be repaid. Clients who are not eligible for legal aid in the Crown Court and pay for their defence privately can apply to reclaim their costs from Central Funds if they are subsequently acquitted. The rules are to be found on the Court Service website at www.hmcourts-service.gov.uk > Legal/Professional > National Tax-ing Team > Costs out of central funds.

Costs assessment guidance

1.14   Ensuring that you will be paid is as important in criminal defence work as in civil and family, mentioned above.

The Integrated Criminal Bills Assessment Manual (CBAM) elaborates many of the principles in the contract. The LSC has updated the January 2008 version of CBAM, using 'track changes' to reflect the change from the General Criminal Contract (Jan 08) to the Standard Crime Contract 2010. It can be found at: www.legalservices.gov.uk > Criminal Defence Service (CDS) > Pay rates and schemes > Guidance on fees and funding. Other guidance on costs is also available from the same page, for example, funding for warrants of further detention, proceeds of crime matters, guidance for funding anti-social behaviour orders, and CDS 6 and 7 billing codes.

CHAPTER 2

Taking on civil and family cases

Introduction

2.1   When a client approaches you with a legal problem, there are a number of considerations to bear in mind in deciding whether you can take the case. These include:

- Is the case within the scope of the legal aid scheme?
- Is it covered by your contract?
- Do you have sufficient matter starts to be able to take it?
- Is the client financially eligible?
- Does the client's case pass the merits test?
- Is there any other reason why you cannot take it?

Only if the case passes all these tests can it be taken on.

Scope of the scheme

2.2   Civil legal aid – formally, Community Legal Service (CLS) funding – is available for all types of civil and family cases that are not specifically ruled out by the Access to Justice Act 1999.

Schedule 2 to the Act precludes funding for cases

in relation to –
(a) allegations of personal injury or death, other than ... clinical negligence,
(aa) allegations of negligently caused damage to property,
(b) conveyancing,
(c) boundary disputes,
(d) the making of wills,
(e) matters of trust law,
(f) defamation or malicious falsehood,
(g) matters of company or partnership law,
(h) other matters arising out of the carrying on of a business,
(i) attending an interview conducted by the Secretary of State with a view to his reaching a decision on a claim for asylum – (but see chapter 7).

It also rules out advocacy

in any proceedings except –
(1) proceedings in –
    (a) the Supreme Court,
    (c) the Court of Appeal,
    (d) the High Court,
    (e) any county court,
    (f) the Employment Appeal Tribunal,

(g) the First-tier Tribunal under any provision of the Mental Health Act 1983 or paragraph 5(2) of the Schedule to the Repatriation of Prisoners Act 1984, or the Mental Health Review Tribunal for Wales,

(gza) the First-tier Tribunal under –
    (i)   Schedule 2 to the Immigration Act 1971,
    (ii) section 40A of the British Nationality Act 1981,
    (iii) Part 5 of the Nationality, Immigration and Asylum Act 2002, or
    (iv) regulation 26 of the Immigration (European Economic Area Regulations 2006),

(ga) the Upper Tribunal arising out of proceedings within paragraph (g) or (gza),

(ha) the Special Immigration Appeals Commission, or

(i) the Proscribed Organisations Appeal Commission,

and limited civil proceedings in the Crown Court and magistrates' court.

However, section 6(8) of the Act allows the Lord Chancellor to issue a direction bringing certain excluded services back into scope. These are known as the exceptions to the exclusions, and include advice on:

- wills, where the client is over 70, disabled, the parent of a disabled person or a single parent making provision to appoint a guardian;
- criminal injuries compensation;
- matters covered by the representation exceptions:
  - business cases that concern serious wrongdoing, abuse of position of power or significant breach of human rights by a public authority;
  - business cases where the client's home is at stake;
  - cases with a significant wider public interest;
  - cases where the liberty of the client is at stake;
  - conveyancing where necessary to give effect to a court order in funded proceedings, or in family cases to an agreement reached to avoid or settle proceedings;
  - trust law matters concerning ownership or possession of the client's home;
  - business cases where the client is reasonably disputing whether he or she was in fact carrying on a business;
  - mixed cases where the excluded part is a minor or incidental part of the case;
  - personal insolvency where the client is resisting a petition;
  - personal injury proceedings arising out of abuse of a child or vulnerable adult or sexual assault;

- proceedings under the Proceeds of Crime Act and quasi-criminal proceedings;
- inquests in death in custody cases;
- the First-tier and Upper Tribunals in respect of banning individuals from teaching or working with children or vulnerable adults;
- the First-tier and Upper Tribunal in respect of income tax or VAT and duties cases where the penalties are criminal in ECHR terms.

Excluded cases that are not within the scope of the direction may be funded on a successful application under section 6(8)(b) of the Act. This section gives ministers the power to fund a case even though it is out of scope. Such funding is rarely granted; most applications are for representation at inquests that do not come within the 'death in custody' exception. Although applications are granted by the Lord Chancellor, applications should be made to the Legal Services Commission (LSC) first, since the Lord Chancellor will only make a grant where recommended to do so by the LSC. More details can be found in section 27 of the Funding Code Decision Making Guidance.

In general, therefore, unless a case is excluded by Schedule 2 and not brought back in by the direction, it will, in principle, be covered by legal aid.

Scope of contracts

2.3   Legal aid cases are divided into categories by the contracts. At the highest level, civil and crime are treated separately, have separate contracts and different funding rules. Within the Civil Contract, the categories are:

- family;
- personal injury;
- clinical negligence;
- housing;
- immigration;
- welfare benefits;
- employment;
- mental health;
- debt;
- consumer and general contract;
- education;

- community care;
- actions against the police etc; and
- public law.

The definitions of each category used to be set out in the Specialist Quality Mark (SQM), along with the supervisor standard applicable to each one. However, they have been removed from the 2010 version. Nor are they to be found in the contracts. The contracts refer to the Category Definitions 2010; this is a separate document that does not form part of the contract but can be found on the LSC website at www.legalservices.gov.uk > Community Legal Service > Civil Contracts > 2010 Standard Civil Contract. This document contains the definitions, and there is a guidance document to be read alongside it (see appendix D).

Case study

We have a contract in social welfare law. My client is a tenant facing possession proceedings. She appears to have a counterclaim because her flat is damp and the landlord has not carried out repairs, although she has asked them to do so. The landlord says it's condensation. Is this covered under our Debt Contract?

Although the debt category covers all proceedings arising out of the occupation of premises, those involving a contested counterclaim are excluded, so you will need to deal with this case as a housing matter, either yourself or by referring it to the member of your consortium who does housing work. (See the Category Definitions 2010.)

Any case that does not fall into one of the above is categorised as 'miscellaneous'.

An organisation can only be funded to conduct civil legal aid cases if it has a Standard Civil Contract with the LSC. The contract will specify what cases the organisation can take on.

Every contract has a schedule, which is the part specific to the organisation. In order to be allowed to take on cases, you must be permitted to work in that category by your schedule. The schedule will specify the number of matter starts of controlled work, and whether licensed work is allowed for each category. Controlled work – Legal Help, Help at Court and Controlled Legal Representation – is funding for advice and some tribunal representation granted by the organisation; licensed work, also known as legal representation and certificated work is funding for representation in courts, granted by the LSC.

The matter starts permitted in your schedule are the maximum number of new controlled work cases in that category of law you are permitted to take on during the life of the schedule (usually a year). If you requested them in your tender for a contract, there will also be a number of tolerance matter starts allowed; these are cases in which you do not hold a contract, but may nevertheless conduct work. Family, immigration, personal injury, clinical negligence, mental health, actions against the police etc, education and public law are excluded from tolerance and therefore such cases can only be taken on by organisations with contracts in the relevant category.

Licensed work is not restricted by matter starts, so there is no limit on the number of certificate applications you may make in a year, in any category, except that you can not take on a case excluded from tolerance without a licence in that category.

Therefore, provided you have a contract or are permitted to do tolerance work in the relevant category, and have sufficient matter starts remaining, you can take on the case, provided the client is eligible.

Financial eligibility

2.4   There are two significant barriers to taking on cases: the means test and the merits test. Every client must qualify financially before their case can be taken on (with very limited exceptions in the family and mental health categories; see chapters 5 and 8), and the case must pass the relevant merits test.

Financial eligibility is assessed on three separate criteria, all of which the client must satisfy, by being below the threshold on capital, gross income and disposable income.

The limits on each of these are set out in the Community Legal Service (Financial) Regulations 2000 (SI No 516), which is amended periodically, usually at least once per year as benefit levels are uprated. Up to date limits can be found on the LSC website (www. legalservices.gov.uk/civil/civil_legal_aid_eligibility.asp). There is also guidance in volume 2, part E of the LSC Manual and volume 3, part D.

In the case of controlled work, you should ascertain the client's resources and calculate eligibility; the decision on whether the means test is met is delegated to you. For licensed work, however, the decision is made by the LSC.

> **Case study**
>
> *Section B6 (6.2) of the Funding Code says that satisfactory evidence of the client's means must be provided before we assess eligibility. Our clients rarely bring this evidence with them to the first appointment. Is there anything we can do about this?*
>
> You need to explain clearly to the client what evidence they will need to bring with them. It is a good idea to have a standard letter which can be sent by a secretary or receptionist to confirm this. Many organisations are now also sending the client a text message the day before the appointment.
>
> However, if you can justify it to protect your client's position then you can start work before the client provides evidence, and in exceptional cases the LSC accepts that it may not be possible for them to provide it at all (Standard Civil Contract Specification, para 3.36).

Where the client has a partner with whom he or she is living as a couple, you should always aggregate the means of both the client and the partner (whether or not they are married or civil partners).

Passporting benefits

2.5 Clients directly or indirectly in receipt of income support, income-based jobseeker's allowance, income-based employment and support allowance or guarantee state pension credit are automatically eligible for all types of legal aid without the need for further assessment of either capital or income.[1] These benefits are therefore referred to as passporting benefits. A client in receipt of support under ss4 or 95 of the Immigration and Asylum Act 1999 is passported, but only for Legal Help and Controlled Legal Representation in the immigration category.[2]

Assessment of capital

2.6 Capital is 'every resource of a capital nature belonging to [the client] on the date on which the application is made',[3] either as money or as

---

1 Community Legal Service (Financial) Regulations 2000 as amended, reg 4(2).
2 Reg 4(3).
3 Reg 26.

the realisable value of an asset.[4] It includes money owed to the client, whether or not recovered,[5] and also includes life insurance and endowments if their security can be borrowed upon.[6]

However, the value of household furniture and effects, clothing and tools of trade is excluded,[7] as is (in the case of controlled work) money the client could realise by selling or borrowing on the strength of any business he or she may own.[8]

Where the client owns property, the value of that property should be taken into account in the calculation. The value is the client's equity – that is, the current realisable market value (guidance is that this means that a deduction of 3 per cent should be made from the value, to allow for the cost of selling the property),[9] less the value of any outstanding mortgage. Deduction for mortgage is capped to £100,000 – so where a property is worth £220,000 and the outstanding mortgage is £120,000, the client's equity should be taken as £120,000, not £100,000. The first £100,000 of equity should also be disregarded.[10]

At the controlled work level, where any property is the subject matter of the dispute, the value of that property is disregarded from the calculation. However, for licensed work applications, the subject matter of dispute disregard is capped to £100,000.[11]

Case study

My client instructs me to advise her regarding divorce and ancillary relief. She and her husband own (as joint tenants) a flat, which has just been valued at £550,000. She wants the flat to be transferred to her. The outstanding mortgage is £150,000. Is she eligible for a) Legal Help; b) a certificate?

The value of the property should be taken as £533,500 – that is, £550,000 minus 3% costs of sale. Disregard the mortgage, capped to £100,000 – so the equity is £433,500.

---

4 Reg 27.
5 Reg 28.
6 Reg 29.
7 Reg 30.
8 Reg 31.
9 LSC Manual, volume 3, para 3D-067.
10 Community Legal Service (Financial) Regulations 2000 as amended, reg 32.
11 Reg 32A.

The client's share of this is £216,750, half of the equity – although the asset is in dispute, there is a presumption of equal shares for the purposes of assessment, and they are joint tenants.

Disregard the first £100,000 of equity – the client's capital is £116,750.

For Legal Help, the entire subject matter of the dispute is disregarded, so her capital is taken to be zero and she is eligible on capital.

For licensed work, only the first £100,000 of disputed property is disregarded, so her capital is taken to be £16,750. This is above the threshold of £8,000 and therefore she is not eligible on capital.

Assessment of income

2.7 Once you have found the client eligible on capital, you should proceed to the next stage, assessment of income. The client must be eligible on both gross and disposable income, and the thresholds are set on the basis of a calendar month. For example, if the client instructs you on 6 March, you should look at all money received since 7 February.

'Gross income' means total income from all sources (apart from housing benefit and some benefits and allowances, most commonly disability living allowance).[12] It will include salary, benefits, maintenance, and any other income.

You should deduct the following expenses from gross income to arrive at disposable income:

- the actual amount of any rent or mortgage payments, net of any housing benefit – but capped to £545 per month if the client has no dependants;[13]
- tax and National Insurance contributions on any earnings;[14]
- childcare costs, but only to the extent that they are incurred because of work;[15]
- where working, a fixed cost of employment allowance of £45 (for both the client and partner if both are working);[16]

---

12 Reg 5a.
13 Reg 24.
14 Reg 18.
15 Reg 23.
16 Reg 23.

- any maintenance being paid in respect of a child or other dependant family member not a member of the client's household;[17] and
- fixed dependants' allowances for the partner and each other dependant relative who is a member of the household (note that it is a common misconception that the dependants' allowances can only be claimed in respect of the client's children, an impression not dispelled by the wording of the forms which refer to 'child'. The regulations are quite clear that the allowance is claimable for any dependant relative who is a member of the client's household).[18]

The LSC's eligibility calculator is helpful as it always gets the arithmetic right and applies any allowances and disregards correctly. It can be used online at www.legalservices.gov.uk/civil/guidance/eligibility_calculator.asp.

Assessment of the means of a child

2.8   You are allowed to accept applications from a child (see LSC Manual, volume 2, part E and volume 3, part D).

When deciding on an application for Legal Help, you should assess the means of the child and those of the person(s) who have care and control or are liable to maintain the child or who usually contribute substantially to the child's maintenance. So, in effect, you will often be assessing the means of the parents, with the expectation that they should fund the case if they are able to do so.[19]

However, you should consider whether it is just and equitable to aggregate the child's means with those of the person(s) liable to maintain them, and if it is not just and equitable you should just assess the means of the child. No guidance is given as to what is 'just and equitable', although the contract says that the presumption is that there should be aggregation but that you can take into account all the circumstances, including the age and resources of the child, and that non-aggregation is more likely to be justified where there is a conflict between the child and the liable person.[20] In the absence of detailed guidance, this is a decision for you as the provider assessing eligibility for Legal Help, and you should therefore keep a detailed file note

17 Reg 21.
18 Reg 20.
19 Standard Civil Contract Specification, para 3.38.
20 Standard Civil Contract Specification, para 3.39.

justifying your decision, especially if it is a decision not to aggregate. You may want to telephone the relevant LSC office that deals with your organisation and speak to someone in the Legal/Means team, if you want to be confident that you have made the right decision. You can find the details from the LSC's 'Where work is processed' document, it can be downloaded from LSC website at www.legalservices.gov.uk > Community Legal Service > Civil Forms.

Where a child applies for a funding certificate, it is only the child's means that are taken into account, not those of the litigation friend or any other person liable to maintain the child, and therefore you should only include the child's finances on the MEANS form.[21]

Reassessment of means

2.9   The means tests are not one-off tests; if clients' circumstances change during a case, their means should be reassessed. In the case of controlled work, you should reassess means yourself, and if the client is no longer eligible, you may need to withdraw the funding. The LSC suggests that it may not be appropriate to reassess the client's means unless they have improved 'dramatically' or the matter is likely to run for some time, suggested as three months or more (LSC Manual, volume 2, para 2E-029). It would be advisable to check the guidance in the light of each client's circumstances, as you do not automatic-ally have to stop work in every case.

In the case of licensed work, you should report the change of circumstances to the LSC for them to reassess the means. Guidance on how to apply a reassessment for licensed work can be found in volume 3, part D of the LSC Manual.

It is the client's duty to report any change of circumstances to you, and therefore you must always advise clients of the existence of this duty at the first meeting. It should be confirmed in your standard letter.

Merits tests

2.10   Each case must satisfy, and continue to satisfy, the merits test. There are a number of different tests, depending on the nature of the case and the type of funding sought, and they are dealt with in the relevant

21 Community Legal Service (Financial) Regulations 2000 reg 11(3).

sections of chapters 3–8. You should always bear in mind that each merits test should be passed at the start of the case, and should continue to be passed throughout its life. If there is insufficient merit in a particular step in the proceedings, you should not take that step; if there is not, or is no longer, sufficient merit in the case as a whole, you should refuse or withdraw funding (controlled work), or report that to the LSC (licensed work).

Other restrictions on taking on cases

Referral fees

! Change from previous rules !

2.11   Although referral fees have been allowed (controversially) as a matter of professional conduct for the last few years,[22] there is an absolute prohibition on them in legal aid work. Clause 6.8 of the Standard Civil Contract Standard Terms makes clear that no payment or benefit may be made to or received from any third party, including another publicly funded provider or member of your consortium for the referral of work or the introduction of clients.

Client has received previous advice

! Change from previous rules !

2.12   The Legal Help form requires the client to certify that they have not previously received advice on the same matter, and where they have done so within the last six months requires you to explain why you took on the case. This is because there are specific rules in the contract to prevent the legal aid fund paying out twice for the same matter, and therefore in order to make a claim the second time you must be able to demonstrate that the case meets one of the exceptions allowing you to do so.

Some of the exceptions apply if you are the client's original provider looking to re-open a case that has been closed; others apply if you are a second provider looking to take over a case from the original organisation.

In the case of controlled work, para 3.47 of the Standard Civil Contract Specification states that a second matter start can only be opened on the same case where:

22 Solicitors' Code of Conduct sub-rule 9.02(h).

(a) at least six months has elapsed since there was a claim on the first matter; or
(b) there has been a material development or change in the client's instructions and at least three months has elapsed since there was a claim on the first matter; or
(c) the client has reasonable cause to be dissatisfied with the first provider; or
(d) the client has moved a distance away from the first provider and communication is difficult; or
(e) the first provider is no longer able to act for the client because of a conflict of interest or other good reason of professional conduct; or
(f) the first provider is not making a claim for the work.

Items (a) and (b) above apply in all cases; (c)–(f) only apply in cases where the client is looking to transfer provider.

Where you are relying on para 3.47(b) (material development or change), you should note that:

• Giving instructions following a failure to give instructions is not a change in instructions.
• A decision or response from any third party to any correspondence, application, appeal, review or other request made in the course of the original matter is not a material development.
• A change in the law that was anticipated in the original matter is not a material development.[23]

However, if you are the first provider, you can instead re-open the original matter and make a further claim (see chapter 3) in some circumstances.

Paragraph 3.51 requires you to make reasonable enquiries of the client as to whether there was previous advice. Where there is a transfer, you should establish that there is good reason, and record that reason on the file.[24]

However, it is not sufficient for you to take the client's word as to the reasons for transfer. You must seek the client's authority to obtain the file from the previous provider, and must then request the file from the previous provider. You cannot start work on the case until you receive the file. Where the client refuses to give you authority, or where you obtain the file and discover that there is in fact no good reason for transfer, you may not make a claim for the case. The sole exception is where there is urgent work that is absolutely necessary

---

23 Standard Civil Contract Specification, para 3.49.
24 Standard Civil Contract Specification, para 3.56.

to protect the client's position or meet a court deadline, in which case you can do the urgent work and claim for it, even if it transpires there was no good reason. See paras 3.52 and 3.53 of the Specification.

If you are the second provider and the client is relying on reasonable cause for dissatisfaction, you must notify the LSC of the alleged poor service on the part of the previous provider, and should also signpost the client to the appropriate regulatory body who can deal with complaints.[25]

In the case of certificated work, there is no specific rule or guidance on transfer of solicitor. However, to transfer, the second solicitor would have to make an application to the LSC to amend the certificate, and the LSC will consider whether the application is justified. The second solicitor must include work done by the first solicitor on the bill at the end of the case, and therefore the LSC (or court) will be able to see all work done by both solicitors, and may disallow on assessment any unjustified duplication.

Permitted work

2.13   So, if your client's case is within the scope of the scheme and your contract, and passes the means and merits tests, you will be able to take it on. However, there are restrictions on what work can be done.

The Funding Code criteria (at s2) set out limitations on the work that can be done at each level of legal aid. The definitions in the criteria are important, as they set out in full what can and cannot be done at each level of funding. Where the client's case needs work that is out of the scope of the current level, you will need to make an application for funding at the next level.

Definitions of permitted work

2.14   The main types of funding common to all areas are:

- **Legal Help**, which allows the provision of advice, negotiation and attempts at settlement and resolution, but not the issuing or conducting of court proceedings or advocacy;
- **Help at Court**, which authorises help and advocacy for a client at a particular hearing without formally being on the court record as acting for the client;

25 Standard Civil Contract Specification, para 3.55.

- **Legal Representation**, which allows the provision of representation in proceedings or contemplated proceedings, including the conduct of litigation and advocacy.

Controlled Legal Representation is a form of legal representation at the controlled work level – that is, which is controlled work rather than licensed work, and therefore granted by the provider rather than the LSC. It allows you to represent clients before tribunals, but only in the mental health and immigration categories.

Family Help is a form of funding only available in the family category, and slots in between Legal Help and Legal Representation. Family Help (Lower) is a form of controlled work, also known as private law level 2 work, and authorises advice and assistance in attempting to resolve a family dispute through negotiation and settlement. It does not include mediation, but does include advice in support of mediation. Family Help (Higher) is licensed work covering all litigation up to but not including a final contested hearing.

Investigative Help is a type of licensed work that allows the LSC to issue a certificate that is limited in scope and costs, permitting the solicitor to investigate the strength of a proposed claim.

More details of the types of work that can be carried out at each funding level can be found in the following chapters.

Conducting a civil case

continued

Introduction

3.1   This chapter deals with most types of civil case, where the procedures are very similar. There are separate chapters on family cases (private and public law), immigration and mental health, as they have their own funding schemes and rules.

In chapter 2, we saw that there are three key stages in providing publicly funded services; to ensure that the matter is within scope, the client is financially eligible and the case meets the merits test. In addition, you need to ensure that forms are completed correctly and funding is obtained.

This chapter explains how these steps are taken successfully in respect of most civil work.

See appendices G and H for a summary of the Legal Services Commission's (LSC's) Costs Assessment Guidance, in respect of the most common queries raised by caseworkers.

Legal Help

Scope

3.2   At the most basic level, work must be allowed under the Access to Justice Act 1999 (see chapter 2 for more information).

Legal Help allows you to provide advice and assistance in relation to a specific matter, but does not cover issuing proceedings, advocacy, or instruction of an advocate (although you can get counsel's opinion, where justified in a complex case; but this would be very rare). It does not cover the provision of mediation and arbitration, although it does allow you to advise your client on issues arising from mediation and arbitration.[1]

For information about clients who are outside England and Wales or who are not from England and Wales, see further below.

Other sources of funding

3.3   The Funding Code[2] states that Legal Help may only be provided if it is reasonable for the Community Legal Service (CLS) fund to pay for it, having regard to any other sources of funding available to the

---

1   Funding Code, criterion 2.1.
2   Criterion 5.1.

client. This means that, for example, you should check whether the client has legal expenses insurance (perhaps as part of home contents cover) or is a member (or the partner of a member) of a trade union.

Forms

3.4 The form is the CW1 Legal Help, Help at Court and Family Help (Lower) form.

The assessment of means and client's details sections must be fully completed, and signed by the client, normally in the presence of someone from your organisation, before you start doing any legal work.[3]

Case study

I don't really want to stick a Legal Help form under the client's nose and ask them to sign, even before we've said 'Good morning'. Does that mean I will not be able to charge for all my time during the initial interview?

You will be covered, as the Standard Contract Specification, para 3.12(i), confirms all the time in an interview will be allowed, when a client signs the CW1 form at any point.

The form must be kept on the file and is not sent to the LSC, unless requested for an assessment.[4]

What if the client cannot sign the form?

3.5 There will be occasions when your client is a child or patient, and you may not be satisfied of their capacity to sign the form and give instructions. Sometimes a client will not be physically able to attend your office. You must not use more than 10 per cent of your matter starts in any schedule period for clients who cannot attend on you (or a member of your consortium) personally.[5]

Whenever you grant Legal Help to a client in the circumstances described below, you should make an attendance note justifying

---

3 Standard Contract Specification, para 3.12.
4 Standard Contract Specification, para 3.13.
5 Standard Contract Specification, para 3.28. This restriction does not apply to organisations conducting family or housing cases under the Unified Contract 2007.

what you did, and tick the appropriate box on page 5 of the Legal Help form.

Applications on behalf of children

3.6   You can accept an application direct from a child, if the child is entitled to bring, prosecute or defend proceedings without a litigation friend or equivalent;[6] or there is good reason why one of the persons listed in Funding Code, criterion B5 (see below) cannot apply on the client's behalf and the adviser is satisfied that the child understands the nature of the work and is capable of giving instructions.

An application can be accepted on behalf of a child from:

- a parent, guardian or other person responsible for the child's care; or
- a litigation friend or guardian ad litem; or
- if neither of the above are available, any other person (except anyone who works in your organisation), provided that the other person has sufficient knowledge of all the circumstances to act responsibly in the child's interests and to give proper instructions.

Applications on behalf of patients

3.7   An application can be accepted on behalf of a patient from:

- a receiver under Part VII of the Mental Health Act; or
- a nearest relative or guardian under Part II of the Mental Health Act; or a litigation friend or equivalent; or
- if none of the above are available, any other person, (except anyone who works in your organisation) provided that the other person has sufficient knowledge of all the circumstances to act responsibly in the patient's interests and to give proper instructions.

Where an application is accepted under these arrangements, and the client is the child/patient, the form should be completed in their name and their means assessed (see below for assessing a child's means). However, the form will be signed by the person applying on their behalf.

Applications by post

3.8   You may grant Legal Help to a client by post where there is a 'good reason'. This is defined in Standard Contract Specification, para 3.15 as 'where the client requests that the application is made in this way

6   Funding Code, criterion B4.

and it is not necessary for the interests of the client or his or her case to attend in person'.

People resident outside the European Union

3.9 You may not grant Legal Help to a client resident outside the European Union if one of the following applies:[7]

a) the client could, without serious disadvantage, delay their application until they had returned to the EU;

b) someone resident in the EU could apply on their behalf; or

c) it would otherwise be unreasonable to accept the application.

This facility is particularly useful in immigration cases where clients have been refused entry to the UK, or have been removed or deported, but have a right of appeal that can be exercised from outside the UK.

The previous government announced plans to amend Schedule 2 to the Access to Justice Act 1999 to remove the right to legal aid from anyone (whether or not a British citizen) who resides outside the EU, British Overseas Territories, the Crown Dependencies, Macao or Hong Kong, or outside a jurisdiction with which the UK has a bilateral agreement allowing access of citizens to each other's legal aid schemes. This would not apply to immigration and asylum, international child abduction, child contact or forced marriage cases or (in the case of those present but not resident in England and Wales) domestic violence, child care, emergency homelessness or mental health detention.[8] At the time of going to print, the coalition government has not stated whether it will adopt these proposals and have not brought forward the necessary legislation. They were not included in the *Proposals for the Reform of Legal Aid* green paper issued in November 2010.

Applications by fax

3.10 You can only accept applications by fax if that is specified in your contract schedule. If it is, you need to follow the rules set out in Standard Contract Specification, para 3.27.

Telephone, webcam and email advice

3.11 You can give, and claim for, advice over the telephone or by email, webcam etc if the client cannot attend your office for a 'good reason'

---

7 Standard Contract Specification, para 3.26.

8 'Legal aid: refocussing on priority cases, response to consultation', Ministry of Justice, February 2010.

as defined in Standard Contract Specification, para 3.15, see applications by post above, provided the client is later found to be eligible for Legal Help and signs the form later. If the client subsequently fails to sign the form, you cannot claim payment.[9]

Financial eligibility

3.12   Clients must be financially eligible on both capital and income. They must inform you of any change in their means and you may have to stop work if their means change significantly (see chapter 2 for more information). However, there are no contributions to be paid in respect of Legal Help.

Criterion B6 of the Funding Code states that you can only carry out work for clients who are financially eligible and that you must obtain satisfactory evidence of their means before assessing eligibility. In practical terms, that means, except in exceptional circumstances, you must obtain evidence of a client's means before starting work.

If it is 'not practicable to obtain it before commencing controlled work', you may start without it; but you need to show that you acted reasonably in assessing eligibility and starting work without evidence. In practice you should record on your initial attendance note:

- **why** it was reasonable to start work without evidence of means (for example, because the client needed advice urgently due to the imminent expiry of a time limit);
and
- **how** you assessed eligibility (eg by making sure that the Legal Help form is properly completed, using the information the client was able to give you from their account of what they have been living on).

You must get the evidence as soon as practicable unless the client's circumstances prevent this at any point in the case, for example due to mental disability, age or homelessness.[10]

If you act reasonably in granting Legal Help to a client before obtaining evidence of their means and you do not claim any disbursement or report any time after the point where the LSC decides it would have been practicable to obtain satisfactory evidence of means, you can still claim payment for the work.

---

9   Standard Contract Specification, para 3.32.
10   Standard Contract Specification, para 3.36.

However, if the LSC decides that you could have obtained evidence of means at any stage of the case, costs will be 'nil assessed' at any audit. Having files 'nil assessed' can have very serious consequences, so it is strongly advisable to get valid evidence of means prior to starting work in all but emergency situations.

Merits test

3.13 The Legal Help merits test is known as the 'sufficient benefit test', and in full states: 'Help may only be provided where there is sufficient benefit to the client, having regard to the circumstances of the matter, including the personal circumstances of the client, to justify work or further work being carried out'.[11]

The general approach to the test is set out in the guidance to the Funding Code (LSC Manual, volume 3). The question is whether a reasonable private paying client of moderate means would pay for the work. At the Legal Help level, the LSC considers that it may well be worthwhile paying for initial advice, including that the case is not worth pursuing further. It is designed to weed out vexatious and non-legal matters. Particular issues have arisen in relation to welfare benefits matters – see below.

The more Legal Help is provided, the more relevant the cost–benefit test becomes. Even when payment is a fixed fee, the costs for the test should be calculated at hourly rates (LSC Manual, volume 3). For a purely financial matter the amount in issue should not be exceeded by the cost of providing Legal Help.

Previous advice

3.14 Clients are generally only entitled to advice on a matter from one LSC provider, so you should always ask the client whether they have taken previous advice before starting work.

! Change from previous rules !

Standard Contract 2010 Specification, paras 3.51–3.57 set out what you must do if the client has received previous advice, whether that is from your organisation or somewhere else.

There is a list of particular circumstances in which a new matter start will not be justified at para 3.59 of the Standard Contract Speci-

---

11 Funding Code, criterion 5.2.

fication. However, it is worth noting that you can open a new matter if a client faces enforcement proceedings because he or she is alleged to have breached the terms of a suspended or postponed order, or the terms on which proceedings were adjourned.[12]

You generally cannot open a new matter for a client who has received advice on the same matter within the last six months, unless an exception applies. Exceptions are listed at para 3.47 of Standard Contract 2010 Specification:

- there has been a material development or change in the client's instructions and at least three months have elapsed since the previous claim was submitted:
  - note that if the client has simply failed to give instructions, that cannot be counted as a change in instructions;
  - any change in the law that was anticipated in the original matter cannot count as a material development;
  - a decision, or other response from another party, arising from the first piece of work cannot count as a material development;
- the client has reasonable cause for dissatisfaction with the previous adviser (this must be justified dissatisfaction with the service, not because the client was not happy about the advice they were given, or wants a second opinion);
- the client has moved away and has difficulty communicating with the previous adviser;
- the first adviser is no longer able to act for a good reason relating to professional conduct, eg conflict of interest;
- the first adviser has confirmed that no claim will be made.

If the client says that he or she is dissatisfied, you must request confirmation of the reasons for transfer, and a copy of the file from the previous organisation. If the client refuses consent, no advice should be given and no claim can be made.[13] No work may be done until the previous file has been received, unless absolutely necessary to protect the client's position or meet a deadline. When you receive the file, if you believe the client was unreasonable in being dissatisfied with the service, you must stop work but can still claim a fixed fee if urgent work was justified before getting the file.[14]

---

12 Standard Contract Specification, para 3.59 below subpara (g).
13 Standard Contract Specification, para 3.52.
14 Standard Contract Specification, para 3.53.

Case study

Can I open a new matter when the client has already received advice on the same problem?

Legal Help forms are also known as 'new matter starts' (see chapter 2 for more information about means and merits tests for Legal Help cases).

Matter claimed	Open new matter?
Up to 3 months ago	No
3–6 months	Yes – if there is a material development or change in instructions
6+ months ago	Yes

Case study

My client says he received advice from Community Legal Advice over the telephone last month. Can I open a new matter start?

It depends how much work they did for him. Ask him to show you the confirmation of instructions, advice and action letter which they will have sent him under SQM requirement F1.1.

If he has not signed a Legal Help form, you can open a new matter, as initial telephone advice is not 'controlled work' under Standard Contract 2010 Specification, para 3.47.

Otherwise, you should treat advice from the Community Legal Advice telephone service as you would advice from any other LSC provider.

Reopening a closed matter

3.15   Although you may not be able to open a new matter, you can (and may be obliged to) do more work on the original matter.[15] The disadvantage is that you cannot claim an additional fixed fee; but there are compensations:[16]

- previous work and additional work after the client comes back, can be counted together towards the exceptional case threshold;
- further disbursements can be claimed.

15 Standard Contract Specification, para 3.67.
16 Standard Contract Specification, para 3.49.

Case study

What is the procedure for reporting a revived Legal Help case to the LSC?

The LSC's online reporting system does not recognise supplementary claims. You send your Relationship Manager an email explaining what you have done. The Relationship Manager will void the first claim so that you do not claim twice for the same matter.

Opening more than one matter

! Change from previous rules !

Separate and distinct

3.16   If a client has problems that are 'separate and distinct',[17] you can open more than one matter. Opening more than one matter for a client must be carefully justified in every case if you are not to fall foul of LSC audits. If your organisation is found to have opened matters incorrectly, significant amounts of money may need to be repaid to the LSC, so it is extremely important to get this right.

It is relatively easy to justify that more than one case is justified as 'separate and distinct' if they necessarily fall under different categories of law. So, if a client has an employment problem and needs a divorce, it is justifiable to open two matters.

It is more difficult to justify opening more than one matter within one overall category of law. The first thing to remember is that the rules contained in the category specific sections of the Specification take precedence.[18] So, if you are considering whether to open more than one matter within a category, you should look up the category specific rules first.

Different causes or events

3.17   If your client's circumstances are not explicitly dealt with, it is worth applying the wording in the general Contract Specification, which states that matters are 'separate and distinct' 'typically because they arise out of different causes or events'. So, it is a good idea to ask yourself whether the causes or events are separate. For example, if your client has a housing disrepair problem and a housing benefit

17 Standard Contract Specification, para 3.42.
18 Standard Contract Specification, para 1.11.

problem, these would be very likely to be separate and distinct, even though they could both fall within the housing category.

It is more difficult if the client has 'more than one separate and distinct legal problem' within a category.[19] You must be able to demonstrate two things:

> If legal proceedings were started, or other appropriate remedies pursued, for each problem it would be appropriate for such proceedings to be both issued and heard separately.
>
> AND
>
> Each problem requires substantial legal work which does not address the other problem(s).

'Substantial legal work' is defined as at least 30 minutes' additional preparation or advice, or separate communication with other parties on legal issues.[20]

Work that does not address the other problem(s)

3.18   If you are going to satisfy the LSC that work on one issue does not address another, this has to be clear in your case recording. If you consistently deal with two or more issues together, it will be very difficult to argue that they were really 'separate and distinct'. You will need to open two separate files and keep separate attendance notes and letters relating to each issue. However, more than one problem may be discussed in one interview with a client as this may be more convenient for them. If so, separate attendance notes should be produced for each and time apportioned between the issues.

If you consider that the test is satisfied, you can ask the client to sign more than one Legal Help form at the initial meeting, or subsequently.[21]

More than one client

! Change from previous rules !

3.19   The LSC says that you should only use one new matter if the problem involves more than one client, unless:[22]

a) if proceedings were issued, each client would be a party to those proceedings;

19 Standard Contract Specification, para 3.42.
20 Standard Contract Specification, para 3.43.
21 Standard Contract Specification, para 3.44.
22 Specific Standard Contract Specification, para 3.50.

b) each client has a separate and distinct legal interest in the problem or issue; *and*

c) in considering whether there is sufficient benefit test for the second or any subsequent client to receive Legal Help, you take into account the fact that Legal Help that is already being provided in relation to the same general problem.

Case study

I have two clients who have been made redundant by the same employer. The employer does not appear to have followed the correct procedure and so we believe both clients have claims for unfair dismissal. Is this one or two matter starts?

This is two matter starts. You would have to check the facts in relation to both clients separately. Even in a situation where it looks as though the employer has acted in the same way in relation to each client, there may be differences between them.

There is also the issue of confidentiality. If each client is unaware that the other has contacted you, you cannot breach confidentiality.

Funding

Fixed fees

3.20   Legal Help is paid under fixed fees, although cases that reach the escape threshold (three times the fixed fee) can be paid in full at hourly rates. Current fees and hourly rates are found in the Standard Contract Payment Annex. You can download the contract from the LSC's website at: www.legalservices.gov.uk > Community Legal Service (CLS) > Civil contracts > 2010 Standard Civil Contracts. See chapter 10 for more information on payment schemes.

Paragraph 3.46 of the Standard Contract Civil Specification states that you must not open more than one matter start for a client unless the client has more than one 'separate and distinct' legal problem.

More than one fixed fee

3.21   In some circumstances, you may be able to justify opening more than one Legal Help file for a client. For more information about this, see 3.16 above; and comments in relation to individual categories of law, below.

Debt – Legal Help key issues

3.22 Reading the general provisions, you might think you could open a new matter start for each separate debt in a multiple debt case. However, the category-specific provisions[23] say not necessarily!

You can open a new matter start for each debt disputed on separate, substantive grounds, and also where proceedings have been issued in respect of more than one debt. An application for a liability notice for council tax counts as the issue of proceedings. If a client faces separate enforcement proceedings (whether or not arising from a judgement in civil courts), that also justifies opening more than one matter start.

Case study

My client has multiple consumer debts and a liability order in respect of council tax. She has received a Default Notice under the Consumer Credit Act 1974 s87 Can I open a second Legal Help matter?

Sorry, no you can't. There has to be *more than one* set of proceedings. If the creditor issues a claim in the county court, you could open a second Legal Help matter.

You can also open a new matter start if a client faces enforcement proceedings because he or she is alleged to have breached the terms of a suspended order, or the terms on which proceedings were adjourned.[24] This may be useful in relation to rent or mortgage debts. Debt advisers should beware referring ongoing rent and mortgage arrears cases to a housing specialist unless there are housing specific issues, such as disrepair, or there are possession proceedings justifying an application for representation. This LSC is likely to say the debt specialist could and should have dealt with them as part of the debt case.

Employment – Legal Help key issues

3.23 Employment advisers will find little comfort in the category-specific provisions for employment.[25] They do not add much to the general provisions, and the chances of being able to open more than one matter start for a client appear slim.

---

23 Standard Contract Specification, para 10.7.
24 Standard Contract Specification, paragraph immediately below para 3.59(g).
25 Standard Contract Specification, para 10.14.

The determining issue is whether the client's claims arise 'from the same set of circumstances'. If they do, the case only merits one matter start, even though you may be dealing with, for example, both wrongful and unfair dismissal claims.

Housing – Legal Help key issues

! Change from previous rules !

3.24   The category-specific provisions[26] are more detailed than most other categories of social welfare law:

- You can open a second Legal Help case when you pursue proceedings under the Environmental Protection Act 1990 and to assist the client with civil proceedings under Legal Help because the case appears likely to be allocated to the small claims track.

- All matters within the course of a homelessness application should be dealt with under a single matter start (including where the local authority remits a decision for further consideration following a Housing Act 1996 s202 review); but additional matter starts can be opened in the following circumstances:
  - when on appeal under Housing Act s204 the decision is subsequently remitted for reconsideration by the local authority (unless an appeal under section 204(1)(b) is compromised on the basis that the local authority completes its review and notifies its review decision);
  - where on appeal under Housing Act s204 the decision of a local authority is varied and Legal Help is required in relation to enforcement of any duty arising from the new decision;
  - to assist the client in requesting a review, under Housing Act s202(1)(f), of accommodation offered by a local authority (but not just to provide general advice about the offer and review process);
  - for advice in relation to the protection of the client's property under sections 211 and 212 of the Housing Act (subject to the usual merits tests);
  - for advice relating to the terms and conditions, in particular alleged rent arrears, of the client's occupation of accommodation provided under Part VII of the Housing Act (although if the work concerns suitability of such accommodation or the dis-

26 Standard Contract Specification, paras 10.24–10.29.

charge of an interim duty of the local authority then it should be dealt with under the substantive homelessness matter start);
– for advice in relation to a decision by a local authority that its duty towards the client has been discharged under Housing Act s193(6) or s195(4), and/or any subsequent fresh homelessness application.

An interim application for judicial review (such as failure of a local authority to accept an application or to provide accommodation pending a decision) would not generally justify a new matter start but would, in an emergency, justify the exercise of devolved powers to grant a certificate.

Housing possession schemes

! Change from previous rules !

3.25   You cannot ask a client to sign a Legal Help form at a court duty scheme, as this work is funded under a separate schedule, and is paid at a fixed fee per client seen.[27]

If the client's case needs further work, you can ask the client to come to your office and sign a Legal Help form (subject to the usual rules in relation to means and merits).

However, you cannot then claim a fee for advising that client under the court duty scheme.[28] It is very important that organisations have systems to prevent double-claiming in error in these circumstances. If you open a housing Legal Help case within six months of having advised the same client on the same case at a duty scheme you will not be entitled to the court duty payment for that client, so your systems will need to allow you to identify such cases and where necessary notify the LSC to rescind a payment already made against your court duty schedule.

Welfare benefits – Legal Help key issues

! Change from previous rules !

3.26   The category-specific provisions[29] are clear that any review, appeal or request for supersession must be dealt with as part of the same matter as any previous advice on the same benefit.

---

27 Standard Contract 2010, Payment Annex, s6.
28 Standard Contract Specification, para 10.39.
29 Standard Contract Specification, para 10.81.

The Standard Contract Specification, para 10.76 refers to circumstances in which it might be justified to carry out welfare benefits checks under the contract. Feedback from practitioners, relating to audits carried out in 2009–2010, suggests that it can be difficult (though not impossible) to justify opening a matter start for advice on claiming benefits, even those previously accepted as legally complex by the LSC. See Point of Principle of General Importance (PoP) CLA51 and its guidance for more information

In relation to separate matter starts for separate benefits, the category-specific provisions simply refer you back to the general provisions at Standard Contract Specification, paras 3.40–3.60. This suggests that you can open a new matter for each benefit if you are advising on a number of benefits at the same time and each required more than 30 minutes' work. For example, a case involving disability living allowance and housing benefit would involve communicating with two different parties, and if you had to appeal (the appropriate remedy), each benefit would have a separate hearing, which would involve different legal and factual issues. However, feedback from practitioners following audits in 2009–2010 suggests that it is difficult to persuade the LSC that legal advice on entitlement to welfare benefits is merited at all. It is strongly advisable to ensure that attendance notes reflect the legal nature of the advice provided. The guidance to PoP CLA51 makes it clear that advice on different benefits must be dealt with under one NMS unless there is more than one appeal.

Case study

I see that Schedule 2 to the Access to Justice Act 1999 does not cover advocacy at welfare benefits tribunals; but I thought I could provide assistance to my client as a McKenzie adviser. What does this mean? I'm confused.

The Standard Contract 2010 Specification for Welfare Benefits (para 10.80) does say that it may in 'very exceptional circumstances' be possible to justify attendance as a McKenzie adviser. The role of a McKenzie adviser is to provide legal advice to a client during a hearing, not to represent him or her, so the client should address the Tribunal. You should also note that the McKenzie adviser's role is to provide legal advice to the client, not general support which should be provided by a friend, relative or support worker.

If your client would not be able to represent himself or herself at the tribunal, due to nervousness, mental health problems or learning difficulties, where justified, you could act as a McKenzie adviser to the client accompanied by a friend or relative who did the actual representation.

For more information about McKenzie advisers, see appendix A.

Disbursements

3.27 You can claim disbursements in addition to the fixed fee,[30] provided that they meet the criteria set out in the contract:

- it is in the best interests of the client to incur the disbursement;
- it is reasonable to incur the disbursement for the purpose of providing controlled work – ie necessary for the purpose of giving advice to the client or progressing the case;
- the amount of the disbursement is reasonable; and
- it is not a disbursement which is specifically prohibited.[31]

Disbursements that may not be claimed under controlled work

! Change from previous rules !

3.28 The Standard Contract Specification, para 4.24 provides a non-exhaustive list of disbursements that may not be incurred in the provision of controlled work. Note that the same disbursements are prohibited for licensed work, save that court fees are an allowable disbursement under a certificate.[32] These disbursements are:

- costs of (or expenses relating to) the residential assessment of a child or treatment, therapy, training or other interventions of an educative or rehabilitative nature unless authorised by the Lord Chancellor;
- ad valorem stamp duties;
- capital duty;
- clients' travelling and accommodation expenses, save in the circumstances prescribed in the costs assessment guidance and unless they relate to treatment, therapy, training or other interventions of an educative or rehabilitative nature or to the residential assessment of a child;

30 Standard Contract Specification, para 4.21.
31 Standard Contract Specification, para 4.24 and subject-specific sections.
32 Standard Contract Specification, para 6.63.

- contact centre fees;
- court fees, unless for a search/photocopying/bailiff service, or as part of controlled legal representation or otherwise permitted by category-specific rules (see below);
- discharge of debts owed by the client, for example, rent or mortgage arrears;
- fee payable on voluntary petitions in bankruptcy;
- fee payable to implement a pension sharing order;
- fee payable to the Office of the Public Guardian;
- immigration application fees;
- mortgagees' or lessors' legal costs and disbursements;
- passport fees;
- probate fees;
- in the family category of law only:
  - costs of or expenses in relation to the provision of family mediation, conciliation or any other dispute resolution including family group conferences (fees for family mediation are claimed direct by the mediator);
  - costs or expenses of risk assessments within Children Act 1989 s16A and undertaken by Cafcass officers or Welsh family proceedings officers, including assessments of the risk of harm to a child in connection with domestic abuse to the child or another person;
  - costs of or expenses relating to any activity to promote contact with a child directed by the court under Children Act 1989 ss11A–11G. See, further, Funding Code Guidance, section 2.5 para 4(b);
- any separate administration fee charged by an expert, where the 'administration fee' includes, but is not limited to, a fee in respect of offices and consultation rooms, administrative support including typing services, subsistence and couriers;
- a cancellation fee charged by an expert where notice of cancellation is given more than 72 hours before the relevant hearing or appointment.

The LSC has limited what it will pay in respect of experts to 45 pence per mile for travelling costs, and £40 per hour travelling time.

Family practitioners should note the Unified Contract Specification, para 10.61, which states that:

> Court fees are an allowable disbursement under Family Help (Lower) only where such fees are incurred for the purpose of obtaining a consent order. In all cases, court fees may only be incurred where they are

a reasonable and proportionate step which satisfies the private Client cost benefit criterion (Funding Code criterion 11.3.2).

This is slightly ambiguous, but it means that consent order fees are the only ones permitted and it must be reasonable to incur them.

This contrasts with licensed work, where court fees are an allowable disbursement, and with Legal Help, where court fees are never allowable.

A full list of allowable and non-allowable disbursements for licensed work can be found in the Funding Code Guidance, LSC Manual, volume 3, para 3C-018.

Help at Court

Scope

3.29   Work must be allowed under the Access to Justice Act 1999 (see chapter 2 and appendix F for more information).

Help at Court is help and advocacy for a client in relation to a particular hearing, without formally acting as legal representative in the proceedings.[33] The Funding Code guidance explains that Help at Court only covers informal advocacy, usually by way of mitigation at individual court hearings. Ongoing representation can only be provided under a legal representation certificate.

Help at Court is particularly useful for cases where a Legal Representation Certificate would not be available, for example where a client does not have a defence to a possession claim; but does need an experienced adviser to set out repayment proposals to the court. Help at Court can also be used to represent the client on an application for enforcement of an order where the client is the applicant.

Financial eligibility

3.30   As Legal Help, see above.

Merits test

The sufficient benefit test (see Legal Help, above)

3.31   The nature of the proceedings and the circumstances of the hearing must be such that representation will be of real benefit to the client.[34]

---

33 Funding Code, criterion 2.1.
34 Funding Code, criterion 5.3.2.

This means the issue(s) must be more complex than the client could have explained to the court himself or herself.

You must apply the test before every hearing and note the file with your justification. 'Sufficient benefit test met' is not an adequate justification.

Case study

I am assisting a client to make a claim against a trader in the small claims court for failing to deliver goods worth £300. The trader has not responded to the claim. Can I represent the client under Help at Court?

A legal representation certificate would be refused as the case has been allocated to the small claims track (Funding Code, criterion 5.4.6). However, it is unlikely that the case would meet the cost–benefit test and it is unlikely that representation would be of real benefit to the client as the issues in the case appear straightforward.

Forms

3.32   The form is the CW1 Legal Help, Help at Court and Family Help (Lower) form (see Legal Help, above).

If the client has already signed a Legal Help form to cover advice and assistance, he or she does not need to sign another form in relation to Help at Court.[35]

Funding

3.33   Advisers without rights of audience may provide informal advocacy and claim payment under Help at Court, as long as advocacy is justified and the court agrees to hear them.

There are no additional fixed fees to cover Help at Court. However, the additional work involved may make it more likely that the case will reach the escape threshold (three times the fixed fee).

Where advocacy is justified, you may claim travel and waiting to/ from and at court, as well as preparation and attendance, where appropriate. See chapter 10 for more information on payment schemes.

---

35 Standard Contract Specification, para 3.14.

Ending a case

3.34 Standard Contract Specification, para 3.82, sets out the circumstances in which you can close your file and claim your costs.

Most are obvious: the client decides not to proceed, or decides to take the matter forward themselves; a funding certificate is granted, or you cannot act further due to a conflict of interest or other professional conduct issue; or the matter simply reaches a logical conclusion.

One is less obvious, which is where the client fails to give instructions for three months (unless the matter is on hold, for example, because you are waiting for a third party to act or you have agreed it with the client). You have to watch out for this, because on a contract compliance audit (see chapter 18) the LSC may say that the case terminated at that point, and disallow all profit costs and disbursements after it. This is important in exceptional cases.

You cannot stop work or close a matter simply because the value of your costs is equal to, or more than, the fixed fee.[36]

You should close and claim for your case as soon as you properly can, as apart from anything else, the date of the claim is when time starts to run to open a new matter start if the client subsequently needs further advice.

You have to submit a claim for the matter within three months of the ending of the matter. If you fail to do this 'persistently', you may receive a contract warning notice, which could lead to contract termination.[37]

Ending a case – monitoring

! Change from previous rules !

3.35 The LSC monitors organisations remotely, using the data they supply as a matter of course when applying for funding or claiming at the end of the case.

The Standard Contract also includes key performance indicators (KPIs). We will deal with all the KPIs in this section for completeness, although some relate to controlled work and some to licensed work. Some KPIs apply to all categories of law and some are category specific. Standard Contract, paras 2.70–2.117 contain the detailed rules.

36 Standard Contract Specification, para 3.67.
37 Standard Contract, clause 14.5.

A key change in the Standard Contract 2010 is that failure to meet KPIs can result in contract sanctions.[38] Therefore, it is important for caseworkers to be aware that their performance under the contract can affect the organisation as a whole.

Key performance indicators

3.36   A summary of the KPIs is as follows.

Standard Contract: KPIs summary – all categories

Civil controlled work – substantive benefit to clients	% varies by category of law – see below
Civil licensed work – substantive benefit to clients (except where varied by category of law – see below)	50% (min)
Judicial Review – substantive benefit to clients – all categories	40% (min)
Alternative Dispute Resolution (ADR) proposed or used (Licensed work) – applies from 1 April 2012	10% (min) (exceptions apply, see below)
Controlled work (non-fixed fee) – assessment reduction	10% (max)
Licensed work – assessment reduction	15% (max)
Fixed fee margin	20% (max)
Matter start usage	85% (min)

Actions against the police etc

Legal Help matters – substantive benefit to clients: does not apply to this category	N/A
Licensed work cases that proceed beyond the Investigative Stage cases – substantive benefit to clients	50% (min)
Certificated cases – substantive benefit to clients	30% (min)
Total net damages recovered for clients must exceed costs – applies from 1 April 2012	2:1

38 Standard Contract Specification, para 2.70.

Clinical negligence

Legal Help matters – substantive benefit to clients: does not apply to this category	N/A
Licensed work cases that proceed beyond the Investigative Stage cases – substantive benefit to clients	60% (min)
Certificated cases – substantive benefit to clients	30% (min)
Total net damages recovered for clients must exceed costs – applies from 1 April 2012	2:1

Community care

Legal Help matters – substantive benefit to clients CA, CB, CC, CD, CE, CF, CI, CG, CH	40% (min)
Certificated cases – substantive benefit to clients	40% (min)

Consumer and general contract

Licensed work cases that proceed beyond the Investigative Stage cases – substantive benefit to clients (professional negligence)	60% (min)
Certificated cases – substantive benefit to clients (professional negligence)	30% (min)

Debt

Legal Help matters – substantive benefit to clients DC, DD, DA, DB, DE, DF, DG, DH, DJ	50% (min)
Certificated cases – substantive benefit to clients	50% (min)

Education

Legal Help matters – substantive benefit to clients EA, EB, EC, ED, EE, EF, EG, EH, EI, EJ	40% (min)
Certificated cases – substantive benefit to clients	40% (min)

Family[39] Not in force – included for information only

Legal Help matters – substantive benefit to clients (does not apply to public family law) FA, FB, FC, FD, FE, FF, FG, FH, FI, FJ	40% (min)
Certificated cases – substantive benefit to clients (private law children)	40% (min)
Certificated cases – substantive benefit to clients (other than public law and private law children)	50% (min)
ADR proposed or used (licensed work) except public family law, domestic abuse – applies from 1 April 2012	10% (min)
Exemption from family mediation justified (confirmed by mediator or LSC) (excludes domestic abuse and child abduction) – applies from 1 April 2012	30% (min)
Level 2 fee claimed (excludes domestic abuse and child abduction) – applies from 1 April 2012	50% (max)
Excludes domestic abuse and child abduction – applies from 1 April 2012 Of level 2 cases, % proceeding under 'other CLS Funding' must not exceed	35%
Excludes domestic abuse and child abduction – applies from 1 April 2012 Of certificated cases, % proceeding to a final hearing or beyond must not exceed	50%

Housing

Legal Help matters – substantive benefit to clients HA, HB, HC, HD, HE, HF, HG, HH, HI, HJ, HK, HL	40% (min)
Certificated housing possession cases – substantive benefit to clients	40% (min)

Immigration

Legal Help matters – substantive benefit to clients IA, IB, IC, ID, IG	15% (min)

39 Following the termination of the tender process, the Standard Contract was not brought in for family work. However the KPIs are included here as guidance on matters the LSC consider important and which may trigger audit or investigation if not met.

Controlled Legal Representation (CLR) – substantive benefit to clients (fast track cases are excluded)	40%

Mental health

Legal Help matters – substantive benefit to clients: does not apply to this category	N/A

Welfare benefits

Legal Help matters – substantive benefit to clients WA, WB, WD, WE, WC, WF	50% (min)
Certificated cases – substantive benefit to clients	40% (min)

Civil contract work – matters and cases providing substantive benefit to clients

3.37   These KPIs require that a specified percentage of your completed cases have outcome codes that the LSC considers demonstrate a substantive benefit to clients. It is therefore extremely important to make sure that the correct codes are identified at the end of each matter. The best person to do this is the caseworker, as he or she will have the best understanding of what happened.

The LSC has published the codes it considers to show 'substantive benefit' at paragraph 2.107 of the Standard Contract Specification. If there is a suitable positive outcome code, you should always select it rather than one that the LSC regards as negative. So, for example, where justified by the case, you should select 'client advised and enabled to plan and manage their affairs better' rather than 'client ceased to give instructions'. Although the Standard Contract did not apply to family or housing with family at the time of writing, it is useful to refer to the codes listed there as they show which the LSC consider show substantive benefit in those categories as well.

ADR proposed or used

3.38   This KPI is designed to encourage people to settle cases outside the court system.

Controlled work (non-fixed fee) – assessment reduction 10 per cent max

3.39   When your exceptional cases are assessed, the costs claimed must not be reduced by more than 10 per cent.

Licensed work – assessment reduction 15 per cent max

3.40   This sets the target in relation to licensed work. The LSC says that its monitoring software gives credit for successful appeals.

Fixed fee margin – 20 per cent max

3.41   The LSC is concerned that some organisations will select clients with straightforward cases that do not require much work, in order to retain a high surplus under each fixed fee case. This KPI can only be met if the total cost of cases under fixed fees when calculated in minutes and items is at least 80 per cent of the appropriate fixed fees.

For example, a provider may have 100 matter starts in debt. The fixed fee for debt cases is £200. If the provider uses all of his or her matter starts and has no exceptional cases, the provider will be paid £20,000. The reported claims made in financial values must be at least £16,000.

Matter start usage – 85 per cent min

3.42   This KPI encourages organisations to use their allocation of matter starts.

CLS Funding Certificates

Scope

3.43   CLS Funding Certificates are also known as certificates for full legal representation. They authorise the conduct of litigation and the provision of advocacy and representation, and include steps preliminary and incidental to proceedings, and steps to settle or avoid proceedings.

Clients in receipt of a CLS funding certificate have a high degree of protection against costs being awarded against them.[40] Failure to advise clients of their ability to seek public funding where available is a matter of professional misconduct[41] (though there is no obligation on any individual solicitor to take on a case on legal aid as opposed to privately as long as the client is aware they could have got legal aid somewhere else).

---

40 Access to Justice Act 1999 s11(1) and the Community Legal Service (Cost Protection) Regulations 2000.
41 Rule 2.03 of the Solicitors' Code of Conduct 2007 para (1)(d): '[You must] discuss with the client how the client will pay, in particular (i) whether the client may be eligible and should apply for public funding.'

Investigative Help

3.44 This is a type of CLS funding certificate which is limited to investigation of the strength of a proposed claim. Investigative Help includes the issue and the conduct of proceedings only so far as this is necessary to obtain disclosure of relevant information or to protect the client's position in relation to any urgent hearing or time limit for the issue of proceedings.

Before you apply for a certificate

3.45 You need to ensure that the general criteria are satisfied:

- The case must concern a matter of England and Wales law, and not in an area excluded by the Access to Justice Act 1999 (see chapter 2 and appendix F).
- The client must be an individual, and a party or proposed party to the proceedings or potential proceedings.
- You must be permitted by contract to carry out the case.
- The client must not have acted unreasonably in this or any other application, or in these or any other proceedings (for example, by concealing information or acting dishonestly to obtain funding – this criterion does not refer to a client's general character or notoriety).
- There must be no alternative funding available to the client, for example through an insurance policy or trade union membership, or through another person or organisation the client could approach to fund the case.
- There must be no alternatives to litigation, or the client must have exhausted available alternatives, such as complaints and ombudsman schemes and alternative dispute resolution mechanisms.
- The application should not be premature – that is, funding under Legal Help or Help at Court would not be more appropriate at this stage.
- It must be necessary for the client to be represented in the proceedings, and funding will be refused if it is not necessary, for example if the case is straightforward and parties would ordinarily not be represented, or if the client does not need to be separately represented.
- Funding will be refused for cases allocated to the small claims track in the county court.[42]

42 See Funding Code, criterion 4, and Funding Code Decision Making Guidance, section 9.

• Representation will be refused if the case is suitable for a conditional fee agreement and the client is likely to be able to enter into a Conditional Fee Agreement (CFA).

Clients abroad

3.46   Although the case must be a matter of England and Wales law, the client does not have to be resident in England or Wales to receive funding. Where clients abroad are entitled to access the courts in England and Wales, they are entitled to legal aid, and it is not uncommon for legal aid to be granted in such cases. However, the Ministry of Justice consulted on taking such cases out of scope in 2010 and it is possible that this right may be amended in future (see above at 3.9).

Clients abroad – procedures

3.47   Where the client is outside the EU (the Channel Islands and Isle of Man counting as part of the EU for these purposes), special procedures must be followed:

• The application must be sent to the London regional office of the LSC and be written in English or French.
• If the client is not a member of UK armed forces posted outside the EU, the application must be sworn before a person authorised under local law to administer oaths or before a British consular official.
• The application must be accompanied by a sworn statement, made by a responsible person who has knowledge of the facts, certifying the client's statement of means as accurate.

However, the additional requirements of this rule may be waived by the LSC if compliance with them would cause serious inconvenience, difficulty or delay.[43]

Clients from abroad

3.48   Under Home Office guidelines,[44] legal aid is not classed as a 'public fund' for the purposes of those with no recourse to public funds. Legal aid is available regardless of immigration status.

---

43 Funding Code Procedures C8.
44 See www.ukba.homeoffice.gov.uk/sitecontent/documents/residency/publicfunds.pdf.

Children

3.49 Where the client is a child, you should note that (unlike controlled work) children cannot apply for funding direct. Where children are parties to litigation in the courts, they should be represented by litigation friends, and it is the litigation friend who should make the application for funding on behalf of the child. However, the application should be in the name of the child. Where the court orders that the child can be a party to the proceedings without a litigation friend, you should make the application on the child's behalf as the child's solicitor.[45]

The child's own means, not those of the litigation friend, are the means to be assessed, and you should therefore put the child's means on the MEANS form. In cases where others might have an interest (for example, in education cases), the LSC can require them to make a financial contribution.[46] Therefore, where you are submitting an application on behalf of a child, you should make clear whether you are seeking to justify non-aggregation of means, and if so, explain why it would be inequitable to aggregate.

Financial eligibility

3.50 See chapter 2. See also 3.63 'Funding from the client's point of view', below. From 15 November 2010, the LSC tightened the requirements for proof of means accompanying applications for certificates. Where the client declares a bank statement on the MEANS form, he or she will be required to provide three months' worth of statements. Where the clients are in employment, they will need to provide three months wage slips (and an L17 will no longer be required unless they cannot do so).[47]

Merits test

3.51 Funding will not be granted unless the case passes the merits test. There are a number of different merits tests depending on the type of case – for those that apply in family and immigration cases, see chapters 4, 5 and 7; for all others, see below.

---

45 Funding Code Procedures C9.
46 Community Legal Service (Financial) Regulations 2000 reg 38(5).
47 See www.legalservices.gov.uk/civil/cls_news_12142.asp?page=1 for more.

The Funding Code Decision Making Guidance is the key reference document for issues relating to CLS Funding Certificates. It can be found in the LSC Manual, volume 3, part C. It can also be downloaded from the LSC website www.legalservices.gov.uk > Community Legal Service (CLS) > Guidance on fees and funding.

The standard merits test is found in the Funding Code Criteria, at criterion 5.7. In relation to Representation Certificates, cases must be put into one of six brackets describing the prospects of success:

(a) Very good – above 80 per cent.

(b) Good – 60 to 80 per cent.

(c) Moderate – 50 to 60 per cent.

(d) Poor – below 50 per cent.

(e) Borderline – where it is not possible to say prospects are better than 50 per cent because of difficult disputes of fact, law or expert evidence.

(f) Unclear.

If prospects are poor or unclear, representation will be refused. If prospects are borderline, representation will be refused unless there is a significant wider public interest (ie the case will benefit a group of individuals wider than the client) or the case is of overwhelming interest to the client (ie it is about life, liberty, or the roof over his or her head).

The Funding Code contains sections on categories of law which contain further guidance on the application of the test to specific cases.

Cost–benefit analysis

3.52   Cases must also meet a cost–benefit test.

Claims for damages

3.53   For claims for damages:

(a) if prospects are very good, likely damages must exceed likely costs;

(b) if prospects are good, likely damages must exceed likely costs by a ratio of 2:1;

(c) if prospects are moderate, likely damages must exceed likely costs by a ratio of 4:1.

Unless there are exceptional circumstances, certificates will not be issued to bring or defend small claims track cases.

Unquantifiable cases

3.54　In unquantifiable cases (including claims other than for damages, and defences to claims for damages), having regard to all the circumstances, including the prospects of success, the likely benefits must justify the likely costs such that the reasonable private paying client would be prepared to bring or defend the case.

Public interest cases

3.55　In public interest cases, having regard to all the circumstances, including the prospects of success, the likely benefits to the client and others must justify the likely costs. Cases involving such issues are referred to the Public Interest Advisory Panel for decision.

Information about the kinds of cases considered appropriate for funding on public interest grounds can be found on the LSC's website at: www.legalservices.gov.uk > Community Legal Service (CLS) > Civil legal aid eligibility > Public Interest Reports.

Changes to prospects of success or cost–benefit

3.56　As the case progresses, inevitably further information and evidence will come to light. If the adviser considers that either limb of the merits test is no longer met, the case should be referred to the LSC for decision. The LSC will issue an embargo, which prevents further work being done, and a notice to show cause as to why the certificate should not be discharged. Either the adviser or the client can reply to the notice to show cause. Similarly, an embargo and notice will be issued if the LSC, on an application to amend, take the view that there is no longer merit in the claim.

The effect of an embargo is that no further work can be done under the certificate, except replying to the show cause notice, until such time as the embargo is lifted. If either the adviser or the client makes representations that the certificate should continue, and the embargo is lifted, the work can continue. If the embargo is not contested or is upheld, the certificate will be discharged.

Forms

3.57　Applications for certificates for legal representation and for Investigative Help are made to the LSC. Except in certain circumstances where urgent work is required (see below), solicitors do not have the power to grant or amend certificates directly.

Special procedures also apply in urgent cases (see below).

You should complete form CLSAPP1 with your client and submit it to the LSC. The form needs to be accompanied by the relevant MEANS form – MEANS 1, MEANS 2, etc – depending on the client's circumstances. Evidence of the client's means covering the last three months will also be required. See chapter 2 for details of financial eligibility; and volume 3, part D of the LSC Manual also has detailed guidance.

The CLSAPP1 contains a statement of case, and this should be completed in as much detail as possible, as this is the part of the application that demonstrates that the criteria for granting a certificate are met. Don't forget that your client's statement is not the same as a statement of case! You have to explain to someone at the LSC, who has not met your client, why what the client says amounts to a cause of action and why it should be funded.

It is also extremely important to ensure that forms are completed correctly: one in four forms is rejected by the LSC because it is not signed. This wastes your time and the LSC's time, and delays the client's case.

See appendix B for an application checklist.

Refusals and appeals

3.58   A refusal of a certificate on the basis of merit can be appealed, within 21 days of the decision, to the Funding Review Committee of the LSC. A refusal on financial grounds cannot be appealed, though a fresh application can be made if circumstances change.

Funding

3.59   Civil CLS Funding Certificates are funded on an hourly rate basis. See chapter 10 for more information.

In almost every case, a CLS funding certificate is only granted subject to two limitations:

- a particular step in the proceedings, such as 'all steps up to the filing of a defence and thereafter obtaining counsel's opinion', or 'all steps up to a case management conference'; and

- a costs limitation, usually £2,500. Costs limitations include profit costs (and any enhancement or uplift), counsels' fees and disbursements, but not VAT.

It is extremely important not to do work outside the scope of either limitation as you will not be paid for it. It is particularly easy to lose track of counsels' fees and disbursements, and it really helps to keep all documents relating to financial issues together in the file.

Limitations can be amended on application to the LSC or under devolved powers in urgent circumstances (see below for more information about devolved powers).

Amendments to scope and costs

3.60   Requests for amendments to either scope or costs limitations are made to the LSC, using form CLSAPP8. In making a request, the adviser will be obliged to demonstrate that the case continues to satisfy both limitations of the merits test, and state what new scope or costs limitation is required. Therefore, there must be merit not only in the case as a whole, but in each step of the proceedings.

Timing the application for an amendment has to be done with care, as the date an amendment takes effect is the date of the decision. If you leave your application until the last minute, you risk exceeding the current limitation and not being paid. On the other hand, you must justify why the work needs to be done at the particular time, as the LSC will refuse any amendment considered to be premature. They will also refuse an amendment that might become redundant due to some other event taking place.

Use of counsel and amendments for a QC

3.61   A CLS funding certificate allows you to instruct counsel; but if the case warrants a QC, you must apply to the LSC for authority. See the LSC's Costs Assessment Guidance for more information.

Disbursements and prior authority

3.62   In many cases, disbursements can be large, and there is a risk to the organisation that they will not be allowed, or allowed in full, on assessment of the bill.

Therefore, the prior authority scheme allows an organisation to apply to the LSC for authority to incur a disbursement in advance, if it is above £100. The application is made using form CLSAPP8, accompanied by a quote for the disbursement and reasons why it is necessary. The advantage of having authority is that no question as to the validity of the disbursement can be raised on assessment of the bill, unless and to the extent that it exceeds the amount or scope of the authority. Prior authority therefore gives a measure of costs protection for expensive disbursements.

Funding from the client's point of view

Contributions

3.63   Clients on passporting benefits or with very limited means do not have to make contributions to the cost of their case during its lifetime; but they may need to make payment at the end of their case if money or property is recovered or preserved, under the statutory charge (see below at 3.65 for more information). It is therefore easy for such clients to be lulled into feeling that their legal aid is going to be free, when it is not, and so it is even more important to ensure they understand the effect of the statutory charge and are given a costs estimate which is revised at every relevant point throughout the case.

If the client's capital is between the lower and upper thresholds, the client is required to pay a contribution. The amount of the contribution is the lower of (a) the amount by which capital exceeds the lower threshold and (b) the total estimated costs of the case.

If the client's disposable income is between the lower and upper threshold, a contribution will be payable. The amount of the contribution depends on the amount by which income is above the lower threshold, but is a fixed sum plus a percentage of the excess each month for the life of the certificate.

If the client fails to pay a contribution, after 21 days you will receive a show cause notice from the LSC, and all work will have to stop until the client makes payment. See 'Changes to prospects of success or cost–benefit' at 3.55 for more information.

Should the amount paid in contributions exceed the final costs as assessed, the client will be entitled to a refund of the difference.

Changes in circumstances

3.64   Clients must be financially eligible on both capital and income. They must inform the LSC of any change in their means. A reassessment will then be carried out.

Statutory charge

3.65 The charge is governed by the Community Legal Service (Financial) Regulations 2000, and the Community Legal Service (Costs) Regulations 2000. The statutory charge under certificates operates at all levels of service, and across all categories except family mediation. It operates on both property recovered and property preserved.

If a matter is funded by Legal Help *only*, the charge does not arise in any category.

If a case is funded initially under Legal Help and goes on to a certificate, if the charge arises, it also applies to the Legal Help costs.

See chapter 4 for information on the way the statutory charge applies in family cases.

If money or property is at issue in the proceedings, then the successful client is at risk of the charge. A claimant client whose claim succeeds recovers property; a defendant client who resists a claim preserves property.[48] Even if title to the property is not in issue, but possession of it is, the charge still arises.[49] Where the proceedings result in payment to someone other than the client, but the payment is for the benefit of the client (eg repayment of a debt; payments to a dependant), the charge arises.[50]

The charge gives the LSC first call on any money or property recovered in the proceedings. It is used to repay the costs of funding the case. So, if a claimant in a housing disrepair case wins compensation of £5,000, and costs under the certificate and Legal Help were £1,500, then (assuming no costs were awarded from the other side) the charge would operate and the client would receive only £3,500 (recovery). On the other hand, if the client was defending a claim for a £5,000 share in property and won the case, if the costs were £1,500, he or she would be liable to pay £1,500 (preservation).

All monies due to a client in legal proceedings must be paid to his or her solicitor if the client is legally aided in any way.[51]

All property is caught by the charge, unless exempt by regulation. Exempt property is currently limited to:

- periodical payments of maintenance;
- interim payments in Inheritance Act proceedings;
- the first 50 per cent of a redundancy award;

---

48 *Hanlon v The Law Society* [1980] 2 All ER 199.
49 *Parkes v Legal Aid Board* [1994] 2 FLR 850.
50 Access to Justice Act 1999 s10(7).
51 Community Legal Service (Costs) Regulations reg 18.

- the client's clothes, household furniture or tools of the trade (except in exceptional circumstances);
- state benefits and pensions, and any other property subject to a statutory prohibition on assignment.[52]

The amount of the charge is calculated to compensate the LSC for funding the case, and is therefore the amount of costs as assessed (less any contribution paid by the client), less costs recovered from the other side. Therefore, the amount is the net amount paid to the supplier by the LSC.

If the charge arises, the client will have a financial interest in the organisation's bill of costs. Clients should be advised of the potential effect of the charge at the outset of the case, given regular costs updates, and at the end of the case be given a copy of the bill and advised of their right to make representations on the bill, including at any assessment hearing. The only element of the bill that does not form part of the charge is the costs of assessment.[53]

Recovery of money

3.66   Costs Regulations reg 18 provides that all monies owing to a funded client should be paid to his or her solicitor, not to the client direct. The only exceptions are maintenance, and money paid into court to be invested for the client's benefit in the limited circumstances set out in reg 18(1) and (2). Costs Regulations reg 20(1)(a) obliges the solicitor to report any recovery or preservation to the LSC straight away.

Once money is received, the solicitor may make a judgment as to whether it is exempt property. If it is, it may be paid to the client. If not, it must be paid to the LSC. In cases of doubt, the best course is to pay to the LSC, which can refund the client. If the solicitor fails to protect the LSC's charge and pays the money to the client without deducting it, the solicitor is liable.[54]

Costs Regulations reg 20(4) entitles the solicitor to apply to the Regional Director for permission to pay to the client money which is not required to satisfy the charge – for example, if £10,000 is recovered and costs will not exceed £5,000, an application can be made to return the extra £5,000 to the client.

Unless an application to defer the charge is being made (see below), the solicitor should send a cheque for the value of the money

52 Community Legal Service (Financial) Regulations reg 44.
53 Community Legal Service (Financial) Regulations reg 40(4).
54 Standard Contract Standard Terms, clause 14.12; Specification, para 5.37.

recovered with the final bill to the LSC. The LSC will assess the bill, pay solicitor and counsel, and return the balance to the client.

Recovery of property, and preservation cases

3.67 In such cases, money is unlikely to be paid to the solicitor. Instead, the solicitor will report recovery or preservation to the LSC. The LSC will pay the costs of solicitor and counsel, and pursue the client for the costs.

Enforcement of the charge – the LSC's powers

3.68 The LSC has no power to waive the charge altogether, except in very limited circumstances (basically, where it was recognised as a wider public interest case from the start and the LSC funded this client but not others to act as a test case; Financial Regulations reg 47).

In certain circumstances, the charge can be deferred under the Financial Regulations reg 52. The conditions are:

- the property is the client's (or his or her dependant's) family home; or in family cases, money to be used to purchase a home for the client or dependants; and
- the LSC is satisfied that the home will provide sufficient security for the charge; and
- the charge is registered with the Land Registry.

If the charge is deferred, simple interest at 8 per cent per annum will accrue from the date of registration. Interest is due on the lower of the value of the charge or the value of the home (Financial Regulations reg 53(3)).

Otherwise, the charge is payable immediately unless the LSC agrees to accept payment by instalment, and the LSC can enforce the charge, if necessary, by enforcement proceedings in the courts.

The solicitor should report to the LSC using the appropriate ADMIN form.

Ending a case

3.69 CLS funding certificates come to an end in one of three ways: being discharged or revoked, or when a final bill is submitted at the end of the case. See 3.35 above for information about LSC contract monitoring and key performance indicators, using data taken from closed cases.

Discharge

3.70   When the LSC decides that a certificate should not continue because changing circumstances indicate that funding is no longer justified on the merits, or because the client is no longer financially eligible, the certificate will be discharged. The effect of this is that the client is no longer in receipt of public funding. If discharge is at the instigation of the LSC, there is a right to appeal to the Funding Review Committee. Once the certificate is discharged, the case is at an end and the file can be billed. At the end of a case, the adviser should usually apply for the certificate to be discharged.

Revocation

3.71   The effect of revocation is not simply to end the funding of a case – revocation retrospectively removes funding from the client, so that he or she never had a valid CLS funding certificate at all. The LSC will only revoke a certificate when information comes to light to suggest that it should never have been issued, for example because a client concealed information about his or her resources because the client was never in fact eligible. The effect of revocation is that the client becomes liable for all costs incurred under the certificate.

Submission of final bill

3.72   See chapter 10.

Urgent cases

Scope

3.73   The LSC defines a case as urgent if it is necessary to carry out work before a substantive application could be made and determined. The LSC aims to process most substantive applications within four weeks. Therefore an emergency certificate is unlikely to be granted unless the work has to be carried out before a substantive certificate could be granted and cannot wait without serious adverse consequences to the client, for example risk to the life, liberty or physical safety of the client or the client's family or the roof over their heads; or the delay will cause a significant risk of miscarriage of justice, or unreasonable hardship to the client, or irretrievable problems in handling the case; and in either case there are no other appropriate options available to deal with the risk.

Other appropriate options could be: contacting the police where life or physical safety are at risk; seeking an adjournment of a hearing or an extension of time; dealing with the urgent work via another level of service (eg Legal Help or Help at Court); or by the client taking urgent steps in person where that was reasonable.

You should also consider whether it would be more appropriate to grant or amend a certificate under devolved powers (see 3.79 below) before you submit an application to the LSC for decision.

Financial eligibility

3.74 See chapter 2. See also 'Funding from the client's point of view', 3.63 above.

Emergency representation may be granted without a full means assessment. This clearly has advantages for the client, but it creates a financial risk for the CLS fund.

Revocation

3.75 The client may turn out to be financially ineligible, may not co-operate with the means assessment, or may not accept an offer, should a contribution be required. In all of those circumstances the emergency certificate will be revoked (ie cancelled and the client treated as though he or she was never in receipt of legal aid).

The client will be responsible for the full costs of his or her representation. In addition he or she will not have the protection from opponents' costs provided by a representation certificate. You must therefore advise the client of this and give a costs estimate. If the certificate is revoked, you should submit a bill in the usual way; the LSC will pursue the client for the costs.

Merits test

3.76 The appropriate merits test (see 3.51 above) must be satisfied, as well as the urgency criteria.

However, as the situation will be urgent, it may often be that only limited information is available. If so, emergency representation may be granted where it appears likely on the information available that the merits test will be satisfied.

Forms

3.77 Emergency applications for civil legal aid certificates are made on form CLSAPP6 and are submitted by fax. Emergency amendments to limitations on existing certificates are made on CLSAPP8.

The LSC Regional Office must receive the substantive application within five working days of the emergency grant. If you fail to submit the application, the emergency certificate only covers work done within the first five working days, and you will not be paid for work beyond that period.

Funding

3.78   Emergency certificates will usually be limited to £1,500 (profit costs, counsels' fees and disbursements, but not VAT).

Emergency certificates only last for four weeks, so you must ensure that you are covered by a substantive certificate from that date, or else you will not be paid. This time limit cannot be extended.

Devolved powers

Scope

3.79   The practice needs to have a Quality Mark and a contract in the relevant category to exercise devolved powers. The Standard Contract Specification (paras 5.4–5.7) lists the devolved powers available. The LSC has announced that it will take a more restricted approach to devolved powers from March 2011. The LSC monitors the use of devolved powers, and may suspend or terminate them if they have been seriously misused. The LSC has issued guidelines in respect of the consequences that will follow if devolved powers are used incorrectly. These are graded to reflect the seriousness of the error.[55]

Certificates can be granted for full Legal Representation in urgent cases. You may not use devolved powers to grant a certificate where there is an outstanding certificate or application at the LSC, or where a previous application has been refused and there is no clear and relevant change of circumstances to suggest that a reapplication would be granted.

Some limitations on substantive certificates can be amended in urgent circumstances. For civil non-family certificates, the following codes can be amended: CV079, CV080, CV081, CV092, CV083, CV084, CV085, CV086, CV091, CV092, CV095, CV096, CV097, CV099; certificates may not be amended to correct mistakes or to change solicitor. The devolved power does not extend to amending

55 LSC Manual, volume 3, part C, Funding Code Decision Making Guidance.

the description of proceedings or adding parties to the proceedings or additional proceedings. Guidance can be found in the LSC Manual, volume 3, part C, Funding Code Decision Making Guidance.

Steps for granting an emergency certificate

3.80   1   Select a matter type code (eg NEMPL – employment).
- See LSC Manual, volume 3, part E for a full list.

2   Identify the wording code for the allowable proceedings (eg EM001: wording code 'To be represented in an action for breach of contract of employment and/or wrongful dismissal against the opponent').
- See LSC Manual, volume 3, part E for a full list.
- If there is no appropriate wording code, the LSC Regional Office must be contacted.

3   Apply an appropriate scope limitation wording (eg CV001: 'Limited to all steps up to and including the hearing on ...').
- See LSC Manual, volume 3, part E for a full list.

4   Apply a costs limitation.
- See LSC Manual, volume 3, part E for a full list.
- Costs limitations include profit costs, disbursements and counsels' fees, but *not* VAT.
- In emergency applications this will generally be £1,500, though the costs limitation can be granted or amended up to £10,000.

5   Submit an application for a substantive certificate within five working days.

Refusals under devolved powers

3.81   There is no right of appeal against the refusal to grant an emergency certificate.[56]

Financial eligibility

3.82   As 'Urgent cases', above.

Merits test

3.83   As 'Urgent cases', above.

---

56 LSC Manual, volume 3, part C, Funding Code Decision Making Guidance.

Forms

3.84   Devolved powers grants are made using CLSAPP1. Devolved powers amendments are made using CLSAPP8. MEANS6 can be faxed to the LSC for a preliminary assessment.

A substantive application must be submitted to the LSC using CLSAPP1, or in the case of an amendment CLSAPP8, within five working days of the exercise of devolved powers.

Funding

3.85   As 'Urgent cases', above.

Very expensive cases

3.86   One of the problems to bedevil public funding for legal services is that individual high-cost cases have historically consumed a high proportion of the budget. In November 2001, the Lord Chancellor issued a Direction that created a limited budget to fund CLS cases expected to cost more than £25,000.

Scope

3.87   The Special Cases Unit (SCU) manages the budget and agrees individual case contracts for cases which fall into five types:

- Individual very high-cost cases: where costs are expected to exceed £25,000, such as Children Act 1989, clinical negligence and judicial review cases.
- Cases which might exceed £75,000 if they proceeded to contested trial, final hearing or the conclusion of any appeal stage before the Court of Appeal or House of Lords.
- Multi-party actions (MPAs): these range from 1,000-claimant actions to 10-claimant actions.
- Exceptional funding cases: when funding is approved outside the Funding Code criteria.
- Exceptional 'one-off' contracts with firms without a Standard Contract (Civil), eg where clients run out of money during a case and the firm does not have a contract.

The SCU can treat more than one set of proceedings or certificates as a single case when deciding whether the cost thresholds are reached, for example in public law Children Act proceedings involving numerous parties.

Cases can be referred to the SCU by the LSC Regional Office at any stage if it appears that they may meet the criteria.

Financial eligibility

3.88 See chapter 2. See also 'Funding from the client's point of view', 3.63 above.

The LSC has a limited power to waive eligibility rules in relation to MPAs.

Merits test

3.89 Only three types of case are automatically entitled to funding:

- special Children Act proceedings;
- proceedings in which the client's life or liberty are at risk;
- judicial review proceedings in which:
  - the court has given permission for the case to continue, and
  - the case:
    - has a significant wider interest or
    - is of overwhelming interest to the client or
    - raises significant human rights issues.

However, in practice, the LSC has stated that every case that passed the normal merits test received funding.[57]

Under the General Funding Code, clinical negligence cases which have moderate prospects of success (50–60 per cent) need a damages-to-costs ratio of only 2:1, which is less than most other cases. However, SCU clinical negligence cases must have a damages-to-costs ratio of 4:1.

Forms

3.90 You need to submit:

- a statement of what the case is about;
- a statement of objectives – what is in issue and what is likely to be secured;

---

57 LSC Manual, volume 3, part C, Funding Code Guidance section 15, release 7, September 2008.

- a case analysis – this must include:
  - issues of law – favourable and unfavourable, setting out how any obstacles will be overcome;
  - issues of fact – favourable and unfavourable, assessing the evidence supporting each;
  - expert evidence required – and why;
  - costs in issue – eg amount of claim for damages – special rules for clinical negligence see below;
  - key events and resources required – likely costs of solicitors, counsel, experts and disbursements;
  - risk analysis – and how to deal with risks identified;
  - statement of prospects of success within the terms of the funding code;
- a funding code assessment – addressing each relevant element of the funding code and stating how each is satisfied;
- case theory – a short statement (five sentences or less) explaining why the client will win the case;
- broadly costed overall case plan, including:
  - when counsel and experts will be instructed;
  - when the case management conference will be held;
  - when the trial will take place;
  - forecast of cumulative costs – at key events and appropriate intervals and at 31 March each year;
  - fully costed plan for the next stage of the case, showing an overall price for the stage – also setting out costs of all elements of work to be performed and costs to be incurred;
  - breakdown of costs to date;
  - details of any costs-sharing agreements;
- of the person managing the case, and of the team (if any) who will be doing the work;
  - names of person managing the case and the team members;
  - what they will be doing;
  - evidence of their suitability;
- evidence of the firm's suitability to handle the work to its conclusion.

There is more information about what to submit to the SCU (including sample case plans) on the LSC's website at www.legalservices. gov.uk > Community Legal Service (CLS) > High cost civil cases.

Funding

3.91 The SCU, which is based in the LSC's London and South Tyneside offices, has produced a guidance pack which is available from the LSC's website at www.legalservices.gov.uk > Community Legal Service (CLS) > High cost civil cases. Funding is agreed as set out in the case plan. There is very little flexibility to move costs from one heading to another once they are agreed. It can also be difficult to get amendments to the case plan accepted.

For a case where inter partes costs are expected to be paid if successful, funding is provided on a risk-sharing basis. If it settles, recovery is at full inter partes rates; but if unsuccessful, the LSC will pay at specified hourly rates with no mark-up (normally £90.00 for senior counsel, £70.00 per hour for solicitors and £50.00 for junior counsel).

There are specific rates of payment for contracted cases, which vary depending on the type of case, prospects of success, and any exceptional circumstances.

Claims can be made on form CLSCLAIM1, at the hourly rates applying, for costs to date at the start of the contract, and at the end of each stage. If a stage lasts longer than six months, a claim for costs can be made every six months. These are applications for payment on account, made on form CLSPOA1.

At the end of the case, claims can be made in the same way as under an ordinary certificate (see chapter 10), though at the hourly rate agreed in the contract. If no costs were awarded, and the statutory charge does not apply, form CLSCLAIM1 should be used. Otherwise, CLSCLAIM2 and the appropriate ADMIN form are required. If costs are recovered from the other side, the LSC is entitled to the recoupment of payments on account. High cost case bills are always assessed by the LSC, not the courts.

Conducting a family private law case

Introduction

4.1   This chapter deals with conducting family private law cases. There are separate chapters on the general rules that apply to all civil cases, as well as family public law, immigration and mental health, as they have their own funding schemes and rules.

In chapter 2, we saw that there are three key stages in providing publicly funded services: to ensure that (i) the matter is within scope, (ii) the client is financially eligible and (iii) the case meets the merits test. In addition, you need to ensure that forms are completed correctly and funding is obtained. This chapter explains how these steps are taken successfully in respect of family private law.

Where appropriate, you will be referred back to chapter 3, as that chapter sets out the general rules.

See appendices G and H for a summary of the Legal Services Commission's (LSC's) Costs Assessment Guidance, in respect of the most common queries raised by caseworkers.

Scope

4.2   Scope is primarily determined by the Access to Justice Act 1999 (as amended). As we saw in chapter 3, Schedule 2 to the Act excludes a number of matters from the scope of Community Legal Service (CLS) funding. However, these do not cause many problems for family lawyers.

It is worth remembering that the then Lord Chancellor made directions in April 2001 to bring some excluded services back into scope (Exceptions to the Exclusions). He issued a direction which allows advice on wills, where the client is over 70, disabled, the parent of a disabled person or a single parent making provision to appoint a guardian. The latter fall within the category definition of family work.

For a full list of the work that can be done in the family category, see appendix D.

Controlled work and licensed work

4.3   Controlled work is granted by the solicitor according to rules under the Standard Contract. It is called 'controlled' because the LSC controls the number of matter starts which are allowed each year. The kinds of controlled work that are relevant to family practitioners are

Legal Help and Family Help Lower. Help at Court is not available in family work.

You need a CLS funding certificate – sometimes known as a legal aid certificate, or full representation certificate – to represent a client in legal proceedings. This is called licensed work, as the firm has a general licence to do such work, and numbers of matter starts are not limited. Certificates may be granted by the LSC, or, in urgent circumstances, granted under devolved powers by the organisation.

Private family law – controlled work

Legal Help – level 1

4.4   Legal Help allows you to provide advice and assistance in relation to a specific matter, but does not cover issuing proceedings, advocacy, or instruction of an advocate (although you can obtain counsel's opinion, where justifiable). It does not cover the provision of mediation and arbitration, although it does allow you to advise your client on issues arising from mediation and arbitration.[1]

Representation is not available in uncontested proceedings for divorce or judicial separation, except in very limited circumstances. Straightforward divorce work, where representation at court is not required, should be done under Legal Help.

Legal Help is also known as level 1 in the family standard fees scheme.

Scope

4.5   See chapter 3 for information on the following:

- whether other funding may be available, and public funding should not granted;
- what to do if your client has received previous advice from another organisation;
- what to do if your client has received previous advice from your organisation;
- clients from abroad or clients who are abroad;
- clients who are children.

Legal Help is designed to cover cases which complete after little work beyond the first meeting with the client, and covers the consequential

---

1 Funding Code, criterion 2.1.

letters to the client and any letters to a third party. If you do more work in relation to children or finance issues, you may well be able to go on to grant Family Help (Lower) funding (see below).

Domestic violence and child abduction cases

4.6   These cases are only included in the standard fee scheme as far as level 1. Level 2 is not designed to cover these cases and you will often find that you need to issue proceedings under a certificate very quickly.

Wills and change of name cases

4.7   Where these cases fall within the scope of legal aid, they are only included in the standard fee scheme as far as level 1. You can make a will for a single parent wishing to appoint a guardian for his or her child, but otherwise wills for people over 70 and people with disabilities are outside the scope of the family category and you would need to use a tolerance matter start (they are always tolerance, since they are in the 'miscellaneous' category, and no 'miscellaneous' contracts are awarded) (see chapter 2) – you will only be able to do this if you have tolerances allowed under your schedule.

Cases that would meet the sufficient benefit test would be to change of name of a child, so that children of the family can have the same last name, or to protect a victim of domestic abuse. Change of a child's name is defined as family work, but adult change of name is out of scope. See appendix D.

Divorce petitioner cases

4.8   There is a 'stand alone' fee which applies to divorce, nullity, judicial separation and proceedings to dissolve civil partnerships. This covers cases where the client requires advice to initiate proceedings, they are issued, and there are no children or finance issues that would justify the grant of Family Help (Lower). We will look at this in more detail later on.

Financial eligibility

4.9   See chapter 2 for more information on the following:

- passporting benefits;
- assessment of capital;
- assessment of income;
- reassessment of means.

See chapter 3 for more information on the following:

- evidence of means;
- when you can start work without evidence of means;
- reassessing the client's eligibility if their means change significantly.

Merits test

4.10 The Legal Help merits test is known as the 'sufficient benefit test', and in full states: 'Help may only be provided where there is sufficient benefit to the client, having regard to the circumstances of the matter, including the personal circumstances of the client, to justify work or further work being carried out'.[2] The general approach to the test is set out in the guidance to the Funding Code (LSC Manual, volume 3, part C). The question is whether a reasonable private paying client of moderate means would pay for the work. In most family cases, the test is met.

Forms

4.11 The form is the CW1 Legal Help, Help at Court and Family Help (Lower) form.

The assessment of means and client's details sections must be fully completed, and signed by the client, normally in the presence of someone from your organisation, before you start doing any legal work.[3]

How many Legal Help forms?

4.12 You can have more than one Legal Help matter open at the same time, but this is very unusual in family work. It may be permissible if your client has entirely separate family disputes.[4] The LSC gives the example of disputes in respect of different family relationships, where any potential proceedings would be separate. This would apply, for example where your client was the mother of children of different fathers each of whom was applying separately for residence.

---

2 Funding Code, criterion 5.2.
3 Unified Contract Specification para 2.11.
4 Unified Contract Specification para 10.156.

Funding

4.13   Legal Help – level 1 is paid as two different standard fees.[5] The high-er fee is only applicable when your client is the petitioner in a divorce and there are no significant children or finance issues. In all other cases, the lower level 1 fee is payable (whether or not combined with a level 2 fee).

Divorce, child abduction and domestic abuse cases that exceed three times the fixed fee when calculated at hourly rates, can be claimed in full (see chapter 10 for more information about claiming exceptional cases).

Other level 1 cases cannot be claimed as exceptional.

There is more information on the standard fees scheme in the questions and answers on the LSC's website at: www.legalservices. gov.uk > Community Legal Service (CLS) > Civil areas of work > Family > Legal guidance and updates.

Family Help (Lower) – level 2

! Change from previous rules !

Scope

4.14   This covers the provision of ongoing assistance with a 'significant dispute'.[6]

The LSC removed the requirement for a second meeting, which was referred to in the pre 9 May 2011 version of the Unified Contract. This was been controversial, as the LSC's training materials did not draw practitioners' attention to the need for a second meeting and LSC staff had suggested that such a meeting was not always required. Point of Principle of General Importance CLS 54 was certified on 20 December 2010, which confirmed that a second face to face meeting was not essential.

Post 9 May 2011, you need to demonstrate that there have been 'substantive negotiations' in relation to a 'significant dispute'.

---

5   Current fees and hourly rates are found in the Standard Contract Payment Annex. You can download the contract from the LSC's website at: www. legalservices.gov.uk > Community Legal Service (CLS) > Civil contracts > 2010 Standard Contract.

6   Unified Contract (Civil) Specification para 10.58.

Family Help (Lower) – children

4.15 This covers all work up to the issue of proceedings. It is not necessary to obtain a consent order to formalise any agreement in respect of children, although if you are claiming a settlement fee (see 4.20 below), it is advisable to record the agreement in writing, so that the LSC can see that it was a 'genuine settlement to conclude that aspect of the case'.[7]

Family Help (Lower) – finance

4.16 This covers all work including the issue of proceedings and all work required to obtain a consent order.[8]

Family Help (Lower) – children and finance

4.17 Where a case involves substantial children and finance issues both the children and finance fees may be claimed.

You claim two Family Help (Lower) fees, one for children and one for finance, where the merits criteria are met[9] (see merits test at 4.27 below).

! Change from previous rules !

Where a case involves more than one issue, the LSC requires time to be apportioned equally between them.[10]

Forms

4.18 You do not need another CW1 Legal Help, Help at Court and Family Help (Lower) form. Simply tick the box at the bottom of page 5 of the original form to affirm that the criteria for level 2 are met.

Funding

4.19 Family Help (Lower) (level 2) is paid under standard fees, although cases that reach the escape threshold (three times the fixed fee at levels 1 and 2 combined) can be paid in full at hourly rates.

For more information about claiming exceptional cases, see chapter 10.

---

7 Unified Contract Specification para 10.65.
8 Unified Contract Specification para 10.67.
9 Unified Contract Specification para 10.59.
10 Unified Contract Specification para 10.59.

Settlement fees

4.20   Settlement fees can be claimed for cases that conclude at this level, without the issue of proceedings (save to obtain a consent order – Unified Contract Specification para 10.59). In order to be considered as 'settled', that aspect of the case (ie children or finance) must be fully resolved at that level and the client actively involved in a decision to accept a settlement. The agreement on financial issues must be recorded in writing or in a consent order. It is advisable to record the agreement in respect of children in writing as well.

If the client ceases to give instructions, dies, or the parties are reconciled, the settlement fee cannot be claimed.[11]

! Change from previous rules !

You must wait for 21 days after the case has been concluded before claiming the settlement fee. In relation to financial issues, if the settlement breaks down, and you become aware of the fact within six months, the settlement fee becomes repayable. In relation to children issues, the period is three months.[12]

For more information about when you can or should close a case, see chapter 3.

Case study

Mrs Brown had been married for 11 years and has two children, James and Jennifer. She came to see us about her divorce. She was on reasonably good terms with her husband.

We referred them to mediation and they came to agreement on how they wanted to divide the assets, maintenance, whom the children should live with and how they should visit, spend holidays, etc.

We drafted the petition on the basis of the memorandum of understanding (MOU) prepared by the mediator, and obtained a consent order. The decree absolute has just come through. Can we claim the level 2 fees for children and finance?

If you provided your client with legal advice on the MOU, and carried out further legal work, the case meets the definition of a 'significant family dispute'. Therefore you can claim:

---

11 Unified Contract Specification para 10.65(c).
12 Unified Contract Specification para 10.65(b).

Legal Help level 1	96.00
Family Help (Lower) (children)	221.00
Family Help (Lower) (finance)	231.00
Settlement fee (children)	132.00
Settlement fee (finance)	139.00
	Total £819.00

Funding from the client's point of view – the statutory charge

4.21 For information about the statutory charge, see chapter 3.

The charge is governed by the Community Legal Service (Financial) Regulations 2000, and the Community Legal Service (Costs) Regulations 2000.

The statutory charge does not apply to cases completing at Legal Help (level 1), but if the case goes beyond level 1, the level 1 costs are included in the costs caught by the charge.

The home is exempt from the charge in cases completing under Legal Help, Help at Court or Family Help (Lower). It does not apply to maintenance payments. However, even where a lump sum is paid, the statutory charge does not apply to standard fee cases. This is a powerful incentive to clients to settle at level 2, as in most cases their legal aid will be free.

However, in exceptional cases, the charge applies, but only to costs above the exceptional case threshold (ie those costs over three times the standard fee).

Where the charge arises only under Legal Help, Help at Court or Family Help (Lower), it is in favour of the firm (and is known as the solicitor's charge). You may apply to the LSC to waive it, if its operation would cause grave hardship or distress to the client, or where it would be unreasonably difficult to enforce.

The firm collects the appropriate sum from the client and claims the net costs from the LSC.

But note that at level 3 (certificated work), the charge applies in favour of the LSC and includes the fees at levels 1 and 2.[13]

---

13 Community Legal Service (Financial) Regulations 2000 reg 45.

Certificates – private family law

Scope

4.22   A CLS funding certificate authorises the conduct of litigation and the provision of advocacy and representation, and includes steps preliminary and incidental to proceedings, and steps to settle or avoid proceedings.

! Change from previous rules !

The LSC introduced a new funding scheme known as the Private Family Law Representation Scheme (PFLRS) from 9 May 2011. Application and limitation procedures and requirements remained the same as under the previous scheme. Under the PFLRS there are two levels of funding:

- Family Help Higher – Level 3: To cover all work up to the preparation for final hearing.
- Legal Representation – Level 4: To cover all work from preparation for a final hearing up to and including all work to conclude a case after the final hearing, eg application to the court of first instance for permission to appeal, and advice on the merits of an appeal against a final order.

The LSC also introduced a new fee scheme for advocacy, the Family Advocacy Scheme (FAS) from 9 May 2011. For more information on the fee schemes see chapter 10. For more on the FAS, see chapter 13.

Before you apply for a certificate, see chapter 3:

- general criteria;
- clients who are abroad;
- clients from abroad;
- clients who are children.

Mediation

4.23   The LSC expects every effort to be made to resolve issues through mediation rather than through contested proceedings. Therefore, you should encourage your client to consider mediation wherever possible. Clients must attend an intake assessment with a mediator, unless one of the following applies:

- Family proceedings are already in existence and the client is a respondent/defendant who has been notified of a court date which is within eight weeks of the date of notification.

- The client has a reasonable fear of domestic abuse from a partner or former partner (see below for more information).
- The client or other party cannot see a mediator (examples given include where bail conditions prevent contact with an ex-partner, or where the client is in custody or hospitalised, or lives more than two hours away, etc).
- The other party is unwilling to attend mediation.
- Emergency representation is required.

Domestic violence and abuse

4.24 The LSC does not consider the fact that domestic abuse or violence has taken place should automatically rule out consideration of mediation. They will accept that it is not reasonable to consider mediation if an allegation of domestic abuse has resulted in a police investigation or the issuing of civil proceedings for the protection of the applicant within the last 12 months. In other circumstances, you will need to justify why it is not appropriate to involve the police, for example where this might jeopardise the long-term financial or other interests of the family, or if you have reason to believe that the police will not be able to assist, or if they have been contacted but have failed to respond or to provide adequate assistance in the past.

It is unlikely that funding will be granted for committal proceedings if criminal proceedings have been instigated by the police. Breach of a non-molestation order became a criminal offence in 2007, and the LSC would ordinarily expect the client to report a breach to the police before seeking an amendment to the certificate for committal.

The LSC normally expects a warning letter to be sent to the respondent. However, this is not an absolute rule, for example if you can show that a warning letter might endanger the client.

See the LSC Manual, volume 3, part C for more information on domestic abuse cases.

Financial eligibility

4.25 See chapter 2.

Waiver in domestic abuse cases

4.26 Regulation 5E of the Community Legal Service (Financial) Regulations 2000 gives the LSC discretion to waive the upper disposable income and capital limits for victims of domestic violence seeking protection from the court. However, any contribution from income or capital that is applicable under the regulations cannot be waived. If granting a certificate under devolved powers, you can assume the LSC will exercise its discretion; but when you submit the substantive application, you should make clear that the case is a domestic violence case, and that you are seeking the waiver. It is best to do this by including it in a covering letter and also by clearly marking the front of the MEANS form.

You should advise your client that, although the upper limit may be waived, the liability to pay contributions is not. The usual rules on contributions will apply, so the client's funding will be revoked in the event of non-payment. Clients with income much above the upper limit who successfully obtain a waiver can find themselves paying quite substantial contributions, so you should clearly advise the client to expect that. You can provide an indication of how much this will be by using the LSC's eligibility calculator at www.legalservices. gov.uk > Community Legal Service (CLS) > Civil legal aid eligibility > Eligibility calculator.

This is particularly important in emergency cases, since if you grant an emergency certificate, the client is offered a full certificate with contributions and declines the offer, he or she will be liable for the full costs you incur on the emergency certificate.

Merits test

4.27   This varies according to the type of case – see below.

Stage 1 – Prospects of success

4.28   On the application form, all cases must be put into one of three brackets describing the prospects of success:

- Average or above.
- Poor.
- Borderline or unclear, where prospects are not poor but it is not possible to say they are better than 50 per cent because of difficult disputes of fact, law or expert evidence.

Determining the prospects of success is stage one of the merits test. If prospects are poor or unclear, representation will be refused. If prospects are borderline, representation will be refused unless there is a significant wider public interest (ie the case will benefit a group of individuals wider than the client) or the case is of overwhelming interest to the client (ie it is about life, liberty, or the roof over his or her head).

Stage 2 – Cost–benefit/successful outcome

4.29   This varies according to the type of case, see below.

Appealing refusals

4.30   A refusal of a certificate on the basis of merit can be appealed, within 21 days of the decision, to the Independent Funding Adjudicator (IFA). A refusal on financial grounds cannot be appealed, though a fresh application can be made if circumstances change.

Private law children cases – merits test

4.31   Private law children cases are proceedings concerning contact, residence, parental responsibility, financial provision for children, and other matters under the Children Act which are not Special Children Act or other public law proceedings.

You need to show that you are likely to obtain a 'successful outcome' – a significant improvement in the arrangements for children.

The merits test is as follows:

- Representation will be refused if prospects of success are poor.
- Representation will be refused unless the likely benefits justify the likely cost, such that the reasonable private paying client would be prepared to take or defend the proceedings in all the circumstances.

Forms

! Change from previous rules !

4.32   The client will be required to attend an appointment with a mediator unless any of the exceptions apply (see above). Therefore, form CLSAPP3 should be accompanied by form CLSAPP7, certifying that the case is not suitable for mediation or that mediation has failed.

Representation will be refused unless the CLSAPP7 has been properly completed. In addition, it will be refused if no reasonable attempts to settle without recourse to litigation (whether by negotiation or otherwise) have been attempted.

Forms will be rejected if the signatures are more than two months old. See the aide-memoire at appendix B.

Financial provision and ancillary relief – merits test

4.33   You need to show that you are likely to obtain a 'successful outcome'
– a significant improvement in financial or other arrangements.
The merits test is as follows:

- Representation will be refused if prospects of success are poor; or
  if they are borderline or unclear, unless the case has overwhelming importance to the client (here, roof over his or her head) or
  significant wider public interest (unlikely unless this is a potential
  test case).
- Representation will be refused unless the likely benefits justify
  the likely cost, such that the reasonable private paying client
  would be prepared to take or defend the proceedings in all the
  circumstances.

Forms

4.34   Again, before applying for funding, the client will be required to attend mediation (unless the exceptions apply) and to have attempted
to settle, by negotiation or otherwise. Forms CLSAPP3 and CLSAPP7
are required, together with the appropriate MEANS form.

Funding

4.35   The LSC introduced a new funding scheme known as the Private
Family Law Representation Scheme (PFLRS) from 9 May 2011.
        It also introduced a new fee scheme for advocacy, the Family
Advocacy scheme (FAS) from 9 May 2011. For more information on
the fee schemes see chapter 10.

Grant and scope of a certificate

4.36   In almost every case, a certificate is only granted subject to two limitations. Firstly, it is very rare for a certificate to be granted to cover
the entirety of proceedings. Usually, it is limited to a particular step
in the proceedings. Secondly, costs will be limited, usually to £2,500
plus VAT in the first instance. A full list of limitation codes is given
in the LSC Manual, volume 3, part E.
        Emergency certificates are limited to 28 days. Costs limitations
include profit costs (and any enhancement or uplift), counsel's fees
and disbursements, but not VAT. It is extremely important not to do
work outside the scope of any limitation as you will not be paid for
it. You should note that payments to counsel under the FAS count

towards the financial limitation on certificates.[14] It is particularly easy to lose track of counsel's fees and disbursements and it really helps to keep all documents relating to financial issues together in the file. If you have devolved powers, you have the power to amend the financial limitation on an emergency (but not full) certificate up to £10,000, but only to allow you to do work that is urgent. If you exercise this power, you should inform the LSC on form APP8 that you have done so.

Domestic violence cases

4.37 Representation is available to apply for, or contest an application for, an injunction under Family Law Act 1996 Part IV.

The merits test (criterion 11.10) is as follows:

- Representation will be refused if prospects of success are poor.
- Representation will be refused unless likely benefits justify likely costs, having regard to the prospects of success and all other circumstances.

See above, and the Funding Code Guidance s20.32 (LSC Manual, volume 3, part C) for detailed guidance.

Applying for a certificate – urgent cases

4.38 You may exercise a devolved power to grant an emergency certificate. See chapter 3 for more information about devolved powers.

If a full certificate is refused (on means or merits), or made conditional on a contribution which the client refuses, the client is liable for all costs incurred under the emergency certificate. The client must therefore be advised of this at or before the time of the grant, and given a costs estimate. In these circumstances, the solicitor should bill the certificate in the usual way; the LSC will pursue the client for the costs.

- **Merits:** Emergency representation may be granted as a matter of urgency where it appears in the interests of justice to do so.
- **Means:** Emergency representation may be provided where there has not yet been a detailed assessment of the client's resources, provided that he or she has provided sufficient financial information to demonstrate that it is likely that he or she will be found to be eligible. In cases of doubt, MEANS6 can be faxed to the LSC for a preliminary assessment. See above for the LSC's power to waive the capital and income limits in domestic abuse cases.

14 Unified Contract Specification para 10.27.

- **Limitations**: You must apply both a scope and a costs limitation (see the standard limitations in volume 3, part E of the LSC Manual). Scope should be limited to the steps that need to be taken urgently. The initial scope limitation can be amended, provided the certificate remains limited to steps that need to be taken urgently. Costs will usually be limited to £1,500 plus VAT in the first instance, though this can be exceeded or amended where justifiable.
- **Submission of forms**: The LSC Regional Office must receive the substantive application within five working days of the emergency grant, and in the event of a devolved power amendment to scope or costs, must receive a CLSAPP8 within five working days of the amendment.

It is important to ensure that your emergency certificate is replaced by a substantive certificate within 28 days, as emergency certificates expire at that point and any further work would not be funded. The time limit cannot be extended.

See chapter 3 for information about:

- amendments to certificates;
- refusals and appeals;
- use of counsel and amendments for a QC;
- changes to prospects of success or cost–benefit;
- disbursements and prior authority;
- contributions;
- high-cost cases;
- ending a case;
- discharge of certificate;
- revocation of certificate.

See chapter 10 for information about getting paid in family cases.

Conducting a family public law case

Introduction

5.1   This chapter deals with conducting family public law cases. There are separate chapters on the general rules that apply to all civil cases, as well as family private law, immigration and mental health, as they each have their own funding schemes and rules.

In chapter 2, we saw that there are three key stages in providing publicly funded services: to ensure that (i) the matter is within scope, (ii) the client is financially eligible and (iii) the case meets the merits test. In addition, you need to ensure that forms are completed correctly and funding is obtained. This chapter explains how these steps are taken successfully in respect of family public law.

See appendices G and H for a summary of the Legal Services Commission's (LSC's) Costs Assessment Guidance, in respect of the most common queries raised by caseworkers.

What is public family law?

5.2   Public family law includes special Children Act proceedings and 'other public law children cases'. These are defined in section 2 of the Funding Code Criteria. The term 'special Children Act' covers applications for funding from a child, parent or other person with parental responsibility in cases under Children Act 1989 ss31, 43, 44 and 45, and applications from a child under s25 (use of accommodation for restricting liberty).

'Other public law children cases' include appeals in Special Children Act cases, and other proceedings under Children Act Parts IV and V, as well as adoption and High Court inherent jurisdiction cases (Funding Code, criterion 2.2). It also includes parties other than the child or person with parental responsibility who are joined (or want to apply to be) to special Children Act cases.

Where appropriate, you will be referred back to chapter 3, as that chapter sets out the general rules.

Scope

5.3   See chapter 3 for information on the following:

- what to do if your client has received previous advice from another organisation;
- what to do if your client has received previous advice from your organisation;

- clients from abroad or clients who are abroad;
- clients who are children.

Controlled work and licensed work

5.4   Controlled work is granted by solicitors according to rules under the Standard Contract. It is called 'controlled' because the LSC controls the number of matter starts which are allowed each year. The kinds of controlled work that are relevant to family practitioners are Legal Help and Family Help Lower. Help at Court is not available in family work.

You need a Community Legal Service (CLS) funding certificate, sometimes known as a legal aid certificate or full representation certificate, to represent a client in legal proceedings. This is called licensed work, as the firm has a general licence to do such work, and numbers of matter starts are not limited. Certificates may be granted by the LSC, or, in urgent circumstances, granted under devolved powers by the organisation.

Public family law – controlled work

Legal Help – level 1

Scope

5.5   This covers initial (ie pre-proceedings) advice and assistance in relation to any kind of public law family case, including the consequential letters to the client and any letters to a third party.

However, it is not designed to cover attending child protection conferences as a matter of course. The LSC believes that legal advice is only required in 'exceptional circumstances'.[1] If you attend a child protection conference, you will need to ensure that this is fully justified on your attendance note.

Merits test

5.6   The 'sufficient benefit test' applies to Legal Help: 'Help may only be provided where there is sufficient benefit to the client, having regard to the circumstances of the matter, including the personal circumstances of the client, to justify work or further work being carried out' (Funding Code criterion 5.2). It is hard to think of circumstances where it would not be met in such cases.

---

1 LSC Manual, volume 3, part C; Funding Code Guidance.

Financial eligibility

5.7   Legal Help is means tested, even in relation to care cases.
See chapter 2 for more information on the following:

- passporting benefits;
- assessment of capital;
- assessment of income;
- reassessment of means.

See chapter 3 for more information on the following:

- evidence of means;
- when you can start work without evidence of means;
- reassessing the client's eligibility if their means change significantly.

Forms

5.8   The form is the CW1 Legal Help, Help at Court and Family Help (Lower) form.
The assessment of means and client's details sections must be fully completed, and signed by the client, normally in the presence of someone from your organisation, before you start doing any legal work.[2]

How many Legal Help forms?

5.9   You can have more than one Legal Help matter open at the same time, but only if they relate to entirely separate family disputes where any proceedings would be issued and heard separately.[3] The LSC gives the example where there is a public law Legal Help matter in relation to concerns raised by the local authority and also a private law matter in relation to a divorce.[4]

Funding

5.10   Legal Help – level 1 is paid as a standard fee.[5] Cases that exceed three times the fixed fee when calculated at hourly rates can be claimed in

---

2 Unified Contract Specification para 2.11.
3 Unified Contract Specification para 10.69.
4 Family Fee Scheme Guidance (excluding advocacy), para 2.4.
5 Current fees and hourly rates are found in the Standard Contract Payment Annex. You can download the contract from the LSC's website at: www.legalservices.gov.uk > Community Legal Service (CLS) > Civil contracts.

full (see chapter 10 for more information about claiming exceptional cases).

Family Help (Lower) – level 2

Scope

5.11   This level of funding covers advice and other work for parents or those with parental responsibility. The LSC intend that the focus of work at this level will be on negotiation with the local authority to resolve disputes under the Public Law Outline. Therefore, it covers cases where the local authority has issued a notice of its intention to issue proceedings; but no proceedings have yet been issued.

The letter before proceedings may suggest that a meeting is held between the client and the local authority to discuss the concerns raised in the letter and level 2 will cover attending this meeting (sometimes called 'a family meeting') with the client.

Extract from the Standard Contract Family Specification

5.12   The Standard Contract Family Specification, para 7.36 states:

Payment for Family Help (Lower)
7.36 Family Help (Lower) may only be granted where all criteria at section 11.3 of the Funding Code are satisfied. In addition, in Public Law Work remuneration for Family Help (Lower) may only be claimed where the following conditions are satisfied:
(a) the Local Authority has given written notice of potential s31 Care Proceedings in accordance with the DCSF/Welsh Assembly government guidance issued under the Children Act 1989 guidance and regulations, Volume 1, but no proceedings have yet been issued (application for an Emergency Protection Order does not count as issue of proceedings for this purpose);
(b) your Client is a Parent (as defined above);
(c) your Client requires advice and assistance with a view to avoiding the proceedings, or narrowing and resolving any issues with the Local Authority.

Merits test

5.13   Family Help (Lower) is not merits tested in public family law, as long as the requirements of para 7.36 (reproduced above) are met.

Financial eligibility

5.14   Family Help (Lower) is not means tested in public family law.

Forms

5.15   The LSC has issued a separate form for level 2 in public family law
        – the CW1PL.
            It is designed to be used in relation to advice after the local author-
        ity has issued its notice of intention to issue proceedings (advice prior
        to this is covered under the CW1 Legal Help form). Key points are:

        •   It is not means tested.
        •   It has a box that allows you to record that the criteria for advice at
            level 2 were met.
        •   The local authority's notice of intention to issue proceedings must
            be attached to it.

        In these cases, you tick the box at the top of page 2 of the Family Help
        (Lower) Public Law form, and attach a copy of the notice to show that
        the criteria are met.

Funding

5.16   Family Help (Lower) level 2 is paid as a standard fee. Whether you
        can claim it depends on the local authority issuing written notice of
        their intention to issue proceedings. This can be in an email, as long
        as the wording is unambiguous.

Exceptional cases

5.17   A case becomes exceptional in public law matters where the costs of
        all levels of advice provided at controlled work, calculated at hourly
        rates, exceed three times the relevant fees. Therefore, where level 1
        and level 2 advice has been provided, costs calculated at an hourly
        rate must exceed three times the level 1 and level 2 fees combined.
        If advice has only been provided at either level 1 or level 2, the excep-
        tional limit will be three times the fees for that level of service.

Closing controlled work matters

5.18   For information about when you can or should close a case, see
        chapter 3.

Certificates – public law cases

Scope

5.19 A CLS funding certificate in family public law can only be granted when the local authority issues proceedings, and is therefore usually granted initially as an emergency certificate under devolved powers. It authorises the conduct of litigation and the provision of advocacy and representation.

Certificates

5.20 An application for funding in Special Children Act cases is granted automatically, without reference to means or merits. An application to extend the scope of the certificate (for example, to make an application for a residence or contact order within the care proceedings, or to include representation in any other related proceedings which are being heard together) must be made, as the usual form of the certificate only covers proceedings under Children Act ss31, 43, 44 and 45, and applications from a child under s25.

Apart from 'related proceedings', certificates in this area are kept completely separate from all other work. Therefore, a separate application must always be made – an ordinary certificate cannot be amended to cover Special Children Act proceedings, and a Special Children Act certificate cannot be amended to cover anything else.

The CLSAPP5 includes a question on whether separate representation is appropriate. Once funding has been granted, you have an ongoing duty to report any new information or changes of circumstance which might affect the terms of the certificate under Procedure 43 of the Funding Code.

Financial eligibility

5.21 Certificates in Special Children Act proceedings are not means tested.

Certificates in other public law Children cases are means tested. See chapter 2 for information about the means test.

Merits test

5.22   Certificates in Special Children Act proceedings are not merits tested.

Certificates in other public law Children cases are subject to a limited merits test:[6]

- Representation will be refused if alternative funding is available (eg in adoption, where the child is placed by the local authority who consent to the adoption, it would be reasonable to expect them to bear the costs of the application).
- Representation will be refused if not necessary (for example, because of the involvement of other parties or a professional guardian).
- Representation will be refused if, in all the circumstances, including the importance of the case to the client, it appears unreasonable for funding to be granted (eg where the client's interests are substantially the same as another party's, there is no need for them to be separately represented).

Forms

5.23   You use CLSAPP5 for Special Children Act proceedings and CLSAPP3 in other cases.

Apart from 'related proceedings', Special Children Act certificates are kept completely separate from all other work. Therefore, a separate application must always be made – an ordinary certificate cannot be amended to cover Special Children Act proceedings, and a Special Children Act certificate cannot be amended to cover anything else.

Funding

5.24   Representation in respect of a child, parent or joined party in care and supervision proceedings (Children Act 1989 s31) and related proceedings[7] is covered by a standard fee scheme. The fees are based on the location of the solicitor's office and the nature and number of parties represented.

Fees refer to the LSC region where the fee earner was based during the case:

---

6 Funding Code, criterion 11.9.
7 Defined in the Funding Code, criterion 11.8.

- Wales;
- London, Brighton, Reading and Bristol – all claim the 'London and South' fee;
- Birmingham, Nottingham and Cambridge – all claim the 'Midlands' fee;
- Newcastle, Leeds, Liverpool and Manchester – all claim the 'North' fee.

The standard fee scheme does not apply to other 'Special Children Act proceedings', ie under s25 (when a child is brought before the court and wishes to be separately represented), s43 (a child assessment order), s44 (an emergency protection order) and s45 (extension or discharge of an emergency protection order).

It does not apply to other public law Family proceedings, including appeals in Special Children Act cases, and proceedings under Parts IV and V of the Children Act, as well as adoption and High Court inherent jurisdiction cases.[8]

In Children Act s31 cases, funding under the Graduated Fee Scheme for Legal Representation certificates covers all stages up to the conclusion of the proceedings in the first instance (including representation on any interim appeal and/or advice on the merits of an appeal against a final order). Where Legal Representation is granted to defend or bring an appeal against a final order, it is paid by way of hourly rates.[9]

Other public law family certificated cases are funded under hourly rates.

Advocacy under standard fees

! Change from previous rules!

5.25 The standard fees do not include advocacy. Where advocacy is provided, whether by counsel or a solicitor advocate, the claim is made under the Family Advocacy Scheme (FAS), which applies to all cases where the certificate is granted following an application made on or after 9 May 2011 (see chapter 13 for more information).

The LSC include the following activities under the definition of advocacy for the purposes of the FAS preparation for advocacy:

- appearances as advocate before the court;
- travel to and from court and waiting time;

---

8 Funding Code, criterion 2.2.
9 Unified Contract Specification para 10.50.

- attendances by the advocate at court, including attendance at advocates meetings.

If you are a solicitor carrying out advocacy, it is helpful to keep a separate file for this aspect of the case as it helps you keep track of the advocacy fees to be charged on top of the applicable standard fee for other work. It also helps you identify when to apply for an increase in the financial limitation on the certificate as this includes all profit costs as well as disbursements, advocacy fees and VAT.

Applying for a certificate – urgent cases

5.26   Under paragraph 10.39 of the Unified Specification you have a devolved power to grant legal representation in Special Children Act cases. The CLSAPP5 should be completed and in addition, the devolved power section on page 5 of that form must be completed, stating the date on which devolved powers were exercised and confirming that the criterion as to separate representation is met.

See chapter 3 for more information about devolved powers, and also about:

- amendments to certificates;
- refusals and appeals;
- use of counsel and amendments for a QC;
- changes to prospects of success or cost–benefit;
- disbursements and prior authority;
- contributions;
- high-cost cases;
- ending a case;
- discharge of certificate;
- revocation of certificate.

See chapter 10 for information about getting paid in family cases.

CHAPTER 6

Family mediation

Introduction

6.1   This chapter deals with mediation; but mainly from the point of view of a lawyer, rather than a mediator or client. There is increased emphasis on resolving disputes through mediation rather than litigation, regardless of the way that cases are funded.

Former Court of Appeal judge Sir Henry Brooke retired at the age of 70 and embarked on a new career as a mediator. 'After 45 years in litigation, I have seen so much money spent, stress caused and delay encountered. Reaching settlement at the door of the court is entirely unsatisfactory', he said.[1]

Lawyers should be aware that the judiciary and the Legal Services Commission (LSC) are likely to increase incentives to mediate and in the Standard Contract 2010, the LSC introduced a new key performance indicator (KPI) to encourage the use of mediation (see below).

Used well, and complemented by legal advice, mediation helps clients find a solution to their problems in a more positive way. Legal aid practitioners need to understand how mediation can work to their benefit as well as their client's.

Scope

6.2   There are two types of mediation that can be funded by the LSC:

- family mediation, where the LSC funds the mediator directly; and
- non-family mediation, which can be funded as a disbursement under both Legal Help and CLS Funding certificates.[2]

Family mediation has its own Specification in the Standard Contract, which can be downloaded from www.legalservices.gov.uk > Community Legal Service (CLS) > Civil contracts > 2010 Standard Civil Contract.

You should note that in private family matters, a CLS funding certificate will not be granted unless suitability for mediation has been considered (see chapter 4).

---

1 *Law Society Gazette*, 18 September 2008.
2 Funding Code Guidance, LSC Manual, volume 3, part C.

Financial eligibility

6.3   In non-family mediation, the means test is carried out as usual for the type of funding – Legal Help or a CLS funding certificate (see chapter 1).

In family mediation, the mediator carries out the eligibility test. If one of the parties qualifies for legal aid, then the cost of the assessment meeting will be met by the LSC. However, if one of the parties is not financially eligible, he or she will have to pay for their own mediation costs.[3] This is likely to be considerably cheaper than contested proceedings.

Merits test

6.4   Mediation beyond the assessment meeting will only be provided where the mediator is satisfied that the mediation is suitable to the dispute and the parties and all the circumstances.[4]

Forms

6.5   There are no forms for non-family mediation as this is claimed as a disbursement.

Family mediators will have the appropriate application forms.

Funding

6.6   Where the parties are willing and the issues are suitable, the mediation should be able to deal with all the issues arising, including explanation of the law (but not advice), and disclosure.

From the client's point of view, family mediation is advantageous, as it is exempt from the statutory charge.

Robert Clerke, solicitor and mediator, has explained the stages of mediation in a typical family case:[5]

•   setting the agenda/identification of the issues;
•   disclosure;

---

3 Funding Code Guidance, LSC Manual, volume 3, part C.
4 Funding Code, criteria, LSC Manual, volume 3, part C and Code Procedures.
5 *Carter survival handbook*, Quay Books, 2007, chapter 5.

- identification and exploration of options;
- impasse, and strategies to break through it;
- reality testing;
- recording the outcome – hopefully a memorandum of under-standing (MOU) and, where appropriate, an open financial statement (OFS).

In family cases, appropriate use of mediation can help to make the fixed fees viable, as if the case can be resolved in mediation, it reduces the amount of time the lawyer needs to spend on the case. However, the lawyer will still be needed to advise on the law and draw up the consent order and statement of information for the court.

Conducting an immigration case

continued

Introduction

7.1 This chapter deals with immigration work. You should read it in conjunction with chapters 2 and 3. Chapter 2 deals with general rules about taking on civil cases, and applies to work in the immigration category as it does to all other work. Chapter 3 deals with the rules that apply to the conduct of all civil cases. The immigration-specific rules in this chapter usually build on, rather than replace, the general rules; where they do replace the general rules we will say so.

See appendices G and H for a summary of the Legal Services Commission's (LSC's) Costs Assessment Guidance, in respect of the most common queries raised by caseworkers.

What is immigration work?

7.2 Immigration work is work done in the immigration category. The 2010 Category Definitions define it as:

> Legal help on matters and all proceedings concerning immigration, leave to enter or remain in the United Kingdom, removal or deportation from the United Kingdom, asylum, nationality and citizenship.
>
> Proceedings before Immigration and Asylum Tribunal and any related proceedings before the Upper Tribunal, High Court, Court of Appeal or Supreme Court.

The Standard Civil Contract Specification has a section devoted to immigration work – section 8 – and that section further divides immigration work into asylum and non-asylum work.

Asylum work is defined as:

(a) a claim, including a fresh claim, under the 1951 Convention Relating to the Status of Refugees and/or Article 3 of The European Convention for the protection of Human Rights and Fundamental Freedoms 1950 that falls to be recorded by the UKBA [UK Border Agency] (whether or not it has yet been so recorded) as a claim for 'asylum' within the meaning of the Immigration Act 1999 and the Nationality, Immigration and Asylum Act 2002; or

(b) an application for further leave to remain by a former asylum seeker who was granted a form of limited leave to remain either as a Refugee (on or after 30 August 2005) or Humanitarian Protection or Discretionary Leave (whenever granted) and the matter is now proceeding as either an active review by the UKBA or the client is making or has made an application for further leave to remain on the basis of the 1951 Convention Relating to the Status of Refugees and/or Article 3 of the European Convention for the Protection of Human Rights and Fundamental Freedoms 1950. This will also include matters where the client is appealing an intention to deport based on the 1951 Convention and/or Article 3 of the ECHR.[1]

All other work in the immigration category is non-asylum.

Who can do the work?

Individual caseworkers

7.3   Immigration work is unique in legal aid in being completely subject to an accreditation scheme. Other areas of legal aid also use accreditation, for example to qualify as a supervisor, and even restrict work by accreditation, for example criminal police station work, but only immigration funding is subject to a category-wide restriction.

Unless you are accredited, you cannot be paid for doing any legal aid work in the immigration category at all.[2] There are several levels of accreditation:

- Level 1 probationer;
- Level 1 accredited caseworker;
- Level 2 probationer;
- Level 2 senior caseworker;
- Level 3 advanced caseworker;
- Accredited supervisor.

What work can be done by caseworkers of each level is defined by the contract and the accreditation work restrictions.

Type of contract work	Level of accreditation/other restriction
Conduct of Legal Help matters	Level 1 accredited and above
Use of devolved powers to grant Controlled Legal Representation (CLR) and conduct of CLR cases	Level 2 accredited and above

---

1 Specification, para 8.7.
2 Specification, para 8.18.

Type of contract work	Level of accreditation/other restriction
All contract work carried out for an unaccompanied asylum-seeking child	Level 2 accredited and above and must hold an enhanced Criminal Records Bureau check carried out within the last 24 months
All work carried out at an immigration removal centre under the detained fast track scheme or at an on-site surgery	Level 2 accredited and above

In this context, 'conduct' means 'having responsibility and control for the progression of the case'.[3] So a level 1 fee earner can carry out delegated tasks on an appeal conducted by a level 2 fee earner, whereas all work on the file of an unaccompanied child must be carried out by a level 2 fee earner.

In addition to that broad rule, you must comply with the work restrictions,[4] which can be found on the LSC website at www. legalservices.gov.uk > Community Legal Service (CLS) > Civil areas of work > Immigration and asylum > The accreditation scheme. The restrictions specify tasks that are restricted by accreditation level. Probationers may only carry out the listed tasks; level 1 caseworkers cannot deal with certain types of cases, such as vulnerable clients or disputed nationality cases.

If work is done outside the accreditation scheme or the work restrictions, you may not claim for it.[5]

! Change from previous rules !

Work done by level 3 caseworkers attracts an uplift of 5 per cent on the payment rates, but only on work paid at hourly rates.[6]

Organisations

7.4 Immigration work is excluded from tolerance, so only those organisations with a contract in immigration can do work in the category (see chapter 2 for a full list of tolerance excluded work).

3 Specification, para 8.17.
4 Specification, para 8.11(c).
5 Specification, para 11.78.
6 Specification, para 8.85.

The LSC has also restricted certain types of work to organisations that have special permission to do it – they hold an Exclusive Schedule in addition to their Standard Contract Schedule setting out the restricted work they can do. Work restricted to holders of Exclusive Schedules is:[7]

- to act in the Early Legal Advice Process (ELAP) operated by the UKBA;
- to represent a client detained at an immigration removal centre (note, the exclusion does not apply to prisons or 'other place of detention'[8]).

The above exclusions do not apply where:

- the client is a close family member of an existing client and knowledge of the family circumstances is material to the new client's case; or
- the client is an existing client on whom you have attended and carried out at least five hours' work (excluding travel and waiting) before the client became subject to exclusive contracting, eg was detained.[9]

Scope

7.5 See chapter 3 for information on the following:

- whether other funding may be available, and public funding should not granted;
- what to do if your client has received previous advice from another organisation;
- what to do if your client has received previous advice from your organisation;
- clients from abroad or clients who are abroad;
- clients who are children.

Structure of immigration work

7.6 Immigration work can be divided into four stages:

1   advice and Home Office/entry clearance applications;
2   appeals to the First-tier Tribunal;

---

7 Specification, para 8.5.
8 Specification, para 8.47.
9 Specification, para 8.6.

3 appeals to the Upper Tribunal;
4 litigation in the higher courts.

Stage 1 is funded by Legal Help. Stages 2 and 3 are funded by Controlled Legal Representation (CLR) (though different rules apply and it helps to think of them as different types of work), and stage 4 is funded by certificate.

The Immigration Specification does not create any additional rules for certificated work in the higher courts, and this is therefore not dealt with to any great extent in this chapter.

The various funding types are consecutive as the case progresses. For example, where a client's application is refused, you should consider whether there is merit for CLR, and if so grant it. CLR should be applied for as soon as practicable after the right to appeal has arisen, and before the appeal is lodged, unless there is insufficient time, for example because the client is in detention and there is not time to arrange a visit. In such circumstances, urgent work could be done under Legal Help, but CLR must be considered as soon as possible.[10]

Once CLR is granted or refused, the Legal Help comes to an end and no further Legal Help work may be done on that matter.[11] Post-appeal work will form part of the CLR.[12]

Similarly, where you take an appeal to the Court of Appeal, the issue of a certificate to conduct the appeal brings the matter to an end. If the Court of Appeal then remits the case back to the Asylum and Immigration Tribunal (AIT), a new matter start will be required to do the remitted appeal.[13]

Fee types

! Change from previous rules !

7.7 Some immigration work is paid as graduated fees, some at hourly rates. Different rules apply to standard fee (SF) work and hourly rates (HR) work, and it is therefore important to determine at the start of the case which is which.

Paragraph 8.83 of the 2010 Standard Civil Contract Specification lists all hourly rates work:

10 Funding Code Guidance, para 29.22.9.
11 Specification, para 8.70.
12 Specification, para 8.72(7).
13 Funding Code Guidance, para 29.8.24.

(a) Work in relation to an asylum application (including 'NAM' or 'Legacy'), which was made prior to the 1 October 2007;

(b) A fresh asylum application where the original asylum application was lodged, whether concluded or not, prior to 1 October 2007;

(c) Advice in relation to the merits of lodging an application for permission to appeal to the Upper Tribunal (where advice has not been received under a stage 2 standard fee);

(d) Controlled Legal Representation in relation to an application for permission to appeal and, where granted, the subsequent appeal before the Upper Tribunal;

(e) Bail applications;

(f) Advice solely in relation to form filling as permitted by Paragraph 8.56;

(g) Advice and applying for a Certificate for Licensed Work, including complying with the pre-action protocol;

(h) Initial advice in relation to an Asylum application prior to claiming asylum e.g. at the Asylum Screening Unit (ASU) where you then cease to be instructed. This will also apply where the client returns after attendance at the ASU but where it is confirmed that the client will be dispersed and will not continue to instruct you;

(i) Exceptional Cases under the Graduated Fee Scheme;

(j) Advice under Legal Help for ELAP cases (CLR is remunerated under standard fees);

(k) Advice in relation to a client who is an unaccompanied asylum seeking child;

(l) Cases remitted from the First-tier Tribunal or Upper Tribunal to the First-tier Tribunal;

(m) Where you hold an exclusive schedule, any matters opened as a result of an on-site surgery at an IRC or for a fast track client.

All other work is payable as graduated fees.

Note the distinction between asylum and non-asylum work: for asylum cases, some 'mainstream' work such as fresh claims are payable at HR, whereas all non-asylum applications are SF, with the exception of form-filling advice.

With the exception of bail and Upper Tribunal/remittal work (which are always paid at HR, even where the substantive matter is SF), whether a case is SF or HR will apply to the whole matter.

Matter starts and separate matters

! Change from previous rules !

7.8   A 'matter' is all work done on a single case for a client. A matter can pass through Legal Help and CLR and still be the same matter.

Where you can justify a separate matter, you can claim a separate SF, or make a separate HR claim.

In deciding whether work should be one or more matters, you should bear in mind the following:

- An application and subsequent appeal is one matter,[14] as is an associated application on human rights grounds.[15]
- A family reunion application following a successful application for refugee status will constitute a new matter.[16]
- A fresh application for asylum is a new matter.[17]
- Work in relation to preparation for and applying for a certificate for licensed work (including compliance with any pre-action protocol) is part of the substantive matter.[18]
- Where a client applies to enter or remain in the UK under more than one category, or applies to switch status while the first application remains outstanding, this will be one matter,[19] but where the first application is at appeal stage and a different *additional* application is made, the second application will be a new matter.[20]
- In general, only one matter start should be used for each case or application – that is, a case treated by the UKBA as a single application or by the Tribunal as a single set of proceedings. Two matters should only be opened where it would be appropriate for them to be considered or issued and heard separately and where each requires substantial legal work which does not address the other.[21]
- Acting for more than one client in the same case should be one matter start, not two (eg an asylum-seeker and a family member whose application is dependent), but were there to be proceedings each client would be a party, each client has a separate and distinct legal interest and there is sufficient benefit to the second

14 Specification, para 8.29.
15 Specification, para 8.30.
16 Specification, para 8.31.
17 Specification, para 8.32.
18 Specification, para 8.33.
19 Specification, para 8.35.
20 Specification, para 8.36.
21 Specification, para 3.42. Para 3.43 defines separate legal work as an additional 30 minutes of preparation or advice, or separate communication with third parties on legal issues.

(taking into account the Help being provided to the first), a second matter may be opened.[22]

A second matter start for the same client would not be justified on the same case unless at least six months have elapsed since the first matter was closed, or unless at least three months have elapsed and there has been a material development or change in the client's instructions.[23] If the client fails to give instructions and you close the file, and then the client returns, that is not a change in instructions. A decision, response, etc from a third party to an application, representations, correspondence etc made in the first matter is not a material development.[24] Where further work is justified, but you cannot start a new matter, new disbursements can be claimed, as can profit costs if the case is an HR case, an exceptional case or the new work plus the old work would make it an exceptional case.[25]

See chapter 3 for further information on how to report further work on a revived case and where a new matter would be justified.

Granting Legal Help

7.9   The Legal Help means test as set out in chapter 2 must be applied. The only difference in the immigration category is that support under Immigration and Asylum Act 1999 s4 or s95 is a passporting benefit.[26] In asylum cases, the Funding Code makes explicit that the means of unaccompanied minors should not be aggregated with those of their social worker, foster carer, etc.[27] Proof of means will be required. Many asylum-seekers who are not in receipt of support will be accommodated and maintained by friends and relatives. Where that is the case, you will need to get proof, usually in the form of a letter signed by the person accommodating the client and setting out the nature of any support (and quantifying it if it includes money).

The merits test is the sufficient benefit test – see chapter 2 for further information on the means test, and chapter 3 for further information on the merits test.

---

22 Specification, para 5.18.
23 Specification, para 3.47.
24 Specification, para 3.48.
25 Specification, para 3.49.
26 Community Legal Service (Financial) Regulations 2000 reg 4(3).
27 Funding Code Guidance, para 29.12.

Granting CLR

7.10 CLR is subject to the means test. The test is the same as for Legal Help, except that the capital limit for non-asylum CLR is £3,000, rather than the £8,000 that applies to all other levels of civil funding.[28] We know of no good reason as to why this provision should exist, but exist it does.

CLR has its own merits test, which should be applied at the start of the case, and kept in mind throughout. The test is in two stages:

1 What are the prospects of success?
2 Do the likely benefits to be gained from the proceedings justify the likely costs?[29]

The merits test must be carried out by a level 2 caseworker or above.[30]

The merits test does not apply to Upper Tribunal appeals, since payment may only be claimed if permission is granted (see below). In such cases, the only merits test is whether there is a significant prospect that the appeal will be allowed.

Prospects of success

7.11 In answering question 1, the prospects of success should be categorised in one of four ways:

- Good – that is, clearly over 50 per cent.
- Poor – that is, clearly below 50 per cent.
- Borderline.
- Unclear.

Where prospects are good, you go on to question 2. Where prospects are poor, that is the end of the process and you should refuse CLR. Where prospects are borderline or unclear, you should refuse unless at least one of the following applies:

- The case is of overwhelming importance to the client – that is, it concerns life, liberty, physical safety or the roof over his or her head. Asylum cases will nearly always meet this test.
- The case raises significant issues of human rights.
- The case has a significant wider public interest – that is, it has the potential to bring real benefits for members of the public other

---

28 Community Legal Service (Financial) Regulations 2000 reg 5(3).
29 Funding Code Criteria, section 13. See also Funding Code Guidance, para 29.22.
30 Specification, para 8.6.

than the client and his or her immediate family. Country guidance cases are an obvious example of the type of case that would
meet this test.

The Funding Code gives guidance[31] on where prospects should be
said to be poor:

> Examples of where the prospects of success will be poor are where:
>
> (a) In light of all the evidence the reasons for applying to remain in
> the United Kingdom are, in the case of an asylum application, out-
> side the criteria laid down in the 1951 Convention relating to the
> Status of Refugees or, in the case of a human rights application,
> outside the criteria in the ECHR.
>
> (b) In a second or subsequent asylum or human rights application,
> where the same facts have already been determined before an
> Immigration Judge or AIT on a previous application and dis-
> missed and there has been no relevant change of circumstance.
>
> (c) The Client's circumstances and/or the circumstances within his/
> her country of origin have changed since the initial application
> was made such that any claim on the basis of asylum or human
> rights would be likely to fail.
>
> (d) The Client's credibility is significantly in doubt and the client is
> unable to provide a satisfactory explanation for any discrepancies
> or provide relevant corroborative evidence of his/her statement.
>
> (e) In light of recent case law based on similar facts the appeal is likely
> to fail.
>
> (f) The Client has unreasonably failed to provide the necessary in-
> formation such as to enable the Supplier to properly prepare the
> case despite the reasonable efforts of the Supplier to obtain that
> information.
>
> (g) The Client has provided false information relating to his or her
> identity or nationality and gives no reasonable explanation for
> this.
>
> (h) The Client has resided for over three months in a safe third coun-
> try and does not dispute the safety of that country on reasonable
> grounds.
>
> (i) The Client is to be removed to a safe third country and does not
> dispute the safety of that country on reasonable grounds (this will
> not be relevant to claims under Article 8 of the ECHR).

Where prospects are unclear, you should only do such work as is
necessary to make them clear, and then re-assess the merits. If they
are then poor, CLR should be withdrawn.[32]

---

31 Funding Code Guidance, para 29.22.8.
32 Funding Code Guidance, para 29.22.12.

Likely benefits

7.12 Question 2 is sometimes referred to as the 'private client test' – would a reasonable private paying client of moderate means be prepared to fund the case? This test will be satisfied in all asylum and most immigration cases, but may not be where, for example, a lot of work would need to be done to achieve a limited form of leave.

Where likely benefits do not justify likely costs, CLR should be refused unless there is significant wider public interest (see above for definition).

Where you are satisfied there is merit, you should sign the CLR form, and it is your signature (the client having already signed the form) that effects the grant.[33]

Refusing and withdrawing CLR

7.13 Where you believe the merits test is not, or is no longer, satisfied, you should refuse or withdraw CLR as appropriate and complete form CW4 setting out your reasons. A copy of the form must be provided to the client within five days of your decision, and you should also advise the client of their right to appeal against your decision. Either the client can appeal direct to the LSC, or instruct you to do so on their behalf. There is no right of appeal against a decision to refuse or withdraw CLR in connection with an application for permission to appeal to the Upper Tribunal, except in detained fast track cases. See paras 8.42 to 8.45 of the Specification.

Notifying the LSC

! Change from previous rules !

7.14 You must notify the LSC of all grants, refusals and withdrawals of CLR, whether in relation to a substantive appeal or bail.[34] There is a standard form to be submitted each month alongside your controlled work claims.

Change of supplier

7.15 The client's remedy against a refusal of CLR is to appeal, not to change solicitor. Where you are asked to take on a transfer following refusal,

---

33 Specification, paras 11.133 and 11.134.
34 Specification, para 8.46.

you should advise the client to appeal. However, where urgent work is required, you can grant CLR as borderline or unclear and take on the case to do the urgent work, such as lodging the AIT appeal within the time limits.

Conducting the case

7.16   Once Legal Help or CLR, as appropriate, has been granted (and assuming there is sufficient merit on an ongoing basis), you can conduct the case.

Generally you are permitted to take instructions, take witness statements, make applications and representations, conduct appeals, and so on.

There are rules that govern certain aspects of the conduct of cases, which we will look at in this section.

Attendance at interviews

7.17   The general rule is that you are not permitted to accompany a client to an interview with the Home Office. However, the contract contains exceptions where attendance is authorised – no prior application for permission is required.[35]

You may attend a screening interview where:

- the client is, or claims on reasonable grounds to be, under 18.

You may attend a substantive interview where:

- the client is, or claims on reasonable grounds to be, under 18;
- the client suffers or appears to suffer from a 'mental incapacity' as defined by the Mental Health Act 2005;
- the client is subject to a detained fast track process;
- the client is to be interviewed by an immigration officer under PACE;
- it is alleged that the client may pose a threat to national security;
- the client is subject to the ELAP and you have an ELAP exclusive schedule;
- it is a non-asylum matter and, having regard to the particular circumstances of the case, it is both reasonable and necessary for a representative to attend the interview, given the nature of the interview and the representative's role within it.

35 Specification, para 8.53.

Where you do attend an interview in an HR case, the costs incurred (including associated travel and waiting) will be included within any applicable costs limit (this is a change from the position under the 2007 contract). Where you attend in an SF case, you can claim the interview additional fee.

Travel to detained clients

7.18 You can claim for travel and waiting costs to visit a client in detention. However, travel time is capped to a maximum of three hours for the return journey. Travel and waiting time and associated disbursements are excluded from any applicable costs limit, and in a SF case payable on top of the relevant fee.[36]

Bail

7.19 Where a client is in detention, you can make a bail application where there is merit to do so.

Bail applications to the Tribunal are covered by CLR funding (applications for temporary admission and chief immigration officer bail are under Legal Help).[37] If you do not already have CLR open for an appeal, you should grant CLR to cover bail. If you are already conducting an appeal, you should extend the scope of CLR to cover the bail application. The merits test for bail is the same for CLR generally, except will be specifically related to the prospects of a successful bail application.

Bail work is always paid at hourly rates.[38] See below for costs limits in bail matters.

Use of counsel and attendance at hearings

7.20 Appeals work is out of scope of Legal Help, but is covered by CLR. You may instruct an advocate to attend any hearing if CLR has been granted.

The advocate's time should be included on your bill as if it were your profit costs and it will be paid at the relevant HR or as part of the SF – in a SF case, their time will count towards exceptionality. Where

36 Specification, para 8.49.
37 Specification, para 8.87.
38 Specification, para 8.83.

an advocate is instructed, you cannot make a claim for time spent accompanying them at the hearing.[39]

You can apply to the LSC to increase the rates payable to advocates (including advocates employed by you) if the case raises an exceptionally complex or novel point of law or if there is a significant wider public interest. Any enhanced rates that may be granted apply to advocacy, attendance and preparation only.[40]

Time spent instructing advocates and in conference is properly claimable if reasonable in the circumstances of the case.

'Form filling' advice

7.21   Certain immigration application forms are deemed by the LSC to be sufficiently straightforward that clients can fill them in unaided, and it would not therefore be claimable work to complete them. The specified forms include travel document, passport, citizenship applications and certificates of authorisation for marriage.[41] However, where an issue of law arises, it may be reasonable to give the client legal advice on the completion of the form, but not to complete it. An issue of law does not arise because the client cannot understand the form through language or other difficulties, nor should you start a matter just to facilitate a disbursement such as an interpreter or expert.[42]

Where such advice is given as part of a matter, those costs are claimable as part of the overall costs of the matter.[43] In an SF matter, since form-filling advice is hourly rates, that advice can be claimed at the appropriate hourly rate on top of the applicable SF and there is a field on the CMRF for it to be claimed.

If the matter is solely form-filling advice, then it will be an HR matter.[44]

Post-appeal work

! Change from previous rules !

7.22   The scope of Legal Help ends at the point of Home Office decision and consideration of CLR merits. Therefore, by definition, Legal

39 Specification, para 8.96.
40 Specification, para 8.97.
41 Specification, para 8.56.
42 Specification, para 8.57.
43 Specification, para 8.58.
44 Specification, para 8.83.

Help cannot be used for post-appeal follow-up work, such as chasing of status papers and advice on status.

The CLR will cover advice on the outcome of the appeal, including on the rights conferred by a grant of status, together with any post-appeal advice and assistance that does not justify a new matter start (see above for rules on matter start boundaries).[45]

Appeals to the Upper Tribunal

7.23 Work on an application for permission to appeal to the Upper Tribunal, and if granted the appeal itself and any subsequent remittal back, is CLR work and part of the ongoing substantive matter. It is, however, outside the scope of the SF scheme and payable at hourly rates. If you apply for permission to appeal and permission is refused, you may not claim any costs related to the application or appeal, but may claim any disbursements incurred, including interpreters' fees. This rule does not apply in detained fast track cases or where it is the UKBA which appeals. See paras 8.99–8.104 of the Contract Specification.

Higher courts litigation

7.24 Onward litigation in the higher courts will usually take the form of an application to the High Court for judicial review, or an appeal to the Court of Appeal against a decision of the tribunal.

In either case, a full representation certificate is required. See chapter 3 for information on applying for a certificate. The main difference in the immigration category to the usual rules on certificate applications is that you do not have devolved powers to grant emergency certificates unless you have specifically been granted that power by the LSC – the reverse of the position in other categories, where suppliers have the power by default.

If you do not have devolved powers but there is an emergency, retrospective funding may be granted. This is only possible in judicial review cases where the court grants permission and where the case has significant wider public interest, significant issues of human rights, or is of overwhelming importance to the client. In such cases, the LSC will issue a certificate backdated to the date of the application, provided the application was made promptly. See section 29.4 of the Funding Code Guidance.

---

45 Specification, para 8.72(7).

For appeals to the Court of Appeal, the application to the Upper Tribunal for permission is funded as part of controlled work.[46] If that application is granted, or if it is refused and renewed to the Court of Appeal, a certificate will be needed to fund proceedings before the Court of Appeal, and the issue of the certificate will end the controlled work matter. Therefore, remittal back to the Tribunal would be a new matter.

Managing costs

7.25   The amount of any costs limit depends on the stage of the case and the type of funding.

SF cases do not have limitations on profit costs, since only the fee is payable, and if they escape the fee they are subject to individual assessment of reasonableness. Therefore, there is only a disbursement limit. HR cases are limited by both profits costs and disbursements. Review and reconsideration cases are not subject to costs limits for either costs or disbursements, since they are in theory subject to assessment on a case-by-case basis by the LSC, though little assessment has been done in practice.

These are the applicable costs limits:

- SF stage 1 (Legal Help):
  - £400 disbursements;[47]
  - no profit costs limits.

- SF stage 2 (CLR):
  - £600 disbursements;[48]
  - no profit costs limits.

- HR Legal Help:
  - £800 profit costs (asylum); £500 profit costs (non-asylum);[49]
  - £400 disbursements.[50]

- HR CLR:
  - £1,600 combined costs and disbursements (asylum)/£1,200 combined costs and disbursements (non-asylum).[51]

---

46 Specification, para 8.62.
47 Specification, para 8.75.
48 Specification, para 8.75.
49 Specification, para 8.86.
50 Specification, para 8.90.
51 Specification, para 8.92.

- Bail work:
  - £500 for all bail work, inclusive of disbursements[52] (where CLR has not already been granted for an appeal; where it has, bail work forms part of the main £1,600/£1200 limit. If CLR has already been granted for bail, when it is granted for a substantive appeal, the costs already spent on bail count towards the £1600/£1200).[53]

Any of the above limits can be extended on application to the LSC. In addition, there are limits for specific case stages:

- Where a client instructs you prior to making an application at the ASU, and following attendance at the ASU you cease to be instructed – £100 including disbursements.
- Where advice is given on the merits of an appeal to the Upper Tribunal under Legal Help (usually because the case has transferred to you at this stage, otherwise such advice would be part of CLR stage 2b) – £100 including disbursements.
- Where you provide initial advice in relation to an asylum application which the client decides not to make or ceases to provide instructions before making – £100 including disbursements.

None of these limits can be extended.[54]
For details of making claims for costs, see chapter 10.

---

52 Specification, para 8.92.
53 Specification, para 8.93.
54 Specification, para 8.88.

CHAPTER 8

Conducting a mental health case

Introduction

8.1   This chapter deals with the funding of mental health cases, and should be read alongside chapters 2 and 3. In this chapter we set out the rules specific to mental health work. You should note that most of those rules are in addition to and build on the general rules applicable to all civil work, set out in chapters 2 and 3. There is no specific costs guidance for mental health work, but see appendix G for a summary of costs issues applicable to all civil work.

The peer reviewer's guide also contains useful guidance on the conduct of work and matters such as the extent to which a client's condition should dictate the level of advice and time in attendance they receive. The guide is available on the Legal Services Commission (LSC) website at www.legalservices.gov.uk > Community Legal Service (CLS) > Quality and Performance > Peer Review > Improving your Quality.

What is mental health work?

! Change from previous rules !

8.2   The mental health category of law is defined as:

1   Advice and help where the primary problem or issue relates to a point of English law concerning mental health or the Mental Health Act 1983,or the Mental Capacity Act 2005, including matters concerning education issues but only where based on mental impairment.

2   All proceedings before the Mental Health Tribunal (MHT) (including those arising from criminal proceedings and any related proceedings before the Upper Tribunal, High Court, Court of Appeal or Supreme Court), all other proceedings under the Mental Health Act 1983 or Mental Capacity Act 2005 and any other proceedings where the primary issue is mental health, but excluding any matters falling within the clinical negligence or personal injury categories.[1]

Mental health work is governed by the general provisions of the 2010 Standard Civil Contract, and by section 9 of the Specification. See chapters 2 and 3 of this book for the general rules.

---

1   Category Definitions 2010.

Who can do the work?

! Change from previous rules !

8.3 The 2010 Standard Civil Contract divides work in the mental health category into two types – standard work, and work in high security hospitals.[2] Mental Health Contracts were let by procurement area, with each procurement area being based on a strategic health authority area.

To do any mental health work at all, you must have a schedule authorisation for at least one procurement area. In addition, to do a case in any of the high security hospitals you must either:

- have a schedule authorising you to work in that hospital;[3] or
- be acting for a client whom you have advised in the last two years (or earlier, if you were the last provider to advise him or her) who has since been transferred to a high security hospital, but only if:
  - the client wishes you to continue to act for him or her;
  - you employ an authorised litigator;
  - you have experience of cases involved restricted patients under Mental Health Act 1983 s79; and
  - all representation before the MHT will be carried out by a member of the Law Society Mental Health Review Tribunal accreditation scheme.[4]

If you rely on the second of these two conditions, you should keep evidence of how you comply with the criteria on that case file.

Use of matter starts

! Change from previous rules !

8.4 Subject to the above rules regarding cases in high security hospitals, you can take on cases as you see fit. However, you must use at least 70 per cent of your matter starts for a procurement area on clients who were physically located in the procurement area at the time the matter start is opened.[5]

---

2 Broadmoor, Rampton, Ashworth – Specification, para 9.1.
3 Specification, para 9.6.
4 Specification, para 9.8.
5 Specification, para 9.7.

Levels of funding

8.5   The following levels of funding apply to mental health work:

- Legal Help – advice and assistance, but excluding representation before the tribunal.
- Help at Court – funding for representation for victims under the Domestic Violence, Crime and Victims Act 2004.
- Controlled Legal Representation (CLR) – representation before the tribunal.
- Legal Representation (certificate) – appeals to the Upper Tribunal and representation in the higher courts, including the Court of Protection.[6]

Legal Help, Help at Court and CLR granted on the same case all form part of the same matter.

Mental health work is covered by standard fees (SF) for almost all controlled (ie non-certificate) work – the sole exception being Help at Court for victims.[7]

There are four fees:[8]

- the non-MHT fee, for all work that does not go to the tribunal;
- MHT fee level 1 – initial advice;[9]
- MHT fee level 2 – negotiation and preparation once an application to the MHT has been made;[10] and
- MHT fee level 3 – representation before the MHT, and follow-up work.[11]

A fee may be claimed for each stage through which the matter passes. Any disbursements incurred are in addition to the fee, but where counsel is instructed, their fees are included in the graduated fee[12] and it is for you to negotiate with counsel which part of the fee you will pay to counsel and which part you will keep. Further fees are payable for adjourned hearings[13] and for travel to any hospital that the LSC has designated on their website as a remote hospital[14] (at the time of writing, none had been designated for the 2010 contract).

---

6 Specification, para 9.3.
7 Specification, para 9.86.
8 Specification, para 9.48.
9 Specification, para 9.64.
10 Specification, para 9.66.
11 Specification, para 9.70.
12 Specification, para 9.43.
13 Specification, para 9.71.
14 Specification, para 9.74.

See chapter 10 for more on payment.

Case study

I have granted CLR to my client. I made an application to the tribunal. I prepared the case and represented him at a manager's review, but he then decided he didn't want to proceed to a full hearing yet. What can I claim?

All work is covered by the level 2 fee. You can claim for preparation work, and for attendance at meetings and reviews, at this level. You only go on to level 3 if there is an MHT hearing.

Granting Legal Help

8.6 The general rules set out in chapter 2 and 3 apply to the granting of Legal Help in the mental health category. Where the client's condition is such that he or she will not sign the application form, and there is no other person who could sign it on their behalf, a supervisor in your organisation can sign it on their behalf.[15] The reasons should be noted on file.

Means

8.7 The usual means test for Legal Help will apply – see chapter 2 for details. However, where the client is a patient whose case is the subject of proceedings or potential proceedings before the MHT, no means test is required[16] – the client is automatically eligible. Where the case covers both MHT and non-MHT issues, it will be all one matter[17] and therefore no means test need be carried out.[18]

Merits

8.8 The usual merits test for Legal Help – the 'sufficient benefit test' – will apply. See chapter 2 for details of the sufficient benefit test.

---

15 Specification, para 9.42.
16 Community Legal Service (Financial) Regulations 2001 reg 3(e); Specification para 9.15.
17 Specification, para 9.21.
18 Specification, para 9.16.

Granting CLR

8.9 CLR is granted by your signature on a form already signed by the client (subject to the same provisions set out above for Legal Help where the client is unable or refuses to sign).[19] Since a grant of CLR is a requirement in any case that goes to the MHT (subject to merit, below), and therefore very much standard practice in most cases, it can become easy to overlook the necessity actually to sign the form and keep it on file. In our experience, some firms have suffered on costs compliance audit as a result. You may wish to consider incorporating a reminder into your file opening checklist.

Means

8.10 CLR for representation before the MHT is available without the need for a means test.[20]

Merits

8.11 The merits test applicable to CLR in the mental health category is set at a very low threshold, given that the client's liberty is at stake. The test is that an application may be refused if it is unreasonable in the particular circumstances of the case for CLR to be granted.[21] The contract makes clear that it would be unusual for it to be unreasonable to grant CLR.[22] However, the prospects of success will govern how much work should be done. CLR is available to the patient, and if the nearest relative is the applicant to the tribunal, to the nearest relative.[23]

Conduct of the case

Non-MHT cases

8.12 All cases that do not concern an application or potential application to the MHT are deemed to be non-MHT cases and attract the non-MHT fee.[24] Only Legal Help is available.

---

19 Specification, para 9.39.
20 Community Legal Service (Financial) Regulations 2001 reg 3(e); Specification, paras 12.46 and 9.15.
21 Funding Code, criterion 12.4.
22 Specification, para 9.37.
23 Specification, para 9.35.
24 Specification, para 9.57.

Where you are acting for a victim, Help at Court for representation is available and claimed at hourly rates on top of the fee.[25]

Initial advice in a Mental Capacity Act case is a non-MHT matter,[26] including making an application for a certificate for representation before the Court of Protection.

MHT cases

8.13   MHT cases divide into three fee stages.

Stage 1 is funded by Legal Help and covers initial advice to the client, including a visit to the client and follow-up work up to and including making an application to the MHT.[27]

Once it becomes clear that the case is to be considered by the MHT, you should grant CLR[28] and continue work at stage 2, but you can only go to stage 2 having passed through (and done at least 30 minutes of work at) stage 1.[29] This stage covers all work up to, but not including, the substantive hearing,[30] including preparation of the case generally and for the hearing, negotiation with third parties, attendance at managers' reviews and other meetings[31] where appropriate,[32] as well as taking instructions from the client and instructing experts.

Stage 3 covers representation at the tribunal hearing,[33] including any adjourned hearings (for which an additional fee is payable[34]). Stage 3 also includes work done in applying to the tribunal for a review of its decision under Tribunals Courts and Enforcement Act 2007 s9, or applying for permission to appeal under s11.[35]

Where the tribunal sets aside its decision, you are still in stage 3 but may claim an additional adjourned hearing fee.[36] However, where an appeal or review goes to the upper tribunal, you will need to apply for a certificate for representation at that stage.[37]

25 Specification, para 9.86.
26 Specification, para 9.29.
27 Specification, para 9.64.
28 Specification, para 9.38.
29 Specification, para 9.67.
30 Specification, para 9.66.
31 Specification, para 9.68.
32 Specification, para 9.69.
33 Specification, para 9.70.
34 Specification, para 9.71.
35 Specification, para 9.87.
36 Specification, para 9.87.
37 Specification, para 9.91.

Separate matters

8.14   Each time a client becomes eligible to make an application to the tribunal they enter a 'period of eligibility'.[38] All work done for a client within a period of eligibility, on both MHT and non-MHT matters, forms one matter start.[39] However, where more than one set of MHT proceedings are running concurrently during a period of eligibility, you can claim separate fees for each set of proceedings.

Where you are advising an informal patient (ie not detained) on a non-MHT matter, and the patient is then sectioned, you can open a separate matter to apply to the tribunal, even if the non-MHT matter continues.[40]

When dealing with a detained client, you must start a new matter for each of the following events (where work on a legal issue is required), even if you have an existing ongoing matter:[41]

- the client has an entitlement to a further MHT due to passage of time;
- there is a change in section type;
- the client is discharged from section;
- the client withdraws from the MHT, and within the same period of eligibility applies again.

However, note that communicating the decision of the MHT, advising the client about it and about aftercare is the same matter as the MHT.[42]

Where a Mental Capacity Act matter is open, and then the client is sectioned or otherwise requires MHT advice, a separate MHT matter should be opened.[43]

Disbursements

8.15   Disbursements may be incurred in the usual way in the mental health category.

You can make a claim for payment on account of disbursements during the life of a case, but only where the matter has been open for

---

38 Specification, para 9.58.
39 Specification, para 9.20.
40 Specification, para 9.22.
41 Specification, para 9.24.
42 Specification, para 9.25.
43 Specification, para 9.31.

at least six months and, if there has been a previous application for payment on account, at least six months have elapsed since that payment was made.[44]

Use of counsel

8.16 You are entitled to instruct counsel to represent clients before the tribunal (but note that it is a condition of conducting a high security hospital case that all advocacy be carried out by a member of the Law Society's accreditation scheme[45]). Where you instruct counsel, you will still only be entitled to the level 3 fee, and it is a matter for you to negotiate how much of that fee to pay to counsel. Counsel are not a disbursement.[46]

In unusually complex cases, you can apply to the LSC to pay counsel at an hourly rate above the standard hourly rates in the contract.[47] The LSC will grant prior authority, specifying the hourly rate and the maximum costs limit if the case poses unusually complex evidential problems, or novel or difficult points of law. The LSC consider it highly unlikely that such issues will arise at MHT level. These provisions do not appear to override the requirement that all advocacy in high security hospital cases be provided by Law Society scheme members.

44 Specification, para 9.50.
45 Specification, paras 9.6 and 9.8.
46 Specification, para 9.43.
47 Specification, para 9.44.

Conducting a criminal case

by Julia Sherriff

continued

Introduction

9.1   The 2010 Standard Contract Standard Terms govern both civil and criminal work, but each has a separate Contract Specification setting out the detailed funding rules that apply.

Criminal work is divided into classes by the contract:

- investigations – work done pre-charge;
- proceedings – post-charge court work that does not fall into any other class;
- appeals and reviews – post-conviction work on appeals and reviews of convictions or sentences;
- prison law – work in relation to parole, treatment or discipline in the prison system;
- associated civil work – judicial review and Proceeds of Crime Act 2002 work.[1]

In addition, VHCCs (very high cost cases – Crown Court trials that last more than eight weeks) can be thought of as extra classes of work.

A case may move through several classes. For example, a client arrested and charged with burglary will start in the investigations class, then move into the proceedings class; if convicted, he or she may have further cases in the appeals and prison law classes. Each of those classes of work has separate rules and funding mechanisms, and we will look at each in turn in this chapter. We will also consider the general rules which apply to all classes of work.

General rules

Unique file numbers[2]

9.2   The contract requires you to assign a unique file number (UFN) to every case. The case will retain the UFN throughout its life as it moves through the classes of work. Where you act for more than one client on the same case, each client will have their own UFN, though where you must submit a consolidated claim (see chapter 11) it will be under one 'lead' UFN. Where you act for one client on more than one case, each case will have its own UFN.

---

1 Standard Crime Contract Specification 2010 (hereafter 'the Specification'), para A1.5.

2 Specification, paras A4.39 and A4.40.

All UFNs must be in the format set out in the contract – DDM-MYY/NNN, where DDMMYY is the date the client first instructed you on that matter and NNN is a unique three digit number. It does not matter what that number is, as long as no two clients or cases have the same number.

So, for example, the first client to instruct you on 1 February 2010 would have the UFN 010210/001, the second might then be 010210/002, and so on.

The purpose of the UFN is to allow the Legal Services Commission (LSC) to track and, where necessary, check all work done for a particular client. You are therefore required to record the UFN on file, use it for all applications and claims to the LSC and, since the LSC will use it when communicating with you, ensure that you can search your database against it.

Disbursements

9.3   Disbursements – that is, expenses incurred in the course of a client's case – are generally permitted where it is in the best interests of the client to incur the disbursement for the purpose of giving advice, and the amount of the disbursement is reasonable.[3]

This amounts to a three-stage test:

1 It is in the best interests of the client.
2 It is for the purposes of giving advice or representation.
3 The amount is reasonable.

The client's best interests will be served by incurring expenditure that is necessary for you to conduct the case, or that will assist (or may assist) in achieving the best outcome. For example, travel expenses may be in the client's best interests, even though the client does not benefit directly, because it is necessary for you to incur them to get to court. An expert report may or may not assist the client's case – that would depend on what the expert says – but where it has the potential to do so it would likely be in the client's best interests to obtain it. This test should not be applied with the benefit of hindsight; the question is, what was reasonable based on what was known at the time.

'For the purpose of advice or representation' describes the nature and purpose of the expense. To use the preceding example, travel expenses to court are justifiable as being for the purpose of providing representation. A medical report to comment on a client's medical situation would be for that purpose, since it is evidence that could be

3 Specification, para A5.39.

put before the court, but paying for the client to see a medical expert to obtain treatment would not, since it is not necessary for the purpose of giving advice for the client to be treated, only for you to know what his or her condition is.

Finally, the amount of the disbursement must be reasonable. The LSC reserves the right to set maximum rates for particular types of disbursement (such as expert reports)[4] and the amount authorised will usually be determined in accordance with Ministry of Justice guideline rates.[5] Although it is not mandatory to obtain prior authority to incur disbursements,[6] doing so is advisable where substantial sums are to be incurred as prior authority ensures that the disbursement will be paid.[7]

Where disbursements are incurred, you should retain a receipt or invoice on file.[8] Where you incur mileage, that can be claimed at the rate of 45 pence per mile.[9]

Witness expenses to attend court cannot generally be funded under the contract, unless the court has directed that they may not be recovered from central funds (the usual source of witness expenses, including fees of professional witnesses) and they are not recoverable from any other source.[10]

Work in the investigations class

9.4   Investigations work is work done pre-charge or in the police station, and covers:[11]

- police station telephone advice;
- police station attendance;
- Advice and Assistance outside the police station;
- Advocacy Assistance:
  - on a warrant of further detention;
  - on an application to a magistrates' court to vary police bail conditions;
  - at an armed forces custody hearing.

4 Specification, para A5.38.
5 Specification, para A5.34.
6 Specification, para A5.33.
7 Specification, para A5.30.
8 Specification, para A5.41.
9 Specification, para A5.50.
10 Specification, para A5.49.
11 Specification, para A1.5.

Police station cases

Scope of work

9.5   Police station work will consist of telephone advice, attendance in person at the police station, or both. It is generally available to anyone attending a police station, whether under arrest or as a volunteer, during the course of a criminal investigation.[12] The exceptions to this rule are:

- where the matter falls within the scope of the Criminal Defence Service (CDS) Direct scheme (eg arrests for non-imprisonable offences);[13] and
- advice and assistance to a witness (which is covered in certain circumstances by the Advice and Assistance scheme).[14]

Police station work is not means tested.[15]

Police station work can also be carried out post-charge, for example to deal with identification procedures, arrest on warrant or for breach of bail, or for caution or re-charge following discontinuance or dismissal. However, only post-charge work carried out at the police station can be claimed under the criminal investigations class of work.[16]

For these purposes, a 'police station' is a place where a constable is present, and a 'constable' is an official with a power of arrest conferred by virtue of his or her office.[17] For example, an officer of HM Revenue and Customs (HMRC) is a constable, but a Department for Work and Pensions (DWP) benefit fraud investigator is not; therefore, a client arrested by HMRC is entitled to police station representation, but a client being interviewed by the DWP is not. However, such a client may be entitled to Advice and Assistance if the relevant criteria are met. See below for more on Advice and Assistance.

---

12 Specification, para B9.1.
13 Specification, para B9.9.
14 Specification, para B9.4.
15 Criminal Defence Service (General) (No 2) Regulations 2001 reg 5(1).
16 Specification, para B9.109.
17 Specification, para A1.13.

Case study

My firm has a criminal department and a welfare benefits department. One of our clients has been invited to attend the DWP to be interviewed about an allegation that he has been working and claiming benefits. What should I do?

This will be an interview under PACE (Police and Criminal Evidence Act 1984) and a criminal lawyer should attend, so you should refer the client to your criminal department. Since an officer of the DWP does not have a power of arrest, your client would not be entitled to police station legal aid. However, subject to means, your client would be entitled to Advice and Assistance. You should get the client to sign a CDS1 and CDS2 and provide proof of means, and then you will be funded to attend the interview with the client. You will have a costs limit of £300, but this can be extended on application to the LSC if necessary.

Sources of work

9.6 In January 2008, the LSC implemented the Defence Solicitor Call Centre (DSCC) and required all requests by detained persons to go through the centre – in its previous incarnation as the Duty Solicitor Call Centre it had only dealt with duty cases.

The call centre records the basic details of an alleged offence before passing the case on to the own solicitor requested, the duty solicitor or CDS Direct. CDS Direct provide telephone advice to clients detained for less serious offences such as drink-driving offences, non-imprisonable offences, breaches of bail and warrants.

Where an attendance is likely to be necessary, CDS Direct will not deal with the matter and the case will be passed to the own solicitor (if requested) or the duty solicitor.

However, you may also be contacted direct by a third party, for example the relative of a client, and requested to take on the case. You may also be contacted by a client direct, for example a client who is aware that the police are looking for him or her and wants to surrender. In such a situation you can take on the case and provide telephone advice and attendance as appropriate, but must report to the call centre that you have taken the case.[18]

---

18 Specification, para B9.20.

Case study

My client's wife phoned to say that he has been arrested for theft, and wants me to go to the police station. Can I go?

Yes. You can attend the police station when instructed to do so by a third party. However, you must notify the DSCC that you have taken the case. You must notify them before you contact the client and obtain a reference number. See para B9.20 of the Specification – you must notify the DSCC in advance for third party instructions and within 48 hours where you are at a police station and instructed direct, or where a client instructs you direct to attend a surrender or bail date.

Permitted work

9.7   Whatever the source of the case, you should consider whether or not to attend the police station. Attendance at the police station is mandatory where:

- the client has been arrested and is to be interviewed;
- there is to be an identification procedure (except a video parade, attendance at which is discretionary[19]);
- the client complains of serious maltreatment by the police.[20]

You cannot claim for payment for attendance at the police station where:

- the client has been arrested solely for non-imprisonable offences;
- the client has been arrested on a warrant for failure to appear or for breach of court or police bail, unless you have clear documentary evidence that would result in the client's release, eg a bail form showing that the client is not in fact in breach of a condition;
- the client has been arrested for offences under Road Traffic Act 1988 ss4, 5, 6, 7 and 7A (driving whilst unfit, drunk in charge of a vehicle, driving with excess alcohol or failure to provide a specimen).[21]

However, attendance in a prohibited case will be permitted (or mandatory, as the case may be) if one of the exceptions apply:

19 Specification, para B9.41.
20 Specification, para B9.39.
21 Specification, para B9.9.

- there is to be an interview or identification procedure;
- the client requires an appropriate adult;
- the client is unable to communicate over the telephone;
- the client complains of serious maltreatment by the police;
- the client is being investigated for an additional offence not covered by the above list;
- you are already at the same police station (but in this case you may only claim the Telephone Advice Fixed Fee);
- the advice relates to an indictable offence;
- the request is identified as a 'Special Request' by the DSCC.[22]

In all other cases, attendance at the police station is at your discretion, and you should consider whether the 'sufficient benefit' test is met. This is the merits test for police station work and states that work may only be done where 'there is sufficient benefit to the client, having regard to the circumstances of the matter, including the personal circumstances of the client, to justify work or further work being carried out'.[23]

The test would be automatically satisfied where the client has a right to advice under the Police and Criminal Evidence Act 1984 (PACE), or where the client is a volunteer, or under equivalent military legislation – but only in relation to initial advice; you must apply the test to determine the extent of advice, and particularly whether attendance (as opposed to telephone advice) is necessary.[24]

Where you intend to attend the police station, and it is not one of the mandatory attendances outlined above, you should be satisfied that the attendance is necessary for the purpose of giving advice that could not be given over the telephone, and is expected to progress the case materially. Specifically, the contract says that it might be reasonable to remain at the police station post-charge to provide advice or make representations on bail, but unless the client is particularly vulnerable it would not be reasonable to stay for photographs, fingerprints and DNA samples.[25]

Who may carry out work?

9.8 Although almost all work comes through the Defence Solicitor Call Centre, there is a distinction between own client and duty work – own

22 Specification, para B9.10.
23 Specification, para A3.10.
24 Specification, para B9.14.
25 Specification, para B9.16.

client being cases where you or your firm were specifically requested, and duty work where the client requested the duty solicitor and the case was allocated to you.

In order to carry out police station work, you must be accredited and registered as such by the LSC. An accredited representative is one who has passed the Police Station Qualification, which is administered by the Solicitors Regulation Authority and consists of a two-part portfolio of cases, an oral examination known as the critical incidents test and a written examination (which need not be taken by a representative who has a legal qualification).

To become a probationary representative you must pass the written examination (if required) and part one of the portfolio; you then have one year to pass the remaining elements to become fully accredited. The accreditation process is no longer bypassed by qualification as a solicitor; everyone must be accredited to do police station work. The training and quality assurance of probationary and accredited representatives must be documented.[26]

Probationary representatives cannot do duty cases, and cannot do cases where the offence under investigation is indictable only; fully accredited representatives can do all cases. See B9.26 to B9.38 of the Contract Specification. See chapter 17 for the obligations of those who manage and supervise representatives.

Starting a case

9.9   Police station work is not means tested, and the client is not required to complete any application form.

A case will be initiated when you are contacted, either by the DSCC or by the client or a third party, and requested to provide advice.

When you take on a case where the client has been arrested and is at the police station, you must make first contact with the client within 45 minutes of being notified of the case.[27] This is a target set out in the contract which should be met in at least 80 per cent of cases, and to enable monitoring of the target,[28] your file should contain a note of the time the case was accepted and the time of first contact, together with a note of why contact was not possible inside the 45 minutes, if applicable.[29]

26 Specification, para B9.33.
27 Specification, para B9.23.
28 Specification, para B9.24.
29 Specification, para B9.25.

Where a client has previously received police station advice on the same matter within the past six months, you cannot provide further advice on the same matter unless:

- there is a gap in time and a material change in circumstances between the first and second occasions; or
- the client has reasonable cause to transfer; or
- the first supplier confirms they will not make a claim.[30]

You should make reasonable enquiries of the client to see if there has been previous advice, and if there has been and the exceptions are not met, should not take the case and cannot make a claim. Reasonable cause for transfer will not be made out where the client finds sound advice unpalatable and wants a second opinion.[31] Where you take on a transfer case, you should note the reason on the file.

Conducting work

9.10   Once you have accepted a case, you can continue to do such work as is necessary and complies with the requirements above. Where the client is bailed to return to the police station, attendance at the bail to return is funded on the same basis as the initial attendance and will be included in the fixed fee – you should ensure that the sufficient benefit test is satisfied and that you are permitted to attend.

There is no costs limitation for police station work.

Police station work will come to an end at the point the client is charged or cautioned, the police decide to take no further action, or the case is otherwise ended. A bill should be submitted at that point – see chapter 11 for details of costs and the billing procedure.

Warrants of further detention

9.11   Where a client is detained and the police seek an extension to the detention under PACE s43 or s44, or under Terrorism Act 2000 Sch 8 para 29 or para 36, you can provide Advocacy Assistance to represent the client at the hearing of the application.[32]

Advocacy Assistance is not means tested[33] and the client is not required to sign an application form, but you should record on the file that you have granted funding.[34] The scope of Advocacy Assistance

---

30 Specification, para B9.70.
31 Specification, para B9.73.
32 Specification, para B9.145.
33 Criminal Defence Service (General) (No 2) Regulations 2001 reg 5(1).
34 Specification, para B9.148.

includes any reasonable preparation and follow-up work.[35] However, counsel may only be instructed in applications before the High Court or a senior judge.[36]

Similar provisions apply to armed forces custody hearings.[37]

Variation of police bail

9.12   In certain circumstances, where the police have the power to impose bail conditions (or 'street bail' conditions), a client can make an application to a magistrates' court to vary the conditions.[38]

You can grant Advocacy Assistance to represent such a client.[39] It is not means tested,[40] and no application form is required, though a note of the grant should be made on the file.[41] The scope of Advocacy Assistance includes any reasonable preparation and giving of any advice on appeal.[42] However, counsel may not be instructed.[43]

Advice and Assistance

9.13   Advice and Assistance can be given to a client who meets the means and merits tests, to advise and assist in respect of a criminal investigation – that is, before the client is charged or summonsed for an offence. It will include representing the client at interviews with non-police agencies, such as the Department for Work and Pensions in a benefit fraud matter, as well as general advice, case preparation and related work.

Means test

9.14   In order to qualify for Advice and Assistance, the client must pass the means test.[44] There are two elements to the test – income and capital – and the client must pass both parts. You are responsible for assessing the client's means and deciding whether the test is met.

---

35 Specification, para B9.151.
36 Specification, para B9.152.
37 Specification, paras B9.158–B9.170.
38 Police and Criminal Evidence Act 1984 ss30BC and 47(1E).
39 Specification, para B9.171.
40 Criminal Defence Service (General) (No 2) Regulations 2001 reg 5(1).
41 Specification, para B9.174.
42 Specification, para B9.176.
43 Specification, para B9.177.
44 Criminal Defence Service (General) (No 2) Regulations 2001 reg 5(5).

Where the client is directly or indirectly in receipt of any of the following benefits, he or she automatically qualifies for Advice and Assistance without the need for an assessment of income or capital:

- income support;
- income-based jobseeker's allowance;
- income-based employment and support allowance;
- guarantee pension credit;
- working tax credit paid with child tax credit and where the gross annual income is below £14,213;
- working tax credit with a disability element or severe disability element where the gross annual income is below £14,213.[45]

A person is indirectly in receipt of a benefit if they are included in another person's claim, eg if a partner receives it on the basis of a couple.

'Capital' means all the client's assets and resources, excluding household furniture and effects, clothes and the tools of the client's trade. Where the client owns property, the value to be taken into account is the equity after disregarding any mortgage, though only up to the value of £100,000. The first £100,000 of any equity is also disregarded, and the remainder is the capital value.[46] Where the client has a partner, the partner's capital should also be taken into account.

Case study

My client has a flat worth £120,000, with a mortgage of £90,000. He has £650 in savings and his wife has £300 in her account. Is he eligible on capital?

The flat is worth £120,000. Disregard up to £100,000 of the mortgage – so the equity is £30,000. Disregard up to £100,000 of equity – so the capital is nil. Aggregate his and his wife's savings, so the total capital is £950, so the client is eligible on capital.

'Income' means all income from any source which the client may reasonably expect to receive within the seven days up to and including the day of his or her application,[47] with the following exceptions:

45 Criminal Defence Service (General) (No 2) Regulations 2001 reg 5(8).
46 Criminal Defence Service (General) (No 2) Regulations 2001 Sch 1 para 7.
47 Criminal Defence Service (General) (No 2) Regulations 2001 Sch 1 para 1.

- any tax and National Insurance paid;
- any contributions paid under Part I of the Social Security Contributions and Benefits Act 1992;
- disability living allowance;
- attendance allowance;
- constant attendance allowance;
- any payment out of the social fund;
- any payment under the Community Care (Direct Payments) Act 1996.[48]

Where the client has a partner, the partner's income should also be taken into account.[49] Where the client has a partner or other dependant member of the household, you should deduct the standard allowance for each member.[50]

The thresholds for capital and income, and the standard dependants allowances, can be found on the keycard at www.legalservices. gov.uk > CDS > Criminal legal aid eligibility. The levels are uprated periodically, usually when benefit levels are increased in April each year, and you should check the website for the most up to date figures.

Evidence of the client's means will be required, and should be retained on file.[51] There is a power to assess means without evidence where it is not practicable to obtain it before the form is signed, but it should be obtained at a later stage and if it is not, any claim should be limited to the equivalent of two hours.[52] In exceptional circumstances, you may dispense with evidence altogether if the client's circumstances make it impracticable to obtain it at any point.[53]

Merits test

9.15   Assuming the client qualifies on means, you should go on to consider whether there is merit. The merits test is the 'sufficient benefit' test – is there 'sufficient benefit to the client, having regard to the circumstances of the matter, including the personal circumstances of the client, to justify work or further work being carried out'.[54]

---

48 Criminal Defence Service (General) (No 2) Regulations 2001 Sch 1 para 8(1).
49 Criminal Defence Service (General) (No 2) Regulations 2001 Sch 1 para 6(1).
50 Criminal Defence Service (General) (No 2) Regulations 2001 Sch 1 para 8(2).
51 Specification, para B9.119.
52 Specification, para A3.7.
53 Specification, para A3.6.
54 Specification, para A3.10.

The sufficient benefit test must be applied throughout the case to determine the extent of the advice required,[55] and the provision of advice must cease if it becomes apparent that the test is no longer satisfied.[56]

The application

9.16   The client must complete and sign the application forms – CDS1 and CDS2 – and you should retain the original copies of them on file. Advice and Assistance is granted by you, with no application to the LSC required, and so the presence of the signed forms on file is sufficient to effect the grant.

The usual rule is that the client comes to you to sign the forms. However, there will be situations where that is not possible, and therefore the contract allows for exceptions where certain criteria are met:

- A **postal application** can be accepted where it is reasonable to do so (for example, where there is good reason why the client cannot attend your offices). However, you cannot accept a postal application where a client is temporarily resident outside the European Union and the matter can be delayed until they return, or another person in England and Wales could apply for Advice and Assistance on the same matter.[57]

- Where the client cannot attend immediately but can telephone you, **telephone advice can be given before the form is signed**[58] and you can claim for that advice. In order to qualify, there has to be good reason why the client cannot attend the office, but the client must later sign the form and be eligible. This power can be combined with one of the others; for example, you could give telephone advice to a client in prison and then post the form to him or her.

- Where the client lacks capacity, you can accept **an application on behalf of a child or person lacking mental capacity**[59] from another person, such as a parent, guardian, deputy or attorney, litigation friend, or any other person where there is good reason why one of the above-named persons cannot make the application. Again,

55 Specification, paras A3.11, A3.15.
56 Specification, para A3.12.
57 Specification, para A4.30.
58 Specification, para B9.125.
59 Specification, para A4.24.

the form will be signed by the authorised person but completed in the name of the client, and it will be the client's means that should be assessed and evidenced.

- You can also accept **an application from a child direct**[60] where the client is entitled to defend proceedings himself or herself (which is true of almost all criminal work), or where you are satisfied that there is good reason why none of the authorised persons in the previous paragraph can make the application and the child is old enough to give instructions and understand the nature of the advice, or where the child is seeking police station advice only.

Where a client cannot attend the office for one of the good reasons outlined above, you may claim for outward travel expenses,[61] and where the client is in custody, detention or hospital travel time[62] for travelling to see the client before the form is signed in order to get the form signed.

Where a client has received previous Advice and Assistance on the same matter within the last six months, there are restrictions on where you can accept a further application that would involve a change of solicitor.[63] You cannot accept such an application unless:

- there is a gap in time and a material change in circumstances; or
- the client has reasonable cause to transfer from the first supplier; or
- the first supplier confirms they are making no claim; or
- previous Advice and Assistance was police station advice only.

You should make reasonable enquiries of the client to find out whether there has been previous Advice and Assistance. If so, and if you can justify the change of solicitor, there should be a clear note to that effect on the file.

Conducting work

9.17   Once you have confirmed that the client is eligible and the form has been signed, you can proceed to work on the client's case.

Advice and Assistance covers all necessary work (other than work in the police station) up to the point at which the client is charged with or summonsed for an offence. It will cover you for attendance

---

60 Specification, para A4.27.
61 Specification, para B9.126.
62 Specification, para B9.127.
63 Specification, para B9.129.

and advice to the client, case preparation, taking witness statements with a view to preserving memory or avoiding charge, and so on. It will also cover attendance at interviews with non-police agencies.

Costs are limited to £300, though an application may be made to the LSC to extend that limit. The limit includes both time and disbursements. Where Advice and Assistance runs alongside police station work, you may not make a separate claim for the Advice and Assistance; all work pre-charge is covered by the police station fixed fee. However, the costs limit will continue to apply and you will need to be within the limit or have a granted extension for Advice and Assistance costs to count towards exceptionality. See chapter 11 for more on claiming for criminal work.

Separate matters

9.18   All work for a client that constitutes one matter will require one application and will lead to one claim. Where, however, work is a genuinely separate matter then a separate application and a separate claim will be required.

All work in respect of a single investigation constitutes one matter and therefore one claim for costs, even if the investigation is subsequently extended to cover other offences. However, work may be treated as a separate matter if it amounts to a generally separate problem requiring separate advice,[64] unless the client requires advice on one occasion only.[65] Where charges are laid at the same time and go on to be one set of proceedings, they will be one matter.[66]

Case study

I had a client who was arrested for theft and taken to the police station, where it was found he was also wanted for a separate incident of criminal damage, and he was further arrested for that. Is that one matter or two?

It depends on the outcome of the case. If he were charged with both offences and bailed to the same court date, that would be one matter and one claim. This is because the two allegations required advice on one occasion only, and resulted in one set of proceedings. However,

---

64 Specification, para A4.42.
65 Specification, para A4.45.
66 Specification, para A4.53.

if he were charged with theft and bailed to return on the criminal damage, that would constitute two matters since they require separate advice on more than one occasion and do not go on to be one set of proceedings. Similarly if he were charged to two different courts on two different dates, that would constitute two matters and two fees, since although only dealt with on one occasion, the allegations go on to form more than one set of proceedings.

Work in the proceedings class

9.19   The proceedings class runs from the point of charge/summons and now includes all magistrates' court work and most Crown Court proceedings.

The main funding types in the proceedings class are:

- Advice and Assistance/Advocacy Assistance as court duty solicitor;
- Representation Orders.

Court duty solicitor work

9.20   A duty solicitor is a solicitor who has passed both the Police Station Qualification and Magistrates' Court Qualification, and has registered as a duty solicitor with the LSC. See the Duty Solicitor Arrangements 2008 for details of the qualification and ongoing obligations required of duty solicitors.

Duty solicitors are entitled to apply to be members of their local court rota, and in certain places additional rotas (see the arrangements for details). Each court house – and in particularly busy courts, each courtroom – will have a duty solicitor available each day, taken from the rota, whose role is to advise and assist otherwise unrepresented defendants.

Technically speaking, two different funding types are available to a court duty solicitor – Advice and Assistance and Advocacy Assistance, to advise the client outside court and represent the client in court respectively. In practice, however, there is no real distinction and a single consolidated claim is made for all work done for all clients on a duty day.

Court duty advice is available to clients whose cases qualify for assistance without regard to their means, and no application form is needed. However, a file note of the details of the client and the case will be needed.

However, clients can only be represented where their case comes within the scope of the scheme:

- The duty solicitor must:[67]
  - advise any client who requests it who is in custody;
  - make a bail application where a client in custody requires a bail application and such an application has not previously been made by a duty solicitor;
  - advise and represent a client before the court in connection with civil orders deemed to be criminal for legal aid purposes:[68]
    - anti-social behaviour orders;[69]
    - parenting orders;[70]
    - football banning orders;[71]
    - closure orders;[72]
    - sexual offences notification orders;[73]
    - sexual offences prevention orders;[74]
    - foreign travel orders;[75]
    - risk of sexual harm orders;[76]
    - restraining orders.[77]

- The duty solicitor may:[78]
  - advise and represent any client who is in custody on a plea of guilty and wishes the case to be concluded that day;
  - advise and represent any client before the court for failure to pay a fine or other sum or to obey an order of the court, and such failure may lead to the client being at risk of imprisonment;
  - advise and represent a client not in custody in connection with an imprisonable offence;

67 Specification, para B10.7.
68 Criminal Defence Service (General) (No 2) Regulations 2001 reg 3(2).
69 Crime and Disorder Act 1998 ss1, 1D, 1G, 1H and 4.
70 Crime and Disorder Act 1998 ss8, 9 and 10; Anti-Social Behaviour Act 2003 ss20, 22, 26 and 28; Powers of Criminal Courts (Sentencing) Act 2000 Sch 1 Part 1A.
71 Football Spectators Act 1989 ss14B, 14D, 14G, 14H, 21B and 21D.
72 Anti-Social Behaviour Act 2003 ss2, 5 and 6.
73 Sexual Offences Act 2003 ss97, 100 and 101.
74 Sexual Offences Act 2003 ss104, 108, 109 and 110.
75 Sexual Offences Act 2003 ss114, 118 and 119.
76 Sexual Offences Act 2003 ss123, 125, 126 and 127.
77 Protection from Harassment Act 1997 s5A.
78 Specification, para B10.8.

- help a client in making an application for a Representation Order, whether the nominated solicitor is the duty solicitor or another solicitor;
- advise and represent a client seeking to vary police-imposed bail conditions pre-charge.
- The duty solicitor must not:
  - represent in committal proceedings;
  - represent at a not guilty trial;[79]
  - advise or represent a client who has had the services of a duty solicitor at a previous hearing in the proceedings (except where they are before the court this time as a result of failure to pay a fine or other sum or comply with an order imposed previously).[80]

As duty solicitor, with the client's permission you are entitled to take on the case and apply for a Representation Order – and indeed court duty slots are a common source of work. However, you should not apply for a Representation Order where the case concludes on the day of the duty.[81]

Representation Orders – magistrates' court

Scope

9.21   A Representation Order is the only method of funding proceedings in the magistrates' court.

! Change from previous rules !

It covers representation to clients charged or summonsed for criminal offences, and also covers proceedings deemed to be criminal for the purpose of legal aid funding, as set out in Criminal Defence Service (General) (No 2) Regulations 2001 reg 3(2):

(a) civil proceedings in a magistrates' court arising from failure to pay a sum due or to obey an order of that court where such failure carries the risk of imprisonment;

(b) proceedings under sections 1, 1D and 4 of the 1998 Act relating to anti-social behaviour orders;

(ba) proceedings under sections 1G and 1H of the 1998 Act relating to intervention orders, in which an application for an anti-social behaviour order has been made;

---

79 Specification, para B10.9.
80 Specification, para B10.10.
81 Specification, para B10.14.

(c) proceedings under section 8(1)(b) of the 1998 Act relating to parenting orders made where an anti-social behaviour order or a sex offender order is made in respect of a child;

(d) proceedings under section 8(1)(c) of the 1998 Act relating to parenting orders made on the conviction of a child;

(e) proceedings under section 9(5) of the 1998 Act to discharge or vary a parenting order made as mentioned in sub-paragraph (c) or (d);

(f) proceedings under section 10 of the 1998 Act to appeal against a parenting order made as mentioned in sub-paragraph (c) or (d);

(g) proceedings under sections 14B, 14D, 14G, 14H, 21B and 21D of the Football Spectators Act 1989 (banning orders and references to a court);

(h) proceedings under section 13 of the Tribunals, Courts and Enquiries Act 2007 (c 15) on appeal against a decision of the Upper Tribunal in proceedings in respect of—
   (i) a decision of the Financial Services Authority;
   (ii) a decision of the Bank of England; or
   (iii) a decision of a person relating to the assessment of any compensation or consideration under the Banking (Special Provisions) Act 2008 or the Banking Act 2009;

(i) proceedings under sections 2, 5 and 6 of the Anti-social Behaviour Act 2003 relating to closure orders;

(j) proceedings under sections 20, 22, 26 and 28 of the Anti-Social Behaviour Act 2003 relating to parenting orders in cases of exclusion from school and parenting orders in respect of criminal conduct and anti-social behaviour;

(k) proceedings under sections 97, 100 and 101 of the Sexual Offences Act 2003 relating to notification orders and interim notification orders;

(l) proceedings under sections 104, 108, 109 and 110 of the Sexual Offences Act 2003 relating to sexual offences prevention orders and interim sexual offences prevention orders;

(m) proceedings under sections 114, 118 and 119 of the Sexual Offences Act 2003 relating to foreign travel orders;

(n) proceedings under sections 123, 125, 126 and 127 of the Sexual Offences Act 2003 relating to risk of sexual harm orders and interim risk of sexual harm orders;

(o) proceedings under Part 1A of Schedule 1 to the Powers of Criminal Courts (Sentencing) Act 2000 relating to parenting orders for failure to comply with orders under section 20 of that Act;

(p) proceedings under section 5A of the Protection from Harassment Act 1997 relating to restraining orders on acquittal;

(q) proceedings before the Crown Court or the Court of Appeal relating to serious crime prevention orders and arising by virtue of section 19, 20, 21 or 24 of the Serious Crime Act 2007;

(r)   proceedings under sections 100, 101, 103, 104 and 106 of the Criminal Justice and Immigration Act 2008 relating to violent offender orders and interim violent offender orders;

(s)   proceedings under sections 3, 5, 9 and 10 of the Violent Crime Reduction Act 2006 relating to drinking banning orders and interim orders.

Case study

My client is in arrears on council tax. She has been summonsed to appear at the magistrates' court. I cannot represent her under my contract. Can I advise her to see the court duty solicitor?

She is in principle eligible to see the duty solicitor, since she is before the court for failure to pay a sum due. Whether she can use the duty depends on whether she is at risk of imprisonment, which is the merits test for court duty work. That will depend on the facts of her case and is more likely if she is in wilful default.

An order also covers advice on appeal, and any related bail proceedings in the Crown Court or High Court.[82]

Financial eligibility

9.22   Representation Orders in the magistrates' court are means tested. With the introduction of Crown Court means testing, committal proceedings and sendings under Crime and Disorder Act 1998 s51 can no longer be treated as non-means tested. Therefore a full application for a Representation Order (including means information) must be completed in all cases.

Applications for Representation Orders are made to the courts, and the court will apply the means test to decide whether the client is eligible. However, you will need an understanding of the test in order to advise clients whether they are likely to be eligible.

The details of the test, together with the eligibility limits applying from time to time can be found in the Criminal Defence Service (Financial Eligibility) Regulations 2006 as amended. The eligibility limits are amended every so often, usually in April, and the discussion that follows is based on the limits applying in August 2010. Up-to-date limits and a calculator can be found on the LSC website at www.legalservices.gov.uk > CDS > Criminal Legal Aid Eligibility > Means Testing.

82 Specification, para B10.35.

Eligibility for a Representation Order is based solely on income – capital is not taken into account. There are three stages to the test:

1 Is the client under the age of 18, or directly or indirectly in receipt of a passport benefit?

2 If not, is the client's gross income below the initial test threshold?

3 If not, is the client's disposable income below the full means test threshold?

If the answer to all three questions is no, the client is not eligible.

The means of the client's partner should always be taken into account, unless the partner has a contrary interest in the proceedings (for example, is a victim or prosecution witness), together with the resources of any other person which have been or are likely to be made available to the client.[83]

The passporting benefits are:[84]

• income support;
• income-based jobseeker's allowance;
• guarantee state pension credit;
• income-related employment and support allowance (ESA).

If the client is directly or indirectly in receipt of any of these, he or she will automatically be eligible for legal aid. Indirectly in receipt means that the client is included as a dependant on another person's claim.

If the client is not passported, you will need to proceed to the two-stage means test. If gross income is below the initial threshold, currently £12,457, then he or she is eligible. If gross income is over £22,325, he or she is not eligible.[85] If gross income is between those two figures, then a full means test to determine disposable income will be required. Following that test, if disposable income is less than £3,398 the client will be eligible. All figures are annual.

'Gross income' is all income from all sources, excluding certain benefits:[86]

• attendance allowance;
• severe disablement allowance;
• carer's allowance;
• disability living allowance;
• constant attendance allowance;

---

83 Criminal Defence Service (Financial Eligibility) Regulations 2006 reg 7.
84 Criminal Defence Service (Financial Eligibility) Regulations 2006 reg 5(4).
85 Criminal Defence Service (Financial Eligibility) Regulations 2006 reg 9.
86 Criminal Defence Service (Financial Eligibility) Regulations 2006 reg 2(1).

- council tax benefit;
- payments out of the social fund;
- direct payments under the Community Care, Services for Carers and Children's Services (Direct Payments) Regulations;
- exceptionally severe disablement allowance;
- service pensions paid under the Naval Military and Air Forces Etc (Disablement and Death) Service Pensions Order 2006;
- independent living funds payments;
- financial support paid for the foster care of a child.

Where the client has a partner or children in the same household, the gross income threshold increases according to the following weighting:[87]

Person	Weighting
Partner	0.64
Child 0–1 years	0.15
Child 2–4 years	0.30
Child 5–7 years	0.34
Child 8–10 years	0.38
Child 11–12 years	0.41
Child 13–15 years	0.44
Child 16–18 years	0.59

To calculate the weighting, add the relevant factors to 1 and divide household income by the result.

Case study

My client earns £25,000 per year. He lives with his partner and their children, aged 6 and 3. Is he eligible for a Representation Order?

The client has a partner and two children, so the weighting is 1 + 0.64 + 0.30 + 0.34 = 2.28. Weighted income = £25,000 divided by 2.28 = £10,964.91. The gross income threshold is £12,457 and the weighted income is below that, so your client is eligible.

---

87 Criminal Defence Service (Financial Eligibility) Regulations 2006 reg 9 and Schedule.

Where the client is not eligible on gross income, but the (weighted) household income is below the upper threshold, you will need to consider whether the client is eligible on disposable income.[88]

'Disposable income' is gross income minus:

- tax and National Insurance paid;
- council tax paid;
- rent, mortgage, etc;
- childcare costs;
- maintenance payments;
- living expenses allowance.

The living expenses allowance is a notional cost of living allowance, currently £5,676 per year. Where the client has a partner and/or children, the allowance is increased using the scale in the table above – so, in the case study, the allowance would be £5,676 x 2.28 = £12,941.28.

Proof of means will always be required to accompany the application, except where the client is in custody, in which case a statement of truth (now incorporated within form CDS15) should be signed instead, or unless the client's sole income is state benefits, in which case the courts can use their direct computer link with the Department for Work and Pensions to check against the client's National Insurance number that the means information is correct.

Where the client is not financially eligible, but can demonstrate that to pay privately would cause him or her real hardship, an application can be made for hardship funding. This application is made on form CDS16 to the LSC rather than the courts, and whether to grant is at the LSC's discretion.

Merits test

9.23　The merits test for the grant of Representation Orders is the 'interests of justice' test. The test is set out in Access to Justice Act 1999 Sch 3 para 5, which says:

> ... in deciding what the interests of justice consist of in relation to any individual, the following factors must be taken into account:
> (a) whether the individual would, if any matter arising in the proceedings is decided against him, be likely to lose his liberty or livelihood or suffer serious damage to his reputation,
> (b) whether the determination of any matter arising in the proceedings may involve consideration of a substantial question of law,

---

88 Criminal Defence Service (Financial Eligibility) Regulations 2006 reg 10.

(c) whether the individual may be unable to understand the proceedings or to state his own case,

(d) whether the proceedings may involve the tracing, interviewing or expert cross-examination of witnesses on behalf of the individual, and

(e) whether it is in the interests of another person that the individual be represented.

Note that this list is not exhaustive, merely examples of what can be taken into account. The Justices Clerks Society has published guidance on the merits test as applied by the courts which contains helpful information about factors that are considered. It is available at www. legalservices.gov.uk > CDS > Criminal Legal Aid Eligibility > Interests of Justice Test.

The application

9.24   Applications for Representation Orders should be made to the court where the case is to be heard. Forms CDS14 and CDS15 should be completed and submitted. Where your client is not in custody, full evidence of means will be required. Where the client is in custody, the declaration in form CDS15 can be signed instead – this is a statement of truth that the information regarding means is accurate.

Court staff have targets for consideration of applications (90 per cent next day, 95 per cent within three days and 100 per cent within six days) but nevertheless an application should be submitted as soon as possible after charge. Orders are deemed to be granted on the date a properly completed application was received.[89]

Where an application is granted, funding for the magistrates' court element of the case is in place and preparation can begin.

Where the application is refused on means, there is no right of appeal, although applicants can ask for a recalculation if they believe an error has been made, and a fresh application can be submitted at any time (if, for example, there is a change of circumstances). Where the application is refused on the merits, there is a right of appeal to the magistrates' court, who will either confirm the original decision or grant an order.[90]

---

89   Criminal Defence Service (General) (No 2) Regulations 2001 reg 6(1).

90   Criminal Defence Service (Representation Orders: Appeals etc) Regulations 2006 reg 4.

Funding in the absence of an order

9.25 The general rule is that no work can be done and no costs claimed until such time as a Representation Order has been granted.

However, an order can be backdated so that a claim can be made for pre-order work where:[91]

- urgent work was required (defined as being a hearing within ten working days of taking initial instructions);
- there was no undue delay in making the application (that is, it was submitted no more than five working days of taking initial instructions);
- an order is subsequently granted.

If all these conditions are granted, you are able to claim for work done from the time of initial instructions onwards – where you acted for a client in the investigations stage, from the point of charge onwards.

Where an order is subsequently refused, you can nevertheless make a claim for work done in certain circumstances:

- Where the application is refused on means, an Early Cover[92] fixed fee of £75 may be claimed if:
  - the application was submitted by 9 am on the sixth working day following initial instructions;
  - you have taken all reasonable steps to assist the client to complete the forms and provide appropriate evidence;
  - no decision had been made on the application by the first hearing;
  - you represent the client at the first hearing, and that hearing moves the case forward and any adjournment is justified; and
  - the eventual decision is that the case passes the interests of justice test but the client fails the means test.
- Where the application has been refused on the merits, a Pre-Order Cover[93] claim, limited to one hour's work at preparation rates, may be made if:
  - a qualified solicitor documents on file why it was believed the interests of justice test was passed; and
  - no claim for early cover is made.[94]

---

91 Specification, para B10.39.
92 Specification, para B10.124.
93 Specification, para B10.117.
94 Specification, para B10.118.

- You can claim a means test form completion[95] fixed fee of £25 where:
  - you complete an application for representation on behalf of the client, whether or not it is actually submitted;
  - you advise the client that although the interests of justice test is in all probability satisfied, the client would fail the means test and the file is marked accordingly;
  - such advice was given within ten working days of charge or summons;
  - the client does not go on to instruct you privately; and
  - you do not make a claim for early cover or pre-order cover.

Disbursements and prior authority

9.26　Disbursements can be incurred in accordance with the general rules – see above.

When you are considering large expenditure, you can apply to the LSC for prior authority to incur the disbursement.[96] The effect of prior authority is that, provided the expenditure does not exceed the terms or amount of the authority, no question can be raised as to it on assessment – in other words, you are guaranteed to be paid.[97] If authority is refused by the LSC, or not granted in full, the application automatically goes before a Costs Assessor, but beyond that there is no appeal – though there is nothing to stop you making a further application at any time.[98]

If authority is refused, that does not prevent you from incurring the disbursement, it merely means that you do not have the security of knowing it will be paid on assessment.

Prior authority will be refused, and so will the disbursement if incurred, where it is a disbursement that should have come out of central funds, for example a court ordered report in consideration of a Mental Health Act disposal.[99]

Where an application for prior authority has been made and refused, and the client nevertheless instructs you to incur the expense, you may accept payment from the client or a third party for that expense.[100] This is the sole exception to the rule that legal aid is

95 Specification, para B10.126.
96 Specification, para A5.28.
97 Specification, para A5.30.
98 Specification, para A5.29.
99 Specification, para A5.36(a).
100 Specification, para A8.52.

complete remuneration for the case and no additional charge may be made to the client or a third party.[101]

Counsel

9.27   A Representation Order for work in the magistrates' court is usually limited to representation by solicitor only. This does not mean that you cannot instruct counsel at all, it just means that counsel is not assigned by the order and therefore the rules regarding unassigned counsel apply. Essentially this means that you are responsible for agreeing and paying counsel's fees.

In more serious cases, you can apply to the court for counsel (or an independent solicitor advocate) to be assigned. Where counsel is assigned, they are entitled to be paid directly by the LSC at the rates prescribed in the contract, though you should submit their bill with your own – see chapter 11.

Whether or not counsel is assigned, you must provide them with the UFN and a copy of the Representation Order when briefing them.[102]

For more details on the instruction of counsel, please refer to chapter 14.

Separate matters

9.28   All work done in the proceedings class is described by the LSC as a case. Only one bill can be submitted per case.[103]

A case is all work done for all clients in respect of:

- one offence; or
- more than one offence where the charges are laid at the same time; or
- more than one offence where the charges are founded on the same facts; or
- more than one offence where the charges form a series of offences.[104]

'Founded on the same facts' covers situations where one charge is withdrawn and replaced by another, or where two charges are laid as alternatives.

101 Specification, para A8.50.
102 Specification, para B10.42.
103 Specification, para B10.58.
104 Specification, para B10.68.

'Series of offences' means offences of a similar nature. For example, where a client is charged with two separate offences which could be tried together, that would constitute one case. Similarly, where two clients are charged with the same offence (assuming you act for both), that would also be one case. There is no hard and fast rule here; the contract does not offer definitive guidance and it is to some extent a matter for you whether you decide there is one case or two.[105]

Co-defendants and conflict of interest

9.29   Note that the regulations say that 'where an individual who is granted a right to representation is one of two or more co-defendants whose cases are to be heard together, that individual must select the same litigator as a co-defendant unless there is, or is likely to be, a conflict of interest'.[106] Therefore, if you are making an application for a Representation Order on behalf of a client whose co-defendant is separately represented, you should ensure that you demonstrate on the application form why there is a potential conflict requiring separate representation.

The Solicitors' Code of Conduct 2007 provides guidance on your obligations in this situation. See paragraphs 23–35 of the guidance to rule 3. The guidance includes a useful discussion of the general principles and the approach to be taken in determining whether there is an actual or potential conflict of interests. Paragraph 33 says:

> ... the regulations are not intended to put solicitors in a position where they are asked by the court to act contrary to their professional responsibilities. If asked by the court for your reasons why you cannot act for both defendants, you must not give information which would breach your duty of confidentiality to your client(s). This will normally mean that you can say no more than that it would be unprofessional for you to continue to act.

Therefore, you do not have to disclose reasons why a potential conflict of interest exists which prevents you from acting for more than one defendant. However, where such a reason exists you should make clear on the application that there is a (potential) conflict, to avoid you being appointed for both defendants, or to avoid delay while the court makes further enquiries.

---

105 Specification, para B10.71.
106 Criminal Defence Service (General) (No 2) Regulations 2001 reg 16A.

Transfer cases

9.30 Just as the court grants a Representation Order, where the client wants to transfer from one solicitor to another, the court must agree to the transfer of the order.

Transfers are governed by regulation, not by the contract. The regulations say that the court may grant an application to transfer where:

- the solicitor appointed under the order considers himself or herself under a professional duty to withdraw;
- there is breakdown in the relationship between solicitor and client such that effective representation can no longer be provided;
- through circumstances beyond his or her control, the authorised solicitor can no longer represent the client;
- there is some other substantial compelling reason.[107]

Matter ends

9.31 A matter ends, and a bill must be submitted, when the case comes to an end in the proceedings class. This will happen when:

- the case has concluded (for example, by acquittal, sentence or committal);
- it is known that no further work will be needed (eg where the client has transferred);
- it is unclear whether further work will be required but at least one month has elapsed since the last work was done;[108]
- the LSC notify you that the case is a VHCC (very high costs case); or
- the Representation Order is withdrawn.[109]

Representation in the Crown Court

9.32 Cases in the Crown Court are generally funded by Representation Orders.

---

107 Criminal Defence Service (General) (No 2) Regulations 2001 reg 16.
108 Specification, para B10.61.
109 Specification, para B10.55.

Means testing

! Change from previous rules !

9.33   Representation Orders in the Crown Court are now means tested. However, the means test is a slightly different one from that applied in the magistrates' court and takes into account both a client's income and capital.

The starting point is that all clients who submit a complete legal aid application will be granted a Representation Order (provided the 'interests of justice' test is satisfied). However, depending on their means, clients may be required to make payments towards the cost of their representation either immediately or following the conclusion of their case, if they are convicted.

Certain clients are still passported. These are the same clients who would be passported in the magistrates' court, ie those under 18 or in receipt of income support, income-based jobseeker's allowance, guaranteed state pension credit or income-related employment and support allowance (ESA).

For those who are not passported, the client's means must be considered. In the Crown Court, unlike in the magistrates' court, this involves assessment of the client's capital as well as income. The means test can be considered in two stages, as follows.

Income

9.34   When the case becomes a Crown Court case, the client may be required to make monthly contributions towards the cost of their representation for the first five months after the case is transferred to the Crown Court. This will apply to clients who have an annual household disposable income of more than £3,398. The income threshold is the same as that in the magistrates' court, so those who passed the means test in the magistrates' court will not be required to pay any contributions from income in the Crown Court.

For those who are required to pay contributions, their annual disposable income will be divided by 12 and they will be asked to pay 90 per cent of the monthly figure each month for the first five months. Alternatively they can pay all five payments up-front in one lump sum.

Late payment of any of the five monthly contributions will result in an additional month's payment, ie the client will have to pay the same amount again for a sixth month.

There is a cap on income contributions which is determined by the type of offence. If a client's contributions reach the maximum level they will be notified and they will not be required to make any further income contributions.

If a client's case concludes within the first five months of being transferred to the Crown Court, they will not be required to continue paying income contributions. However, if they have been convicted they may become liable for payments from their capital if their income contributions do not cover the full costs of their representation (see below).

Assuming the case continues beyond five (or six) months from transfer to the Crown Court (committal or sending under section 51) the client will not be required to make any further contributions until the conclusion of their case.

If the client is acquitted, they will not be required to make any further payments at all and their income contributions will be refunded in full with interest (currently set at a rate of 2 per cent annual compound interest). (Note that any costs associated with late payment may be deducted, and very occasionally a client may be required to make a contribution towards their defence costs where, for example, they have misled the prosecution or the court or brought the prosecution on themselves by their conduct. This would be a matter for the judge to decide.)

However if the client is convicted, their position will depend on the costs of their case. If the client's income contributions have exceeded the actual costs of their case, the overpayment will be refunded with interest (again subject to any deduction associated with late payment). However, if the income contributions are less than the actual costs incurred, the client's capital will then be considered.

Capital

9.35 A client will only be required to contribute from their capital at the conclusion of his or her case if:

- the client is convicted;
- any payments already made from income do not cover the client's defence costs; and
- the client has more than £30,000 of assets (eg savings, equity in property, shares or Premium Bonds).

A client with less than £30,000 worth of assets will not be required to make any further contribution even if the client's income contributions have not covered his or her defence costs. (Note, however, that this threshold may be removed if evidence of the client's assets has not been provided.)

A client with more than £30,000 worth of assets whose income contributions have not accounted for the full costs, will be required to make up the shortfall from their assets. The costs may be recovered in various ways. For example, the LSC may apply an interest-bearing or non-interest-bearing charge to a property or, as a last resort, apply for an order for sale.

Applications

! Change from previous rules !

9.36   The introduction of Crown Court means testing means that a complete application for a Representation Order (forms CDS14 and CDS15) must be submitted for every non-passported client, even if the application is made after the case has been transferred to the Crown Court. The application should still be submitted to the magistrates' court at which the case originated.

The same rules apply in the Crown Court as in the magistrates' court regarding applications from children and vulnerable adults.

There are important new rules on the provision of evidence of means with an application. A major difference between applications for funding in the magistrates' court and in the Crown Court, is that clients who are in custody cannot self-declare as to their means when their case is in the Crown Court.

This does not mean that all evidence (payslips, bank statements, tax returns, share certificates and so on) must be provided with the initial application, although the CDS15 must contain all of the required information. Provided the completed forms have been submitted, a Representation Order will be issued. The client then has 14 days in which to provide the required documentary evidence. If the required documents are not provided in this time, sanctions may be imposed with respect to both income and capital:

- if evidence of income is not provided, the client's monthly contribution could increase to £900 or 100 per cent of the client's monthly disposable income, whichever is higher;
- if evidence of capital is not provided (or the information provided is subsequently found to be incorrect), the LSC may remove the £30,000 capital threshold and require a client who has less than this amount in capital to pay towards the costs of their defence.

Where the evidence required is over and above what would normally be required for a magistrates' court legal aid application, you may be able to claim an evidence provision fee for helping the client to provide this evidence. For standard applications a fee of £45 plus VAT can be claimed. For more complex applications involving two or more pieces of evidence, or a self-employed client whose application is referred to the National Courts Team, a fee of £90 plus VAT can be claimed.

When the completed application has been assessed, the client will be issued with a Contribution Notice or Order alongside the Representation Order, detailing how much they will be required to pay and the sanctions for late or non-payment.

A client can also apply for a review on the grounds of hardship if they feel they have higher than usual outgoings or would suffer financial hardship as a result of the means assessment. A completed form CDS16 must be submitted. This can be submitted either at the same time as the CDS14 and CDS15 forms, or afterwards.

Assessing case costs

! Change from previous rules !

9.37   Case costs in the Crown Court will vary considerably, depending on the type of case, the volume of evidence, the need for expert witnesses and so on. Therefore at the outset of a case it may be difficult to foresee whether a client's contributions will match the actual case costs.

The cap imposed on income contributions is intended to prevent clients from paying substantially more than the likely case costs up front, although it should be noted that according to the LSC figures, the cap is well above the average cost to trial in all categories of cases.

The actual case costs will be calculated at the end of the case and will include the total litigator and advocate fees, including any payments to expert witnesses. At the end of the case this amount will be compared with the amount the client has already paid in income contributions: if the client has already paid more than the actual costs, the difference will be refunded with interest; if the client has paid less, they may be required to contribute further from capital as described above. The Collection and Enforcement Agency will notify the client of the position and any amount they owe once the full costs have been established at the end of the case.

Effects of Crown Court means testing

! Change from previous rules !

9.38   Because of the potentially high costs of Crown Court cases and the obligation to keep the client informed of the potential costs (Code of Conduct, rule 2.03) it is now essential that the cost implications of any step in the proceedings are thoroughly considered. This will be particularly important in cases where, for example, expert evidence is required: the client should be advised of the cost implications prior to the instruction of any expert and cost considerations may have an impact on the conduct of the case.

Clients may also be more reluctant to instruct a solicitor at all, and therefore it will be important to advise clients at the outset as to the potential costs (given the type of case), the advantages of being represented and, if appropriate, the possibility of a hardship application.

Finally, the supporting evidence requirements for a Crown Court legal aid application are more onerous than those in the magistrates' court. Therefore where a case is committed or sent to the Crown Court and evidence has not already been provided, it is essential that this evidence is obtained as quickly as possible, as failure to provide this evidence within 14 days may have serious financial consequences for the client (see above).

The merits test

9.39   The merits test for a Crown Court Representation Order is the interests of justice test, just as in the magistrates' court – see above. All cases that have been committed or sent to the Crown Court will automatically satisfy the test.[110]

Where a case goes from the magistrates' to the Crown Court, the magistrates' court Representation Order will automatically continue into the Crown Court,[111] and no application to extend or amend the order is required (although additional supporting evidence as to means may have to be provided). Even if counsel were not assigned under the order in the magistrates' court, once the case goes to the Crown Court the order is deemed to include representation by one junior advocate (that is, any advocate other than a QC) automatically.[112]

---

110 Specification, para B10.146.
111 Criminal Defence Service (Representation Orders and Consequential Amendments) Regulations 2006 reg 4.
112 Criminal Defence Service (General) (No 2) Regulations 2001 reg 14(1).

For more information on the instruction of counsel in the Crown Court, see chapter 14.

Disbursements

9.40　Disbursements may be incurred in exactly the same way as in the magistrates' court. The test as to whether they are justified is the same, and applications for prior authority may be made.[113] The process is exactly the same as for magistrates' court cases: applications are made directly to the LSC.

Where the disbursement exceeds £100, you have prior authority and have in fact incurred the disbursement, you can make an application for payment on account of that disbursement at any time. Provided that the amount and scope of the prior authority have not been exceeded, payment should be made.[114]

See also chapter 11.

Prescribed proceedings in the Crown Court

9.41　Some civil proceedings have been deemed to be criminal for the purposes of legal aid[115] (designated 'prescribed proceedings'), and indeed where orders are imposed in the magistrates' court, the appeal lies to the Crown Court. Examples include stand-alone anti-social behaviour orders, parenting orders, football banning orders, and Sexual Offences Act orders. The full list is given above in the section covering magistrates' court work.

Where orders are sought on conviction, dealing with the application for an order (or the appeal against its imposition by the magistrates' court) will be done in the usual way on a Representation Order.

Where a stand-alone order is made by the magistrates' court, and the client wants to appeal it to the Crown Court, this will also now be funded by way of a Representation Order.

As for other Representation Orders in the Crown Court, funding for such cases is means tested and therefore the client will need to submit completed forms CDS14 and CDS15 (if non-passported).

There is an upper limit to the costs that can be claimed for such work. This is £1,500.

113 Criminal Defence Service (General) (No 2) Regulations 2001 reg 19.
114 Criminal Defence Service (Funding) Order 2007 para 14.
115 Criminal Defence Service (General) (No 2) Regulations 2001 reg 3(2).

Appeals to the Crown Court

9.42   Appeals to the Crown Court from the magistrates' court, whether against conviction, sentence or order (ie prescribed proceedings), now require a fresh application for funding. The means test is similar to that applied in the magistrates' court, but with an extra £500 allowance to cover the average cost of an appeal.

Clients who are passported or pass the means test will not be required to pay any contribution towards the cost of their appeal.

Clients who do not pass the means test will be required to pay a contribution in the following circumstances:

- £500 if an appeal against conviction is dismissed or abandoned;
- £250 if an appeal against conviction is dismissed but sentence is reduced;
- £250 if an appeal against sentence or order is dismissed or abandoned.

All applications for funding will also be subject to the interests of justice test.

Recovery of defence costs orders

9.43   Prior to the introduction of Crown Court means testing, Recovery of Defence Costs Orders (RDCOs) were the mechanism used to recover the costs paid out to wealthy defendants who were convicted. RDCOs no longer apply in cases where funding is subject to the Crown Court means testing rules (ie all new cases).

However, in cases that started prior to the introduction of Crown Court means testing, RCDOs may still be imposed to recover defence costs. Therefore a brief discussion is included here.

At the end of such a case, the judge should consider whether to impose a RDCO. Orders are governed by the Criminal Defence Service (Recovery of Defence Costs Orders) 2001, and reg 4 says:

(1) The judge hearing the case shall make an RDCO against a funded defendant except as provided in paragraph (2), (3) or (4).

(2) An RDCO shall not be made against a funded defendant who–

(a) has appeared in the magistrates´ court only; or

(b) is committed for sentence to the Crown Court.

(3) Subject to regulation 13, an RDCO shall not be made against a funded defendant who –

(a) has been acquitted, other than in exceptional circumstances;

(b) is directly or indirectly in receipt of –

(i) guarantee credit;

(ii) income support;

(iii) income-based jobseeker's allowance; or

(iv) income-related employment and support allowance;

(c) has none of the following assets –

　(i) capital over £3,000;

　(ii) equity in that defendant's principal residence over £100,000;

　(iii) gross annual income over £22,235; or

(d) is under the age of 18.

(4) Subject to regulation 13, an RDCO shall not be made where the judge hearing the case is satisfied that –

(a) it would not be reasonable to make such an order, on the basis of the information and evidence available; or

(b) the payment of an RDCO would, owing to the exceptional circumstances of the case, involve undue financial hardship.

For cases starting before the introduction of Crown Court means testing, the court enquired into the defendant's means by requiring a means form to be completed following committal. Where a defendant has complex means, the court can refer the enquiry to the LSC's Special Cases Unit. Where a defendant has refused to provide information or further information regarding means, the court should make the order.[116] The client's partner's resources are taken into account, unless the partner has a contrary interest[117] (for example, is a victim or prosecution witness).

The amount of the order is any amount up to the full cost of representation, and the order can specify immediate payment or payment in instalments.[118] Payment is made to the LSC,[119] and the LSC can enforce payment as if it were a civil debt.[120]

It should be noted that RDCOs can be made in any case except where the defendant appears solely in the magistrates' court; so, for example, the Court of Appeal has the same powers as the Crown Court.

116 Criminal Defence Service (Recovery of Defence Costs Orders) 2001 reg 13.

117 Criminal Defence Service (Recovery of Defence Costs Orders) 2001 reg 9.

118 Criminal Defence Service (Recovery of Defence Costs Orders) 2001 reg 5.

119 Criminal Defence Service (Recovery of Defence Costs Orders) 2001 reg 16.

120 Criminal Defence Service (Recovery of Defence Costs Orders) 2001 reg 17.

Appeals and reviews

Scope

9.44   Work in the appeals and reviews class covers representation in the High Court on an appeal by way of case stated, advice on an application to the Criminal Cases Review Commission, and advice on appeals to the Court of Appeal.

Case stated

9.45   Where the client seeks an appeal to the High Court by way of case stated, the appeal is funded by Representation Order. The original order in the magistrates' court (or as the case may be, the Crown Court) covers advice on appeal,[121] including the application to the magistrates' court to state a case.[122]

Once the case is lodged at the High Court, an application for representation in the appeal should be made to the High Court.[123] It is an application for a criminal Representation Order. There is no means test, and the merits test is the interests of justice test.

Where disbursements are needed, you can make an application to the LSC for prior authority.[124] Counsel may be instructed under the order.[125]

Advice and Assistance in the appeals class

9.46   Advice and Assistance may be granted to assist a client with an application to the Criminal Cases Review Commission, or to appeal against conviction and/or sentence.

The Representation Order in the magistrates' or Crown Court includes the provision of advice on appeal,[126] up to the point where an appeal is lodged, and therefore where you represented a client in the magistrates' or Crown Court under legal aid, the advice on appeal should be done under the order. It would not be appropriate to grant Advice and Assistance for that.

Similarly, where a Representation Order is available from the Court of Appeal, Advice and Assistance should not be used as an alter-

---

121 Specification, para B11.3.
122 Specification, para B11.46.
123 Specification, para B11.49.
124 Specification, para B11.59.
125 Specification, para B11.52.
126 Specification, para B11.3.

native to, or to supplement, the Court of Appeal's powers to grant a Representation Order where only counsel has been authorised.[127]

Therefore, the primary use of Advice and Assistance is in cases where the client was not represented, or was represented and seeks a second opinion on the appeal. This would apply whether the client is entitled to go direct to the Court of Appeal or would make an application to the Criminal Cases Review Commission.

The general rules on Advice and Assistance (see the investigations class, above) will apply. The work is means tested[128] and subject to the sufficient benefit test.[129] Costs are limited to £300 (£500 in the case of a Criminal Cases Review Commission (CCRC) application) but may be extended on application to the LSC.[130]

When you are dealing with a CCRC case, the LSC recognise that substantial work may be required, particularly where you are not the solicitor who acted at the trial. This may include obtaining the prosecution and defence files, considering transcripts,[131] commissioning further expert evidence and conducting further investigations. However, you should screen the case at as early a stage as possible, and where there is no reasonable prospect it will meet the CCRC's criteria, refuse to carry out further work.[132]

Representation Orders in the Court of Appeal

9.47   The Court of Appeal has the power to grant a Representation Order, but not until leave to appeal has been granted, or until the application to appeal has been submitted.[133]

The court can grant a Representation Order to an advocate alone,[134] and indeed this is usual practice. Applications for litigators will usually only be granted to undertake some specific step in the proceedings, such as to interview a witness, rather than for the appeal as a whole.

---

127 Specification, para B11.7.
128 Specification, para B11.9.
129 Specification, para B11.8.
130 Specification, para B11.42, Payment Annex.
131 Specification, para B11.23.
132 Specification, para B11.22.
133 Criminal Defence Service (General) (No 2) Regulations 2001, Reg 10(5), as interpreted in *Revenue and Customs Prosecution Office v The Stokoe Partnership* [2007] EWHC 1588 (Admin).
134 Criminal Defence Service (Recovery of Defence Costs Orders) 2001 reg 15.

Court of Appeal Representation Orders are subject to the interests of justice test. There is no means test, but Recovery of Defence Costs Orders may be made.

Prison law work

! Change from previous rules !

9.48   Work in the prison law class is divided into two funding types: (i) Advice and Assistance and (ii) Advocacy Assistance.

Assistance under these two categories may be provided to prisoners (including those on remand and those released on licence or parole where appropriate) in the following types of cases:

- treatment cases;
- sentence cases;
- disciplinary cases;
- Parole Board Cases.[135]

The general rules on Advice and Assistance apply (see above in the investigations class), including the means test[136] and the sufficient benefit test.[137]

Advice and Assistance is limited to a fixed fee of £220 unless profit and waiting time costs (calculated at specified hourly rates) exceed £660, in which case the costs will be assessed.[138]

Advocacy Assistance for Disciplinary cases and Parole Board cases is paid under a standard fee scheme. This is similar to the fee scheme for magistrates' court cases, in that you may claim a lower standard fee, a higher standard fee or a non-standard fee depending on whether your profit and waiting time costs (but not travel) fall below, between or above two standard fee limits.[139] Details of the limits are given in the Payment Annex.

Both Advice and Assistance and Advocacy Assistance may be granted by you, rather than by application to the LSC.[140] However, prior approval must be obtained from the LSC before commencing a

---

135 Specification, para B12.4.
136 Specification, para B12.14.
137 Specification, para B12.6.
138 Specification, para B12.75 and Payment Annex.
139 Specification, para B12.76.
140 Specification, para B12.23.

Treatment case (subject to the introduction of a system limiting the number of new matter starts).[141]

The client must complete the relevant forms (CDS1 and CDS2 or CDS3), and must pass the means test. Means are limited by both capital and disposable income, and the eligibility levels can be found on the LSC website at www.legalservices.gov.uk > CDS > Criminal Legal Aid Eligibility in the current keycard. 'Disposable income' means all income received by the client and his or her partner, less tax, National Insurance and the dependants allowances set out on the keycard. The limits and allowances are amended periodically, usually when benefits levels change.

The sufficient benefit test must be satisfied in all cases, and in addition Advocacy Assistance must not be provided in Disciplinary cases where:

- it appears unreasonable to grant in the particular circumstances of the case; or
- (where required) permission to be legally represented has not been granted.[142]

In all cases you should record on the file how the merits test has been and continues to be met.[143]

Counsel may be instructed under Advocacy Assistance, but you may not claim for accompanying them to a hearing.[144] If you instruct counsel, you are responsible for agreeing a fee with them and paying them directly. Any fee must not exceed the hourly rate payable to a solicitor.

Associated CLS work

9.49   Associated Community Legal Service (CLS) work is civil work arising out of criminal proceedings, for example judicial review or habeas corpus, or civil work under the Proceeds of Crime Act 2002 (POCA). Although you are permitted to do this work if you have a Criminal Contract, even if you don't have a Civil Contract, it is fundamentally civil work and the usual civil rules apply.[145]

See chapters 2 and 3 for more details of civil funding.

141 Specification, para B12.5.
142 Specification, para B12.116.
143 Specification, para B12.7.
144 Specification, para B12.57.
145 Specification, paras B13.2, B13.19.

Criminal offences under POCA are dealt with in the same way as all other Criminal offences. Confiscation as part of criminal proceedings forms part of the criminal case, so where confiscation is sought against a defendant you can deal with that under the Representation Order.

Where confiscation is sought as part of criminal proceedings but which affects a third party (for example, someone who jointly owns property with a defendant), that party can apply for civil legal aid to be represented in the confiscation, notwithstanding that it is part of criminal proceedings in the Crown Court.

Section 23 of the Funding Code Guidance – see volume 3 of the LSC Manual – is a useful discussion of the funding available for POCA matters and the circumstances in which civil or criminal legal aid should be applied for.

Very high cost cases

9.50   Criminal proceedings where the trial in the Crown Court is expected to last more than 60 days are deemed to be very high cost cases (VHCC).

VHCCs are subject to individual case contracts. If you have such a case, you are obliged to report it to the LSC Complex Crime Unit within five working days of the Plea and Case Management Hearing, or becoming aware that it would be a VHCC.

You can only continue with the case if you enter into a contract with the LSC in relation to the individual case.

Further information on the arrangements for VHCCs can be found in the VHCC arrangements 2010, the standard contract terms and the 2010 VHCC Guidance document, all published on the LSC website at www.legalservices.gov.uk > CDS > Very high cost criminal cases > VHCC accreditation.

Getting paid for civil and family work

continued

Introduction

10.1 This chapter deals with billing and payment for civil and family work. You should refer to chapters 3–8 for information on conducting cases.

This chapter does not deal with contract management (which is covered in part C), but with the rules and processes for billing individual cases.

See appendices G and H for a summary of the Legal Services Commission's (LSC's) Costs Assessment Guidance, in respect of the most common queries raised by caseworkers.

Controlled work

10.2 Controlled work cases are billed individually, but they are not directly paid. Instead, each organisation, or office, has a fixed monthly payment set by the LSC. Each month, the organisation submits claims which are off-set against a standard monthly payment (SMP), with the aim that bills and payments balance each other out over the course of the financial year. See chapter 18 of this book for more information on this process (known as reconciliation) and on the management of Civil Contracts generally.

Standard fees are paid for controlled work. These are shown net of VAT and disbursements which may be claimed in addition. Exceptional cases (defined as those where costs exceed three times the fixed fee) may be claimed in full.

Standard fees are claimed by submitting an online claim within 20 days of the end of each month.

In exceptional cases, you need to submit an EC1 claim form with your file in order to be credited with the balance above the fixed fee. If costs are reduced on assessment, you can appeal (see costs appeals, 10.8 below).

Although the basic systems for claiming immigration/asylum and mental health controlled work fees are the same as other civil and family work, they have more complex fee schemes. Family cases also have their own schemes. There is more information about these below.

The fixed fees and underlying hourly rates for all civil and family work are set out in the Standard Contract 2010 or Unified Contract Payment Annex.

CLS funding certificates

Payments on account

10.3   The Standard Contract 2010[1] allows you to claim on account profit costs incurred not earlier than three months after the issue of a CLS funding certificate. Thereafter, you can apply for further payments on account, provided that you make no more than two applications in any 12-month period. The application is made using form CLSPOA1, which can be submitted using the LSC's online facility: www.legalservices.gov.uk/lsconline.asp. You will be paid the amount to bring the total payments on account made to 75 per cent of your profit costs to date.

See below for information about payments on account under the family law fee schemes.

Prior authority and payment on account for disbursements

10.4   You can apply to the LSC for authority to incur a disbursement in advance, if it is above £100. The application must include a quote for the disbursement and set out the reasons why it is necessary. The application is made using form CLSAPP8.

Payments on account of disbursements can be claimed at any time, subject to disbursements being individually or cumulatively above £100. The form is the POA1, as for profit costs above.

Assessment of the final bill

10.5   Once a case has concluded, the final bill should be submitted to the court or LSC for assessment, as appropriate (see below). It should be noted that both the LSC and the court require authority to assess the bill. The authority to assess is either a discharged certificate, or a final order requiring costs to be assessed. Therefore, if the final order makes no mention of costs, a discharge should be sought before submitting the bill.

! Change from previous rules !

For civil licensed work, where the court is responsible for assessment, you must first submit your claim for assessment by the court;

---

1   Standard Contract 2010 Specification, para 6.24.

and when that is complete, make a claim for payment from the LSC within three months of receipt of the final assessment certificate received from the court.

Where the LSC is responsible for assessment you must submit a claim within three months of the right to claim accruing.[2] Frequent submission of late claims may lead to contract sanctions, even termination.[3]

Enhanced rates

10.6 In certain circumstances, you can apply for payment at an enhanced rate. The LSC will consider whether enhancement is justified, and if so will increase the hourly rates for some or all of the work done on the case. It would be very unusual for enhanced rates to be allowed on routine items such as travel and waiting (where payable) or letters and telephone calls.

The test for enhancement is that:

- the work was done with exceptional competence, skill or expertise; or
- the work was done with exceptional dispatch; or
- the case involved exceptional circumstances or complexity,

compared with the generality of proceedings.

Where the test is met, the LSC will allow a percentage increase to the relevant hourly rate not exceeding 100 per cent, or in cases in the High Court or above 200 per cent. The amount of the percentage increase will be determined by having regard to:

- the degree of responsibility accepted;
- the care, speed and economy with which the case was prepared;
- the novelty, weight and complexity of the case.

Assessment of costs by the LSC

10.7 Assessment of costs is governed by the Community Legal Service (Costs) Regulations 2000.

Where proceedings have been issued, the LSC assesses all bills up to £2,500 (excluding VAT). Bills in excess of £2,500 are assessed by the court. The exception to this is where there is an element of costs between the parties, where the bill is assessed by the court regardless

2 Standard Contract 2010 Specification, paras 6.34–6.36.
3 Standard Contract 2010, clause 14.5.

of the size of the claim. There is provision in the Standard Contract for the LSC to take over assessment of all claims, but the LSC have stated that this will not be brought into force immediately – no definite date for this has been given.

Claims to the LSC are made on form CLSCLAIM1, which must be completed in full and accompanied by the certificate, fee notes and invoices, orders and the full file of papers.

Costs appeals

10.8   If costs for exceptional controlled work or licensed work are reduced on assessment, you can appeal. You may want to do this, even if the effort of preparing the appeal seems disproportionate to the reduction in fees, if a successful appeal would improve your key performance indicators (see chapter 17).

Appeals must be made in writing and accompanied by the file. An LSC Internal Reviewer will carry out a formal and detailed review of the original decision. If dissatisfied, there is a further right of appeal to an Independent Costs Assessor. The Independent Costs Assessor is an experienced solicitor in private practice, and not a member of the LSC's staff. The Independent Costs Assessor may confirm, increase or decrease the amount assessed.

Any appeal to an Independent Costs Assessor is considered on paper, although in exceptional circumstances either party can apply to the Assessor for an oral hearing.

See the Standard Contract 2010 Specification, paras 6.68–6.76 or Unified Contract Specification paras 8.48–8.66 for more information on costs appeals.

Points of principle of general importance

10.9   At any point after the submitting of an appeal to the Assessor, but not later than 21 days after receipt of the final decision, the LSC or the provider can seek clarification on the costs rules and provisions. This is done by applying for a certificate of a point of principle of general importance (POP). POPs are the LSC's equivalent of costs case-law, and are binding on regional offices and Independent Costs Assessors when assessing bills. They are not binding on the courts. Applications can be made to the LSC or direct to an Assessor if one has been appointed. The application must set out the exact wording of the POP sought. The LSC's Legal Director will decide whether the matter should progress to the Costs Appeals Committee, which will decide whether a POP should be certified.

Assessment of costs by the courts – legal aid only

10.10 Bills to be assessed by the courts must be drawn up in the form prescribed by the Civil Procedure Rules and the Senior Court Costs Office Guide. A costs draftsman's fee can be claimed on the bill. The bill should then be submitted to the court using the appropriate notice, and accompanied by the relevant fee. Each court and costs office has its own local practices; some will require just the bill, certificate, orders and fee notes and invoices, others the full file of papers.

The forms to be used, the Guide, and a list of fees for different types of case, are available on the Court Service website at www.hm-courts-service.gov.uk > Legal/Professional. Unless a hearing before a district judge or costs officer is requested, assessment will be on the papers. On receipt of the returned assessed bill, the time limit for appealing the assessment begins to run. Solicitors should notify counsel of reductions to their costs within seven days, and all appeals should be submitted within 14 days. Solicitors appeal on behalf of counsel.

For full detail of the procedure, see the Senior Court Costs Office Guide (available on the Court Service website: www.hmcourts-service.gov.uk > Publications > HMCS Frameworks and Guidance > Senior Court Costs Office); and the Civil Procedure Rules parts 47 and 52.

Once the assessment process is completed, you should draft the Costs Certificate, and return to the court for sealing with the appropriate fee. The sealed Costs Certificate, the assessed bill, the funding certificate, and fee notes should then be sent to the LSC with form CLSCLAIM1 for payment. You can also submit CLSCLAIM 1 via the LSC's online facility: www.legalservices.gov.uk/lsconline.asp.

Assessment of costs by the courts – inter partes, and legal aid where the client has an interest in the assessment

10.11 Where the bill is entirely inter partes, or mixed inter partes and legal aid, the bill must be served on the other side before assessment proceedings begin. The other side has three weeks to accept the bill or serve points of dispute, to which you should respond. If agreement cannot be reached, the bill should be sent to the court for assessment. In disputed cases, a hearing before a district judge or costs officer is usual. The procedure then follows that outlined above.

The client has an interest in the assessment if the statutory charge arises, or if a contribution has been paid. The client has the same right to dispute the bill, and to be represented on the assessment, as any other paying party. If the client does not respond, or chooses not to exercise that right, the solicitor should certify accordingly on the bill.

Following assessment, the sealed Costs Certificate should be submitted to the LSC as above, but using form CLSCLAIM2, which is used to report to the Commission in all cases where another party is liable for all or part of the costs. You can also submit CLSCLAIM2 via the LSC's online facility: www.legalservices.gov.uk/lsconline.asp. If the other party cannot or will not pay, the solicitor can either take enforcement proceedings, or assign the costs to the LSC. In this scenario, the LSC will pay the costs, but only at prescribed rates, not inter partes rates, and then pursue the paying party for the costs.

For full details, see the Senior Court Costs Office Guide and the LSC's Civil Assessment Manual.

Inter partes costs and legal aid only costs

10.12   In cases where inter partes costs are possible, it is not uncommon for costs to be ordered or negotiated on the basis of payment of part of the costs of the case. If that is the case, it is important that you are clear as to the terms of the order or agreement, as in some cases but not others you may be able to claim the balance from the legal aid fund. The Standard Civil Contract 2010 allows you to claim from the legal aid fund any costs not payable by another party (legal aid only costs), but only if certain conditions are met – see paras 6.52 and 6.53 of the Specification.

The Specification defines 'legal aid only' costs – costs that can be claimed from the legal aid fund even where inter partes costs are recovered – as:

- costs of completing legal aid forms and communicating with the LSC;
- certain limited types of costs disallowed or not agreed;
- costs of work not covered by a costs order or agreement.

Where a costs order or agreement specifies that another party should pay a proportion of the client's costs (but not a fixed sum), the same proportion of the total work that is not covered is legal aid only costs.

To take a practical example, say total costs on the case are £2,000 at legal aid rates and £4,000 at inter partes rates. If the other side agree to pay your costs in the sum of £2,000, that could be expressed in one of three ways:

- £2,000 as the total agreed costs of the case;
- agreement to pay costs between x and y dates, totalling £2,000; or
- agreement to pay 50 per cent of the costs, being £2,000.

In each case, you receive £2,000 from the other side. In the first case, that £2,000 represents the total costs of the case, so there are no legal aid costs (apart perhaps from £100 or so for filling in the APP1 and so on). In the second case, costs outside the agreed dates are not subject to the costs order, so you can claim those costs from the LSC in addition to the inter partes costs you have received. In the third case, the other side have agreed to pay 50 per cent of your costs, so the other 50 per cent are legal aid only costs, so you can claim £1,000 (50 per cent of £2,000 at legal aid rates) from the LSC, in addition to the £2,000 from the other side.

Family

Controlled work

10.13 Claims for Legal Help and Family Help (Lower) in both private and public Family schemes are paid and claimed as other civil categories, described above.

Family – controlled work exceptional cases

10.14 The escape threshold for Legal Help and Family Help (Lower) in both private and public Family schemes is that profit costs calculated on an hourly rate basis must exceed three times the fixed fee.

Licensed work

10.15 The general rules and procedures for claiming licensed work costs are described above.

Family cases started prior to 9 May 2011, those excluded from the standard fee schemes and exceptional cases

10.16 In Family Proceedings Court (FPC) cases, the LSC assesses all bills. In cases in the county court and above, if the case ends before proceedings have been issued, the LSC assesses the bill.

Where proceedings have been issued, the LSC assesses bills up to £2,500 (excluding VAT). Bills in excess of £2,500 are assessed by the court. The exception to this is where there is an element of costs between the parties, where the bill is assessed by the court regardless of the size of the claim. In the case of public law matters, the £2,500 refers not to total costs, but to assessable costs – that is, disbursements, solicitor advocacy or an exceptional claim.

Where a section 31 public law children case is started in the FPC but concludes in the county court or the High Court, the county court/High Court assessment procedure applies.

Family cases covered by standard fee schemes started on or after 9 May 2011

10.17   Bills for cases that conclude in the Family Proceedings Courts will be assessed by the LSC regardless of the amount of the claim, even where part of the proceedings may have taken place in higher courts. Where a case concludes in the county Court or High Court, the whole bill will be subject to the county court/High Court assessment procedure even where part of the proceedings may have taken place in the Family Proceedings Court. Where assessment is by the court, the court will assess all the costs of the case in one exercise (including costs in the Family Proceedings Court). The costs of the Family Proceedings Court will no longer be assessed separately.

For cases that conclude in the county court or High Court the £2,500 limit for assessable costs continues to apply – ie if the amount of assessable costs is less than £2,500 the costs will continue to be assessed by the LSC. However, where the case attracts a standard fee and the £2,500 limit for assessable costs is exceeded solely by virtue of the claim for disbursements and/or payments under the Family Advocacy Scheme or Family Graduated Fee Scheme, the bill should be submitted to the LSC for assessment. Bills should only be submitted to the court where the profit costs (not covered by standard fees) exceed £2,500.

Claims for advocacy under the FAS must be made on an appropriately completed Advocates attendance form (EX506). If such form(s) are not submitted the claim(s) will not be paid.

Claims covered by family standard fees are made on CLSCLAIM1A You can also submit CLSCLAIM1A via the LSC's online facility: www.legalservices.gov.uk/lsconline.asp.

Family – public law standard fee scheme: exceptional cases

10.18   The escape threshold for Family Help (Higher) in the public family scheme is that profit costs calculated on an hourly rate basis must exceed twice the fixed fee. Don't forget that advocacy is claimed separately and in addition to the fixed fee, so advocacy costs do not count towards reaching the escape threshold.

Family – private law standard fee scheme: exceptional cases

10.19   The escape threshold for Family Help (Higher) in the private family scheme is that profit costs calculated on an hourly rate basis must exceed three times the fixed fee. As above, advocacy is excluded when calculating the escape threshold.

Family – public and private law standard fee schemes: enhancement of hourly rates

10.20   At level 3 – Family Help (Higher), you cannot take any enhancement of hourly rates into account in deciding whether a case escapes from the standard fee, including the 15 per cent uplift that would otherwise be available for panel membership.[4]

If the case escapes when calculated at the normal hourly rate, you can apply for an enhancement where justified. An enhancement may be justified where the work was done with exceptional competence, skill or expertise; the work was done with exceptional speed; or the case involved exceptional circumstances or complexity.[5] However, an enhancement may never exceed 100 per cent.

In exceptional cases, you can claim an enhancement of 15 per cent for membership of the following panels:

- the Resolution Accredited Specialist Panel;
- for work done under a Certificate which includes proceedings relating to children, the Law Society's Children Panel; or
- the Law Society's Family Law Panel Advanced.

Family – public and private law standard fee schemes: client transfers

10.21   If your fees on an hourly rates basis are equal to or greater than the standard fee, you claim the standard fee.[6] If your fees on an

4 Unified Contract Specification para 10.52.
5 Section 12 of the LSC's Costs Assessment Guidance 2007.
6 Unified Contract Specification para 10.44.

hourly rates basis are less than the standard fee, you claim half the standard fee.

! Change from previous rules !

If you are instructed for less than 24 hours, where you are instructed at the same time as another solicitor, or where your client's application to be joined to proceedings is refused, you will be paid by way of hourly rates (Family Specification para 7.17).

Family – public law standard fee scheme: advocacy

! Change from previous rules !

10.22   The standard fees for care proceedings under Children Act 1989 s31 do not include advocacy. The LSC widens the definition of 'advocacy' to include not only appearances as advocate before the court, but also any associated travel and waiting time and attendance as advocate at advocates meetings in public law children matters.

See chapter 13 for information on the Family Advocacy Scheme.

Immigration and asylum

Standard fee cases

! Change from previous rules !

10.23   The scope of the standard fee scheme (SFS) is not defined in the contract, except by exclusion. Paragraph 8.83 of the Specification simply states that 'standard fees apply to all other contract work', prior to a listing of hourly rates cases. Therefore, standard fees apply to all cases other than:

- cases where an asylum application (including legacy cases and fresh claims) is made before 1 October 2007;
- fresh asylum claims where the original asylum claim was lodged prior to 1 October 2007;
- advice on the merits of applying to the Upper Tribunal, the application for permission and if permission is granted, the appeal;
- bail applications;
- advice on form-filling (where allowed under para 8.56);
- applying for a legal aid certificate;
- advice prior to attendance at the Asylum Screening Unit (ASU), where instructions cease at or before the ASU;

- Legal Help in Early Legal Advice Process (ELAP) cases;
- advice to a client who is an unaccompanied asylum-seeking child;
- cases remitted to the First-tier Tribunal
- where you have an exclusive schedule, cases opened following an on-site surgery at a removal centre, or for a fast track client.

Exceptional cases are paid at hourly rates rather than through the SFS.

Immigration and asylum fee stages

10.24 Fees are split into three main stages: 1, 2a and 2b. Different fees apply at each stage in asylum and non-asylum matters, but the stages are the same for both. The fees include travel and waiting.

There are additional fees on top of the basic fee for extra work at each stage (see below).

Stage 1 covers the Legal Help stage of the case, and ends when Controlled Legal Representation (CLR) is granted or refused, or when the matter ends, whichever is earlier.

Stage 2 covers the CLR stage of the matter. Either – but not both – the 2a or 2b fee will be payable, depending on the point at which the matter ends. The 2a fee will be payable where the case does not proceed to – or, at least, representation is not provided at – a substantive hearing; 2b is payable where the case does proceed to a substantive hearing. Stage 2 will end when CLR is granted or refused to lodge an application to the Upper Tribunal, or when the matter ends, whichever is earlier. Where CLR is granted for an application to the Upper Tribunal, the case will be paid at hourly rates from that point onwards.

See the Specification, paras 8.63–8.73 for full definitions of each stage and examples of what work is included.

A claim for stage 1, and either stage 2a or stage 2b, must be submitted within three months of the end of the stage. A claim for exceptional payment should be made at the end of the case once all costs are known.

Immigration and asylum – additional fees

10.25 Additional fixed fees are payable on top of the relevant graduated fee in the following circumstances:

- attendance at a Home Office interview where permitted by para 8.53 specification;

- representation at a Case Management Review Hearing (CMRH) – different fees are payable depending on whether it is an oral or telephone hearing;
- representation at a substantive tribunal hearing;
- representation at a part-heard or relisted hearing.

Immigration and asylum – counsel

10.26   Where counsel is instructed for representation at a hearing, the relevant additional fee will be added to the graduated fee paid to the solicitor.

Immigration and asylum – disbursements

10.27   All disbursements, including interpreters and travel expenses, are payable on top of the graduated fee, subject to the relevant disbursement limits. Disbursements at the Legal Help stage should not exceed £400. Where the case is a graduated fee, disbursements for the CLR should not exceed £600; where the case is payable at hourly rates, costs and disbursements together should not exceed £1,600 (asylum) or £1,200 (immigration).

An application may be made to the LSC to extend any or all of these limits.

Immigration and asylum – exceptional cases[7]

10.28   The calculation for determining whether exceptional payments can be made is relatively complicated. The calculation is made at the end of the case, and covers costs for the whole case – Legal Help plus CLR. Where total profit costs at hourly rates, minus any additional payments made, are more than three times the graduated fee, then an exceptional case payment may be claimed. The amount of the exceptional payment is total profit costs, minus additional payments, minus graduated fee already paid. Therefore:

- stage 1 and 2b fees, plus Home Office interview, plus CMRH, plus substantive hearing, already paid: £450 + £600 + £290 + £175 + £320 = £1,050 SF plus £785 additional fees;
- total profit costs at hourly rates = £4,025;
- total profit costs minus additional fees = £4,025 – £785 = £3,240;

---

7 Specification, para 8.68.

- three times graduated fee = (£450 + £600) x 3 = £3,150;
- costs (£3,240) are greater than three times SF (£3,150), therefore an exceptional payment is due;
- payments made = £1,050 + £785 = £1,835. Therefore exceptional payment due is £4,025 – £1,835 = £2,190.

Claims for exceptional cases should be made at the end of the case – that is, following the completion of both the Legal Help and CLR, where relevant. When making a claim for an exceptional payment, any previous claims under the SFS should be reconciled against the payment sought.[8]

Immigration and asylum – hourly rates cases

10.29   All cases excluded from the SFS (see above) are payable by hourly rates.

In hourly rates cases (except those that become hourly rates cases by escaping from the SFS) there are costs limitations which may be extended on application to the LSC.

For Legal Help, the limit (excluding VAT and disbursements) is £800 in asylum cases and £500 in non-asylum cases.[9]

For CLR, the limit (excluding VAT, but including disbursements[10] and counsel) is £1,600 for asylum cases, £1,200 for non-asylum cases and £500 for stand-alone bail applications (where a substantive appeal includes a bail application, bail is included in the £1,600/£1,200).[11]

Legal Help claims must be submitted within three months of submission of a fresh application for asylum (fresh claim cases only), or within three months of the Home Office decision (all other cases), and then within three months of the end of the case. CLR claims should be submitted within three months of the first tribunal decision, and then within three months of the end of the case.

Upper Tribunal cases

10.30   Upper Tribunal cases are not subject to costs limits, either in respect of costs or disbursements. Instead 'reasonable costs'[12] will be allowed, though may be assessed. Where the application for review was made

8 Specification, para 8.81.
9 Specification, para 8.86.
10 Specification, para 8.92.
11 Specification, para 8.93.
12 Specification, para 8.93.

by the Home Office, or the client is detained under fast track procedures, you may always claim your costs. The rates set out in table 8(a) of the Payment Annex to the contract should be claimed.

In all other cases, no claim for costs may be made if permission to appeal is refused (Specification, para 8.99). Therefore, costs in these cases are at risk, and the higher rates set out in table 8(b) of the Payment Annex may be claimed. Disbursements will always be claimable (para 8.102).

Mental health

Mental health fee scheme

10.31   The mental health fee scheme applies to all controlled work in the mental health category of law, except for Help at Court for Victims (which is paid at hourly rates), and is divided into:

(a) a fee for all non-MHRT (Mental Health Review Tribunal) matters ('non-MHRT fee'); and
(b) three fees for MHRT matters ('MHRT fees') as follows:
  (i)   MHRT fee level 1 (initial advice);
  (ii) MHRT fee level 2 (negotiation and preparation); and
  (iii) MHRT fee level 3 (representation before the Mental Health Review Tribunal).[13]

You cannot claim both the non-MHRT fee and any level of MHRT fee in the same matter for a client.

Help at Court for Victims[14] is not remunerated under the mental health fee scheme but is paid at hourly rates.

Mental health – disbursements

10.32   In general, the cost of all time spent in travel and waiting is included in the fees payable. However, the LSC intends to designate some hospitals as 'remote', and where work is done at these hospitals a remote travel payment will be claimable. Payment of remote travel payments will be generated by completing the appropriate box on the Consolidated Matter Report form (CMRF).

Other disbursements are paid in addition to the fees.

13 Specification, para 9.70.
14 Help at Court – funding for representation for victims under the Domestic Violence, Crime and Victims Act 2004. See Specification, para 9.86.

Mental health – transfers

10.33   Where a client transfers his or her case to you, you are entitled to claim the full mental health fee for each of the levels of work you undertake, including initial advice and negotiation/preparation.[15]

Mental health – adjourned hearing fees

10.34   When a hearing is adjourned or is postponed or cancelled on the day at the request of the tribunal or Responsible Medical Officer, or in circumstances where you make a request to adjourn, postpone or cancel, and where you could not have otherwise reasonably avoided making such a request, and you have actually attended the place of the tribunal, you can claim this fee for each additional hearing that is adjourned on the day.[16]

Mental health – exceptional cases

10.35   Where the amount of any claim as calculated on the basis of hourly rates exceeds three times the mental health fee(s) payable, it becomes an exceptional case and is paid at hourly rates.

   For work covered by the non-MHRT fee or the MHRT fee level 1, the relevant hourly rate is that for Legal Help.

   For work covered by MHRT fee Level 2 and MHRT fee level 3, the relevant hourly rate is that for CLR.

   When calculating whether a matter or case qualifies as an exceptional case, if the case qualifies for remote travel payment(s) and/or adjourned hearing fee(s), then in order for it to become exceptional its costs need to exceed the total of three times the total of all fee levels payable *plus* the total of all additional payments payable.[17]

   The LSC provides the following example:

> In an MHRT case with work at levels 1, 2 and 3 and two adjourned hearings, in order to become exceptional the costs would need to be greater than:
>
> (3 x (Level 1 Fee + Level 2 Fee + Level 3 Fee)) + (2 x Adjourned Hearing Fee).[18]

---

15 Specification, para 9.86.
16 Specification, para 9.71.
17 Specification, para 9.80.
18 Specification, para 9.82.

Exceptional cases will be remunerated on the basis of the relevant hourly rates set out in rule 12.35. These rates will apply to work carried out by either solicitor or counsel.

Mental health – counsel's fees

10.36   Counsel's fees do not count as a disbursement and you are responsible for agreeing and paying counsel's fees.

In an unusually complex case you may request prior authority from the LSC for a higher hourly rate. The LSC says this will be highly unusual in MHRT cases. Where it is allowed, an hourly rate and a maximum cost limit will be specified. These may not be exceeded without further authority (which will not be granted retrospectively). Where authority is granted but the matter start does not qualify as an exceptional case, then the LSC will pay an additional sum equal to the difference between counsel's fees as authorised by the prior authority and the applicable fees which would have been payable.

CHAPTER 11

Getting paid for criminal work

by Julia Sherriff

Introduction

11.1   This chapter deals with billing and payment for criminal work.

Most criminal work is paid for through the monthly contract payment, the biggest exception being work done in the Crown Court.[1]

Although contract cases are billed individually, they are not directly paid. Instead, each firm, or office, has a fixed monthly payment set by the Legal Services Commission (LSC). Each month, the firm submits bills which are off-set against the payment, with the aim that bills and payments balance each other out over the course of the financial year. See chapter 15 for more information on this process (known as reconciliation) and on the management of Criminal Contracts generally. Crown Court bills in cases funded by Representation Orders are individually paid.[2]

This chapter does not deal with contract management (which is covered in part C), but with the rules and processes for billing individual cases. For information about conducting criminal cases, see chapter 9.

Investigations class work

11.2   A bill should be submitted at the end of the investigations class, even if the case continues into proceedings. One bill should be submitted for all work done in the class (subject to the exceptions set out below).

Police station telephone advice only

11.3   Where a client is at the police station and you provide telephone advice but do not attend, you can claim the telephone advice fee.[3]

The fee is not claimable in a case in which Criminal Defence Service Direct (CDS Direct) were involved,[4] and is triggered by a telephone call during which you speak to the client. Only one fee is payable per investigation.[5]

The value of the fee is set out in the Payment Annex of the contract, and is currently £30.25 (£31.45 for London firms).

---

1   Standard Crime Contract Specification 2010 (hereafter 'the Specification'), para A5.21.
2   Specification, para A5.26.
3   Specification, para B9.115.
4   Specification, para B9.114.
5   Specification, para B9.116.

Advice and Assistance

11.4 In cases where you provide Advice and Assistance to a client outside the police station, but do not attend the police station with the client, you can claim for the costs of the Advice and Assistance at the hourly rates set out in the contract. Where the case also involves attendance at the police station, the costs of Advice and Assistance are included within the police station fixed fee.[6]

A single claim for all work done (except Advocacy Assistance, which should be claimed separately) in the investigations class should be submitted when:

- the investigation has concluded, whether by charge, summons or other disposal; or
- it is known no further investigations work will be undertaken for the client; or
- it is unclear whether further work will be required but at least one month has elapsed since the last work (unless the client has an outstanding bail back); or
- post-charge work at the police station has been undertaken (in circumstances in which this work is not funded by a Representation Order).[7]

Where you have acted for more than one client in the same investigation, you should make a separate claim for each client, apportioning the work between them if necessary.[8]

The hourly rates applicable to this work are set out in the Payment Annex of the contract. You should apply the rates to all work done, subject to any costs limit. The costs limit for Advice and Assistance is £300 for both profit costs and disbursements; this limit can be extended on application to the LSC.[9]

Police station attendance

11.5 All work done at the police station is subject to fixed fees. The fee is triggered whenever there is attendance at the police station. This includes aborted attendance, such as where you are notified the client no longer requires advice whilst still en route to the station. However,

---

6 Specification, para B9.139.
7 Specification, paras B9.108, B9.140.
8 Specification, paras B9.112, B9.141.
9 Specification, para B9.143.

it does not include attendance for an ineffective bail to return if you did not check whether it would be effective prior to attending.[10]

Where triggered, the fee will cover all work done in the investigations class except Advocacy Assistance. Therefore, where, for example, you carry out Advice and Assistance outside the police station, such as between bails to return, that work will also be covered by the fixed fee.

There is a separate fee for each duty scheme area, and the fees are set out in the Payment Annex to the contract.

Only one fee is payable per client per case (even if you attend the police station on more than one occasion).[11] Where, however, work is a genuinely separate matter then a separate claim may be made. It will be a separate matter if the client has genuinely separate legal problems requiring separate advice,[12] or if the offences alleged lead to two separate sets of proceedings. If, for example, the client is charged with one offence and bailed to return to the police station on another, separate fees could be claimed in relation to each offence.[13]

A file note should be made setting out any justification for claiming more than one fixed fee[14] and separate Defence Solicitor Call Centre (DSCC) reference numbers should be obtained.

Case study

I had a client who was arrested for theft and taken to the police station, where it was found he was also wanted for a separate incident of criminal damage, and he was further arrested for that. Is that one matter or two?

It depends on the outcome of the case. If he were charged with both offences and bailed to the same court date, that would be one matter and one claim. This is because the two allegations required advice on one occasion only, and resulted in one set of proceedings. However, if he were charged with theft and bailed to return on the criminal damage, that would constitute two matters since they require separate advice on more than one occasion and do not go on to be one set of proceedings. Similarly if he were charged to two different

---

10 Specification, para B9.2.
11 Specification, para B9.89.
12 Specification, para B9.83.
13 Specification, para B9.85.
14 Specification, para B9.83.

courts on two different dates, that would constitute two matters and two fees, since although only dealt with on one occasion, the allegations go on to form more than one set of proceedings.

Payment rates and exceptionality[15]

11.6 Although police station work is payable by fixed fee, you should record all the time spent on the case and report the value of that time at the appropriate hourly rates to the LSC. The applicable rates are set out in the Payment Annex of the contract. Where the value of the case at hourly rates exceeds the Exceptional Threshold fee for the appropriate area, the case is deemed to be exceptional, and you can apply to the LSC for an additional payment.

There are different hourly rates depending on whether the case is a duty or own solicitor case, whether work was done in social or un-social hours, and depending on the offence. The categories of rates for attendance are:

- own solicitor or duty solicitor;
- duty solicitor unsocial hours;
- duty solicitor serious offence social hours;
- duty solicitor serious offence unsocial hours.

Similar categories (except those for serious offences) apply for travel and waiting time.

For these purposes, social hours are between 9.30 am and 5.30 pm on a business day – that is, any day other than Saturday, Sunday, Christmas Day, Good Friday or any bank holiday.[16]

Serious offences are:[17]

- treason;
- murder;
- manslaughter;
- causing death by dangerous driving;
- rape;
- assault by penetration;
- rape of a child under 13;
- assault of a child under 13 by penetration;

---

15 Specification, paras B9.98–B9.100.
16 Specification, para A1.13.
17 Specification, para B9.102(a).

- robbery;
- assault with intent to rob;
- arson;
- perverting the course of justice;
- conspiracy to defraud;
- kidnapping;
- wounding/GBH – both ss18 and 20 of the Offences Against the Persons Act 1861;
- conspiracy, solicitation, incitement or attempt of any of the above;
- any offence if the client is also accused of possession of a firearm, shotgun or imitation firearm;
- any offence if the client is detained under Terrorism Act 2000 s41.

In order to claim duty rates, the case must be a duty case – that is, referred as a duty case by the call centre or done during a duty period, and the work done by an accredited fee earner.[18] To claim serious offences rates, the case must be a duty case and the work done by a duty solicitor,[19] and you must not be a confirmed category 3 firm.[20]

To calculate whether the case is exceptional, you calculate the value of all time spent at the appropriate hourly rate. This will include any Advice and Assistance outside the police station. You should also include a telephone advice fixed fee[21] or a CDS Direct acceptance fee[22] (where a former CDS Direct matter was referred to you for police station attendance). This will give you a total value for the case. If the total value is more than the relevant Exceptional Threshold set out in the Payment Annex, then you can make an application to the LSC to treat it as an exceptional case.[23]

In order to do that, you should complete the form (form CDS18) and submit it to your processing centre (see www.legalservices.gov. uk > Criminal Defence Service > Forms > Where Work is Processed). The LSC will assess the claim, and if following assessment it is confirmed that the case is worth more than the Exceptional Threshold, the case will be treated as exceptional.

---

18 Specification, para B9.101.
19 Specification, para B9.102.
20 Specification, para B9.103.
21 Specification, para B9.87.
22 Specification, para B9.97.
23 Specification, para B9.98.

However, you will still not be paid the full value of the case. Instead, you will only be paid the fixed fee, plus the amount by which the case exceeds the threshold.[24]

Case study

I represented a client at West End Central Police Station on a case of murder over a weekend. It was a duty case, and I spent in total 15 unsocial hours in attendance at the police station, plus six hours' travel and waiting (all unsocial). I also incurred a telephone fee. What will I be paid?

West End Central is on the Central London scheme, so the fixed fee is £260.00 plus VAT. It was a duty case and a weekend so London duty unsocial serious case rates apply: £80 per hour for attendance and £69.50 for travel and waiting, and CDS Direct fee of £8.00.

Your time is worth £(80 x 15) + (69.50 x 6) + 8 = £1,622.30. The fixed fee is £260.00, and the threshold is £880.86. Therefore you are over the threshold and the case is exceptional.

You will be paid (subject to assessment) the value of the fixed fee plus the amount by which the threshold is exceeded: £260.00 + (1,622.30 – 880.86) = £1,001.44.

You should send your exceptional claim to the LSC who will assess the bill.

Exceptional cases will not be paid direct. Instead, the value allowed on assessment will count towards your contract claims.

Advocacy Assistance

11.7   Advocacy Assistance – of whatever type – is the exception to the rule that all investigations work be billed together. Any claim for Advocacy Assistance should be submitted separately. This work is not subject to fixed fees, and the hourly rates set out in the contract will apply subject to a Costs Limit of £1,500. A single claim for all Advocacy Assistance on a case should be made[25] at the end of the investigations stage.[26] Where Police Station Advice and Assistance, or freestanding Advice and Assistance, has already been provided, the same

---

24 Specification, paras B9.99–B9.100.
25 Specification, paras B9.153, B9.166, B9.178.
26 Specification, paras B9.154, B9.167, B9.179.

unique file number (UFN) must be used, although the work must be claimed separately.[27]

Proceedings class work

Court duty claims

11.8   You should claim any work done as court duty solicitor at the end of the duty session. You should make one claim per session, rather than one claim per client.[28] The applicable payment rates are set out in the Payment Annex to the contract.

You cannot claim for travel time or expenses to get to court, except where you are acting on a non-business day (eg a Saturday or bank holiday sitting), or where you are called to court having not been on the rota or having attended on a rota and been released and then asked to return.

Representation Orders

11.9   See chapter 9 for details on conducting work under a Representation Order.

Magistrates' court work should be billed at the end of the magistrates' court stage of the case. There is no provision for interim payments, so the bill will be submitted when one of the defined end points occurs:

- the case has concluded;
- it is known that no further work will be required;
- it is unclear whether further work will be required and at least a month has elapsed since the last work was undertaken;[29]
- a warrant of arrest was issued and at least six weeks, but not more than 19 weeks, have elapsed since.[30]

The exception to this is where sentence is deferred; you may submit a bill when sentence is deferred and another when the client returns to be sentenced.[31] Bills must be submitted within three months of the end of the case.

27 Specification, paras B9.168, B9.180.
28 Specification, para B10.17.
29 Specification, para B10.61.
30 Specification, para B10.66.
31 Specification, para B10.65.

Where you act for more than one client in a case, you should submit a single bill covering work done for all clients,[32] though you will need a separate Representation Order for each one.[33]

Standard fees

11.10 Most magistrates' court work is covered by the standard fee regime. There are three categories of fees – 1, 2 and 3 – and in each category a lower and a higher standard fee.

There are two types of fee:

- if your office is in an area specified by the contract, or if it is not but the court is, you should claim the designated area standard fee;[34]
- if not, you should claim the undesignated area standard fee.[35]

The designated areas[36] are:

- Greater Manchester, London, West Midlands and Merseyside criminal justice areas;
- the local authority areas of
  - Brighton and Hove;
  - Bristol;
  - Cardiff;
  - Derby and Erewash;
  - Kingston upon Hull;
  - Leeds and Bradford;
  - Leicester;
  - Nottingham;
  - Portsmouth;
  - Newcastle-upon-Tyne and Sunderland;
  - Sheffield;
  - Southampton.

The difference between the two is that in a designated area, the fees are slightly higher but you cannot claim for any travel and waiting

---

32 Specification, para B10.59.
33 Specification, para B10.64.
34 Specification, para B10.78.
35 Specification, para B10.79.
36 Specification, para A1.13.

time,[37] whereas in an undesignated area you can claim travel and waiting[38] but the standard fees are lower. Even if you cannot claim travel and waiting, you are still required to record the waiting time (though need not record travel).[39]

In either case, the structure of the fees is the same. Whatever the category of your case, you calculate your core costs (all profit costs except travel and waiting time).[40] If the core costs are below the lower limit for the category of case, you claim the lower standard fee. If core costs are between the lower and higher limits, you claim the higher standard fee. If core costs are above the higher limit, you claim a non-standard fee – that is, you claim your costs in full as incurred.[41]

You should decide which category of fee to claim based on the outcome of the case:

- Category 1 includes:
  - guilty pleas;
  - uncontested breach proceedings;
  - proceedings (other than committals) which are discontinued, withdrawn or where no evidence is offered;
  - bind-overs;
  - deferred sentences;
  - uncontested civil orders designated as criminal by Criminal Defence Service (General) (No 2) Regulations 2001 reg 3(2) (see chapter 9).

- Category 2 is:
  - contested trials;
  - cracked trials where the client pleads guilty on the day of trial;
  - proceedings (other than committals) which are discontinued, withdrawn or where no evidence is offered on the day of the trial;
  - contested breach proceedings;
  - cases where mixed pleas are entered;
  - contested civil orders designated as criminal by Criminal Defence Service (General) (No 2) Regulations 2001 reg 3(2) (see chapter 9).

---

37 Specification, paras B10.81, B10.86.
38 Specification, para B10.84.
39 Specification, para B10.88.
40 Specification, para B10.80.
41 Specification, para B10.89.

! Change from previous rules !

- Category 3 is committal proceedings, but limited solely to those that are discontinued or withdrawn or discharged.

Note that cases committed or sent to the Crown Court under Crime and Disorder Act 1998 s51 are treated as being Crown Court cases from charge – all work should be claimed on the Crown Court bill and no magistrates' court claim can be made (except in the event of a remittal back or a bail application).[42] This is now the case for committals as well as those cases sent under section 51: a category 3 fee can only be claimed when committal proceedings are discontinued or withdrawn at the committal hearing.[43]

Where proceedings have not concluded but a warrant of arrest has been issued, the proceedings will be treated as category 1 proceedings.[44]

Bail applications (including to the Crown Court) and appeals against bail, and contempt, are included in the standard fee of the substantive case.[45]

Where more than one category is possible, you should select the one that will pay the highest fee.[46]

On a change of solicitor, the old firm should claim a category 1 fee unless the case falls into category 3, and the new firm should claim in the usual way. The exception to this is where the conducting solicitor moves firms and takes the case – if this happens, only the new firm can claim, but should claim for both firms.[47]

Where you have claimed a fee and then a further claim is required – for example, claimed a category 1 fee when a client absconds and a warrant is issued, and then continue to represent the client following arrest on the warrant – you should calculate the total costs due for the whole of the case, deduct the amount previously claimed, and claim the balance.[48]

---

42 Specification, para B10.75.
43 Specification, para B10.91.
44 Specification, para B10.95.
45 Specification, para B10.72.
46 Specification, para B10.92.
47 Specification, paras B10.93, B10.94.
48 Specification, para B10.98.

> **Case study**
>
> *My office is in Manchester. My client was charged with theft, indicated a not guilty plea and elected summary trial. He was convicted following trial, and sentencing was deferred for six months. What should I claim?*
>
> Manchester is in a designated area, so you should be claiming the designated area standard fee. Your client took the case to a trial, so the case is in category 2. You should calculate your core costs (all time excluding travel and waiting) to see whether a lower, higher or non-standard fee is claimable.
>
> When your client comes back to be sentenced in six months' time, you can claim a further category 1 standard fee.

Counsel

11.11   Unassigned counsel are treated as you are, and you should include their times on your bill as if they were your profit costs.

Where counsel is assigned, their costs are separate from yours. Rates for assigned counsel are set out in the Payment Annex of the contract, and counsel should prepare a bill at those rates.[49] They will be paid direct by the LSC, but you should submit their bill alongside yours.[50]

Separate matters

11.12   One standard fee is payable per case. A case consists of all work for all clients in respect of:

- one offence; or
- more than one offence, where:
  - they are charged at the same time; or
  - they are founded on the same facts; or
  - they form part of a series of offences.[51]

Offences 'charged at the same time' is a straightforward test. 'Founded on the same facts' is intended to cover situations where two charges are brought as alternatives, or where one charge is substituted for another – common examples include theft and handling stolen goods, or ABH and common assault.

49 Specification, para B10.43.
50 Specification, para B10.44.
51 Specification, para B10.68.

A 'series of offences' refers to offences which have similarities or form a pattern of offending, that could be tried together. Each potential series of offences has to be considered on its own facts and definitive guidance cannot be given. However, there is a useful discussion at section 6.3 of the Criminal Bills Assessment Manual (January 2008 edition). The key principle is that the offences are sufficiently related. For example, offences that are based on a system of conduct, are similar in nature, or where evidence of one is admissible at the trial of another, will all form part of a series. Even though some hearings may be held at different times, or in different courts, that would not prevent a series being established.

Enhanced rates

11.13 In certain circumstances, you can apply for payment at an enhanced rate. The LSC will consider whether enhancement is justified, and if so will increase the hourly rates for some or all of the work done on the case. It would be very unusual for enhanced rates to be allowed on routine items such as travel and waiting (where payable) or letters and telephone calls.

The test for enhancement is that:

- the work was done with exceptional competence, skill or expertise; or
- the work was done with exceptional dispatch; or
- the case involved exceptional circumstances or complexity,

compared with the generality of proceedings.[52]

Where the test is met, the LSC will allow a percentage increase to the relevant hourly rate not exceeding 100 per cent,[53] or in the case of serious fraud 200 per cent.[54] The amount of the percentage increase will be determined by having regard to:

- the degree of responsibility accepted;
- the care, speed and economy with which the case was prepared;
- the novelty, weight and complexity of the case.[55]

Enhancement of the hourly rates takes the case out of the standard fee regime, so you should submit an individual bill to the LSC, accompanied by a note setting out why you believe the criteria for

52 Specification, para B10.100.
53 Specification, para B10.103.
54 Specification, para B10.104.
55 Specification, para B10.102.

enhancement are met and justifying the percentage sought. It is important to remember that what seems obvious to you may not be so to an assessor. So, for example, you should not assume that because the court granted a certificate for counsel that you will automatically get an uplift, having decided to do the advocacy yourself. You will need to address the criteria explicitly and show how your advocacy was exceptional.

Other contract work

11.14   Advice and Assistance in the appeals and prison law classes is claimed under the contract in the same way as free-standing Advice and Assistance in the investigations class (see above, and see also sections B11 and B12 of the contract), as is Advocacy Assistance in the prison law class (see section B12 of the contract). The Payment Annex of the contract provides details of the fixed fees and standard fees applicable to prison law cases.

Representation in judicial review or habeas corpus proceedings, or civil proceedings under the Proceeds of Crime Act 2002, is claimed as all other civil legal aid; see chapter 10. See section B13 of the contract.

Representation in other civil proceedings associated with criminal proceedings (eg where papers from a civil case are relevant to a criminal case) is funded by Representation Order and requires prior authority. However, it is claimed under the same remuneration provisions as apply to civil Legal Representation. See sections B10.152–B10.163 of the contract.

Representation on an appeal by way of case stated is funded by Representation Order (issued by the High Court) and claimed in the same way as in the proceedings class, except that there are no standard fees. See section B11 of the contract.

The claiming process

11.15   Contract work is claimed by submitting details of the bills to the LSC.

With the exception of magistrates' court non-standard fees, you do not need to send in the file of papers and bills will not be individually assessed.

Each month, you should submit form CDS6 to the LSC using LSC online: www.legalservices.gov.uk/lsconline.asp. Each line on the

CDS6 represents one bill. There is a series of codes you should use to differentiate between different types of cases, different offences and scheme areas (for police station fee purposes). The LSC then set off each bill against your contract payments, with the overall aim being that payments match claims, within acceptable reconciliation boundaries – see chapter 18. The codes can be found on the LSC website at www.legalservices.gov.uk > Criminal Defence Service > Forms.

Non-standard fees in the magistrates' court are subject to individual assessment by the LSC. You should complete form CDS7 with details of the case and the amount claimed, plus justification for the costs, and send it to your LSC processing office with your file of papers.[56] The LSC will assess the bill and return the file to you with details of the amount allowed, which will be credited to your contract account rather than paid to you direct. CDS7 can also be submitted as an e-form through LSC online.

If you disagree with the assessment, there is a right of appeal to an Independent Costs Assessor, who is a solicitor independent of the LSC. The Assessor will consider the file, the LSC assessment and your representations and will reduce, confirm or increase the amount allowed by the LSC. There is a 28-day time limit to appeal, and appeals will generally be dealt with on the papers. Full details of the appeal process are set out at section A8 of the Specification.

There is no right of appeal beyond the Assessor, unless you can show a point of principle of general importance. These are very rarely established. See section A8 of the Specification.

Crown Court – litigator fees

11.16   Although all Crown Court work is included within the scope of the contract, the payment rates and rules are governed by the Criminal Defence Service (Funding) Order 2007.

From January 2008, the previous system of payment by hourly rates was abolished and replaced with a graduated fee scheme. It was intended to be a transitional scheme, with the ultimate aim of introducing a combined single fee scheme for all work, both litigation and advocacy. However, at the time of writing the schemes remain separate.

56 Specification, para B10.73.

The scheme makes a distinction between fixed fees and graduated fees. There are fixed fees for cases that do not involve trial on
indictment, such as committal for sentence, breaches and appeals,
and graduated fees for indictment cases.

Graduated fees are determined by a number of factors:

- the classification of the offence – offences are classified into 11
  classes (A–K);

- the outcome – whether a guilty plea (plea entered before or at
  plea and case management hearing), a cracked trial (guilty plea
  entered after plea and case management hearing) or trial (including Newton hearings); discontinuances are paid at the same rate
  as guilty pleas;

- the length of the main hearing – the trial or hearing at which
  pleas were entered;

- the number of pages of prosecution evidence (excluding unused
  material) served;

- the number of defendants represented by you.

To calculate the fee, you should first categorise your case by the
offence. Where there is more than one charge on the indictment,
select the one which would result in the higher fee.

For each outcome type, there is a basic fee which varies depending
on the classification of the offence, and to which an uplift is added
depending on the number of pages of evidence and the length of the
main hearing.

As a result, there are thousands of variables and the tables set out
in Schedule 2 to the Funding Order are lengthy and complex. However, the LSC has made available a spreadsheet into which the classification, trial length, page count and outcome can be entered, and
which then calculates the appropriate fee – see www.legalservices.
gov.uk > Criminal Defence Service > Pay Rates and Schemes >
Litigator Graduated Fee Scheme.

All work done on a case is covered by the graduated fee; the sole
exception is work done in connection with confiscation or forfeiture
following conviction, which is payable at hourly rates in addition to
the fee.

Claims for litigator fees can be made through the LSC Online
billing system, and if you use it to submit claims the website will also
calculate the relevant fee.

Claims are assessed item by item by the LSC, who will compare
the information on your claim with that held by the Court Service.

There is a right of appeal against assessment provided for in para-graph 29 of the Funding Order. Appeals must be made in writing within 21 days of receipt of the assessment. You cannot challenge the fee scheme itself, but can challenge the calculation in any individual case, such as by appealing the classification of the offence or the allowed page count. On redetermination, the fee may be confirmed, reduced or increased.

If you remain dissatisfied with the assessment, you can apply for written reasons within 21 days, and then within 21 days of receipt of the reasons request a hearing before a costs judge.

Payments on account

11.17 Where you have been granted prior authority by the LSC and have incurred a disbursement of more than £100 you can apply for a pay-ment on account of the disbursement at any time.[57]

There is no provision for payment on account of profit costs un-less you can show financial hardship, and even then only if it has been at least six months since the start of the case and it is unlikely that payment will be received for at least three more months. You will have to provide evidence of hardship, usually in the form of a bank statement or letter from your bank.[58]

Crown Court – advocates' fees

11.18 The scheme for advocates is similar to that applying to litigators. The applicable rules and fees are set out in Schedule 1 to the Funding Order.

Each case will have an instructed advocate, who is the advocate named in the brief and is responsible for claiming fees on behalf of all advocates instructed in the case and then passing payment on.

The scheme provides for a basic fee based on the classification of the offence to which is added uplifts for pages of evidence, length of trial, number of witnesses and additional fees for features such as conferences. There is a higher basic fee for a trial and a lower for a guilty plea case. The basic fee includes payment for attendance at a plea and case management hearing and four other hearings during the case; additional fees can be claimed for other hearings.

57 Criminal Defence Service (Funding) Order 2007 reg 14.
58 Criminal Defence Service (Funding) Order 2007 reg 21.

Very high cost cases

11.19   Cases accepted by the LSC as very high cost cases (VHCC) (ie, where the trial is expected to last longer than 40 days or between 25 and 40 days in certain circumstances) are subject to individual case contracts. The rates will depend on the category of case (seriousness) and the level of fee earner (dependent on experience). Standard rates for each category and level of fee earner are set out in the Specification to the 2010 VHCC Standard Contract.

For further information refer to the LSC website at www.legalservices.gov.uk > CDS > Very high cost criminal cases > VHCC accreditation.

Legal aid advocacy

CHAPTER 12

Advocacy in civil cases

Introduction

12.1   This chapter deals with the conduct of and payment for advocacy in civil cases and the general rules applying to both civil and family cases.

In general, we use the term 'advocate' to refer to anyone who has a right of audience to appear in the relevant court or who the court is willing to hear where the scheme makes no distinction between solicitor and counsel. Where there is a difference according to whether advocacy is conducted by solicitor or by counsel, we will use the terms 'solicitor' and 'counsel' as appropriate.

This chapter only deals with the advocacy aspects of cases. For more information on the conduct of litigation, see part A of this book. For information on the particular rules applying in family and criminal cases, see chapters 13 and 14.

General principles

12.2   Advocacy can only be conducted under the following levels of service:

- Help at Court;
- Controlled Legal Representation (CLR) (immigration and mental health only);
- Legal Representation (certificated work);
- specific contracts, such as a housing court duty possession scheme contract.

Advocacy can only be carried out by a person who has a general right of audience or who has been given permission to be heard by the court in the specific case.

Advocacy funded by legal aid can only be carried out in matters before a court and before certain limited tribunals. The full list is set out in Schedule 2 to the Access to Justice Act 1999, reproduced at appendix F. Where justified, you may attend other tribunals as a McKenzie friend (see chapter 3 of part A, and appendix A for more details).

Help at Court

Scope

12.3 Work must be allowed under the Access to Justice Act 1999 (see chapter 2 and appendix F for more information).

Help at Court is help and advocacy for a client in relation to a particular hearing, without formally acting as legal representative in the proceedings or being on the record at the court (Funding Code, criterion 2.1). The Funding Code guidance explains that Help at Court only covers informal advocacy, usually by way of mitigation at individual court hearings. Ongoing representation can only be provided under a Legal Representation certificate.

Help at Court is particularly useful for cases where a Legal Representation certificate would not be available, for example where a client does not have a defence to a possession claim, but does need an experienced adviser to set out repayment proposals to the court. Help at Court can also be used to represent the client on an application for enforcement of an order where the client is the applicant. It is not a stand-alone level of funding, but can only be granted as an add-on to a pre-existing Legal Help matter.

Merits test

The sufficient benefit test

12.4 The nature of the proceedings and the circumstances of the hearing must be such that representation at that hearing will be of real benefit to the client.[1]

This means the issue(s) must be more complex than the client could have explained to the court himself or herself.

You must apply the test before every hearing and note the file with your justification. 'Sufficient benefit test met' is not an adequate justification.

There are no additional fixed fees to cover Help at Court. However, the additional work involved may make it more likely that the case will reach the escape threshold (three times the fixed fee).

Where advocacy is justified, you may claim travel and waiting to/from and at court, as well as preparation and attendance, where appropriate. See chapter 10 for more information on payment schemes.

---

1 Funding Code, criterion 5.3.2.

Specific areas of work

Housing cases

12.5   The Funding Code Guidance, at section 19.3, provides specific guidance on the use of Help at Court in housing cases.

Before making an application for a full certificate, you should consider the availability of Help at Court, and if it is more appropriate a certificate may be refused. Help at Court may be more appropriate where:

- a client is a defendant to possession proceedings, where the arrears are not in dispute, it is unlikely an immediate possession order would be made, and in the absence of a defence the only issue is the terms of a suspended order for possession;
- a client is a defendant to possession proceedings, where the claim for possession is not disputed but there is a dispute over the amount of the arrears;
- the case is an application to suspend or further suspend a warrant for possession or execution where no substantial issue of fact or law is raised.

Help at Court should not be used in any case where a certificate would be more appropriate (unless one has been applied for and refused) – in the above, for example, where the client does have a substantive defence to the possession proceedings, or where there is a substantial issue of fact or law.

Neither should Help at Court be used where it is not justified, for example because it would achieve no more than would explaining to the client what steps they could take themselves or writing a letter on their behalf under Legal Help.

Debt cases

12.6   It will generally be rare for a certificate to be granted in a debt case, since either the client has no defence – in that there is no dispute that they are liable for the debt, the only issue is the terms of repayment – or the case is on the small claims track, or both. However, it may be justified to grant Help at Court where the merits test is met, to allow attendance at a particular hearing.

Who can provide advocacy?

12.7   Solicitors can attend court under Help at Court in circumstances where they have rights of audience – since it will almost always be the county court, that will be most cases. Advisers without rights of audience may provide advocacy and claim payment under Help at Court, as long as advocacy is justified and the court agrees to hear them. Counsel may not be instructed under Help at Court.[2]

Payment for advocacy services

12.8 Advocacy under Help at Court – and associated preparation, attendance, travel and waiting – is claimable as part of the main Legal Help matter. The costs are included within the fixed fee, and may be taken into account in determining whether the case is exceptional – if it is, the costs will be payable at hourly rates.

Controlled Legal Representation

12.9 CLR is only available in the immigration and mental health categories, and advocacy under those levels of service is dealt with in chapters 7 and 8, and payment in chapter 11.

Representation certificates

12.10 Where a certificate is issued to a solicitor covering proceedings before a court, it will in principle be possible to provide and claim for advocacy services under the certificate at all hearings in the case, though like every other step in the proceedings attendance at hearings is subject to there being merit in taking that step. You should also make sure that the particular hearing is within the scope of the certificate; final hearings, for example, are generally not within scope of a certificate as first issued.

Advocacy under a certificate can be undertaken by a solicitor (subject to rights of audience in the higher courts) or by counsel. An advocate can be employed by your organisation or be in independent practice.

There is general authority to instruct one junior advocate under a certificate;[3] the instruction of more than one junior, or of Queen's Counsel acting as such, requires an application for prior authority to be made.[4] Unless the authority is granted, no claim can be made by a

---

2 Specification, para 3.78.
3 Specification, para 5.27.
4 Specification, para 5.25.

second advocate appearing at any hearing or by Queen's Counsel for acting as such (it is always open to Queen's Counsel to accept instructions to appear as a junior and to be paid on that basis).[5] In a case where the statutory charge applies, you also require the informed consent of your client to the incurring of the extra costs of instructing QC or second counsel,[6] and costs officers will be looking to see that on your file.[7]

Where you instruct counsel, the brief must include a copy of the certificate and a copy of any prior authority to instruct counsel.[8] Where the certificate has not yet been issued, you should provide with a copy within 14 days of receipt.[9]

You can instruct a solicitor not employed by your organisation to provide advocacy services.[10]

Payment for advocacy services

Work done by a solicitor

12.11 Advocacy work, and associated preparation, attendance, travel and waiting, done by a solicitor is payable at the hourly rates set out in the Payment Annex to the contract. This is true whether the solicitor is employed by your firm or whether they are acting as an independent solicitor-advocate. Their times should be included on your bill along with all other profit costs and will be assessed in the usual way. See chapter 11 for details of the assessment process. The fact that a solicitor has undertaken the advocacy themselves rather than instruct counsel, especially in a complex case, will assist in justifying an enhancement to the hourly rates.

Work done by counsel

12.12 The legal aid scheme does not provide prescribed rates for counsel in independent practice (counsel employed by a solicitors' firm is treated as a fee earner of the solicitors' firm and therefore solicitors' rates will apply).

5 Specification, para 6.61(d).
6 *Re Solicitors: Taxation of Costs* [1982] 2 All ER 841.
7 Civil Costs Assessment Guidance, para 13.8.
8 Specification, para 5.28.
9 Specification, para 5.29.
10 Specification, para 2.7.

The Civil Procedure Rules provide for fixed fees to be paid for trials in fast track cases. The LSC has adopted these fees in cases where the rule applies,[11] and these are the amounts that counsel can claim in any case falling within the rule:

- claim value up to £3,000: £485
- claim value £3,001–£10,000: £690 (this fee also applies to cases where the remedy is other than damages)
- claim value £10,001–£15,000: £1,035
- claim value over £15,000: £1,650[12]
- separate trial of an issue: up to two-thirds of the main fee, capped to £485[13]

There is no uplift for representing more than one party, but their claims are to be added together for the purpose of calculating the value. The fees apply to representing both claimants and defendants.

The Senior Court Costs Office issues guidance on the rates claimable by counsel in certain limited circumstances:[14]

	1 hour hearing	Half-day hearing
Queen's Bench		
Junior up to 5 years' call	£259	£450
Junior 5–10 years' call	£386	£767
Junior 10+ years' call	£582	£1,164
Chancery Division		
Junior up to 5 years' call	£291	£556
Junior 5–10 years' call	£497	£931
Junior 10+ years' call	£757	£1,397
Administrative Court		
Junior up to 5 years' call	£381	£582
Junior 5–10 years' call	£698	£1,164
Junior 10+ years' call	£989	£1,746

11 Specification, para 6.21.
12 Civil Procedure Rules (CPR) 46.2.
13 CPR 46.3(3).
14 See www.hmcourts-service.gov.uk/publications/guidance/scco/appendix_ 2.htm.

However, it is stressed that such rates are not recommended rates, merely a 'helpful starting point', with the actual fees being more or less than this as the circumstances merit.

Beyond this, there are no prescribed or recommended rates applicable to counsel. The LSC's Costs Assessment Guidance says: 'Unfortunately there is little specific guidance as to the assessment of the proper brief fee. The points made in *Re H* are relevant. "There is ... no precise standard of measurement. The Taxing Master, employing his knowledge and experience, determines what he considers the right figure." It is largely a matter of experience and comparison of one case with another.'[15]

Counsel will generally charge a brief fee for preparation and advice and the first day of the trial, fees for pre-trial hearings, and refreshers for trial days beyond the first day.

Counsel's fees are included in the solicitor's bill, and claimed by the solicitor on behalf of counsel. See chapter 11 for information on the assessment process. Counsel's fees are also included in the costs limit on the certificate. It is therefore important that counsel deliver regular fee notes to the solicitor – both so that the solicitor can monitor and if necessary extend the costs limit, and so that the solicitor can submit the bill promptly at the end of the case.

Payment on account of counsel's fees

12.13   Counsel can apply direct to the LSC on form CLSPOA1 for a payment on account of their costs.[16] An application can be made on each anniversary of the issue of the certificate, with a window of two months before and four months after the relevant date.

An application can also be made at any point if:

- the proceedings have continued for more than 12 months;
- it appears unlikely that an order will be made for the costs of the case to be assessed within the next 12 months; and
- delay in the assessment will cause hardship to counsel.

An application can also be made if:

- the proceedings have concluded or counsel is otherwise entitled to payment; and
- six months have elapsed since then and counsel has not been paid.

15 Costs Assessment Guidance, para 13.21.
16 Specification, para 6.88.

On application, the LSC will pay 75 per cent of counsel's reasonable fees. If the final payment is less than the amount of any payments on account, the outstanding balance will be recouped from counsel.[17]

Case study

I am instructed in a case where my solicitor's certificate was issued on 1 April 2009 and the case is still ongoing. When can I make a payment on account application?

You can apply on the anniversary of the issue of the certificate, but there is a window either side to allow some flexibility – two months before and four months after the date. So you could have applied for a payment on account at any point between 1 February and 1 August 2010. If the case continues into 2011, you can apply again at any time between 1 February 2011 and 1 August 2011, and so on into 2012 if applicable.

At any time, you should put your total costs to date on the POA1, and the LSC will pay 75 per cent of that (subject to reasonableness), less any payment you have already received. So, for example, if you were paid £1,000 on account in 2010 and by 1 February 2011 your costs have reached £5,000, you should put £5,000 on the form and will be paid £2,750 (75 per cent of £5,000 = £3,750, less £1,000 already received).

High cost civil cases

12.14 Where the case is a high cost case (see chapter 3), any advocacy work will also be part of the individual case contract.

Any contract will be with the solicitor, but where an external advocate is instructed, they will need to agree to the payment rates and case/stage plans.

The rates payable to counsel depend on the classification of the case. Where there is a possibility that, if successful, inter partes costs will be recovered, the case is deemed to be 'at risk' and the rates will be £50 per hour for junior counsel and £90 per hour for senior counsel. Where prospects of success are only borderline but the case is nonetheless being funded because of its overwhelming importance to the client, wider public interest or significant human rights issues, the rates will be £65 and £117 respectively. Where there is no

---

17 Specification, para 6.90.

prospect of inter partes costs, standard remuneration rates will apply, but in determining the level of the brief and refresher fees, the LSC will take into account the number of hours agreed, the seniority of counsel and the complexity of the case.[18] The first £5,000 of counsel's fees will always be paid at standard rates rather than high cost case contract rates.

See chapter 11 for claiming costs in high cost civil cases.

Unpaid fees

12.15   Counsel can only claim fees through solicitors. In certificated cases, solicitors must include counsel's fees in the bill and must submit the bill to the court or LSC for assessment within the three-month time limit. See chapter 11 of part A for details of the process.

Where the solicitor fails to submit the bill, counsel will not be paid. There is no direct remedy, since there is no provision for counsel to bill the LSC directly. The standard terms of business and withdrawal of credit scheme of the Bar, set out at Annex G1 of the Bar Code of Conduct,[19] provide that if no satisfactory explanation for non-payment is received, a barrister should report the solicitor to the Chairman of the Bar, who will write to the solicitor. The text of the letter is included in the Annex, and requires an explanation as to the non-payment; if none is forthcoming, the Chairman will place the solicitor on the withdrawal of credit list (which means that no barrister will accept instructions from the solicitor in a private case unless the fee is paid up-front, or in a legal aid case unless the barrister can claim direct from the LSC). The Chairman will also report the solicitor to the Law Society. At the time of writing the Bar Council was consulting on a new scheme,[20] but which does not appear to be substantially different in respect of legal aid work.

So counsel cannot directly enforce costs against solicitors who fail to submit bills for payment. Counsel can to some extent protect themselves by using the payment on account scheme to recover 75 per cent of their costs.

It is a term of the Standard Civil Contract that bills be submitted within the three-month time limit; failure to do so is a breach of

---

18   'A barrister's information pack', www.legalservices.gov.uk > Community Legal Service > High Cost Civil Cases.

19   See www.barstandardsboard.rroom.net/standardsandguidance/codeofconduct/section2-annexestothecode/annexeg1-thetermsofworkonwhichbarristersoffer theirservicestosolicitorsandthewithdrawalofcreditscheme1988/.

20   See www.barcouncil.org.uk/news/newsarchive/535.html.

contract, and repeated failure may lead to sanctions up to and including termination. Counsel may wish to draw a solicitor's failure to submit a bill to the attention of the LSC.

Inter partes costs and legal aid only costs

12.16 In cases where inter partes costs are possible, it is not uncommon for costs to be ordered or negotiated on the basis of payment of part of the costs of the case. If that is the case, it is important that you are clear as to the terms of the order or agreement, as in some cases but not others you may be able to claim the balance from the legal aid fund. The Standard Civil Contract 2010 allows you to claim from the legal aid fund any costs not payable by another party (legal aid only costs), but only if certain conditions are met – see paras 6.52 and 6.53 of the Specification.

The Specification defines 'legal aid only' costs – costs that can be claimed from the legal aid fund even where inter partes costs are recovered – as:

- costs of completing legal aid forms and communicating with the LSC;
- certain limited types of costs disallowed or not agreed;
- costs of work not covered by a costs order or agreement.

Where a costs order or agreement specifies that another party should pay a proportion of the client's costs (but not a fixed sum), the same proportion of the total work that is not covered is legal aid only costs.

To take a practical example, say total costs on the case are £2,000 at legal aid rates and £4,000 at inter partes rates. If the other side agree to pay your costs in the sum of £2,000, that could be expressed in one of three ways:

- £2,000 as the total agreed costs of the case;
- agreement to pay costs between x and y dates, totalling £2,000; or
- agreement to pay 50 per cent of the costs, being £2,000.

In each case, you receive £2,000 from the other side. In the first case, that £2,000 represents the total costs of the case, so there are no legal aid costs (apart perhaps from £100 or so for filling in the APP1 and so on). In the second case, costs outside the agreed dates are not subject to the costs order, so you can claim those costs from the LSC in addition to the inter partes costs you have received. In the third case, the other side has agreed to pay 50 per cent of your costs, so the other 50 per cent are legal aid only costs, so you can claim £1,000 (50 per cent of £2,000 at legal aid rates) from the LSC in addition to the £2,000 from the other side.

Advocacy in family cases

Introduction

13.1   This chapter deals with the particular rules that apply to conduct of and payment for advocacy in family cases. See chapter 12 for the general rules applying to both civil and family cases.

Advocacy can only be conducted under Legal Representation certificates in family work as Help at Court and Controlled Legal Representation (CLR) are not available in the family category.

In general, we use the term 'advocate' to refer to anyone who has a right of audience to appear in the relevant court or who the court is willing to hear where the scheme makes no distinction between solicitor and counsel. Where there is a difference according to whether advocacy is conducted by solicitor or by counsel, we will use the terms 'solicitor' and 'counsel' as appropriate.

This chapter only deals with the advocacy aspects of family cases. For more information on the conduct of litigation, see part A of this book. For information on the rules applying in criminal cases, see chapter 14.

Merits test

13.2   See chapter 3 for the merits tests relevant to legal representation.

Family cases started prior to 9 May 2011

13.3   The Family Graduated Scheme (FGS) continues to apply to these cases. The provisions of the scheme are set out in the Community Legal Service (Funding) (Counsel in Family Proceedings) Order 2001 (SI 2001/1077) as amended.

Scope of the FGS

13.4   The FGS applies only to counsel. Solicitor advocates claim under the appropriate standard fee or hourly rate scheme, depending on whether the case is public or private law, and whether the case started prior to 1 October 2007.

Payments under the FGS are essentially fixed or standard fee payments with a range of base fees for different pieces of work. These fees are set according to the nature of the proceedings, the work to be done, whether junior or leading counsel is employed, and venue.

There is also a range of additional payments that may be added to the fee due, to reflect special features and complexity. The permutation of possible payments is quite complex. There is a helpful guidance paper on the LSC's website at: www.legalservices.gov.uk > Community Legal Service (CLS) > Pay rates and schemes > Family Graduated Fees.

Family cases started on or after 9 May 2011

13.5 The new Family Advocacy Scheme (FAS) apply to cases where the certificate is granted following an application made on or after 9 May 2011. It will be very important for advocates (especially counsel) to check the certificate to see which scheme applies.

The provisions of the scheme are set out in the Community Legal Service (Funding) (Amendment No 2) Order 2010 (SI 2010/1109) and in section 7 of the 2010 Standard Civil Contract Specification.

Scope of the FAS

13.6 The new fees apply to most advocacy, and the majority of fees can be claimed equally by solicitors or counsel, although the fees for providing opinions or advising in conference can only be claimed by counsel. The LSC uses the term 'advocate' when any advocate can claim a payment and 'counsel', when only the latter (or a self-employed FILEX equivalent) can claim.[1] The LSC states that self-employed solicitors, for example consultants, do not meet their definition of 'counsel'. There will no longer be the need to seek prior authority for counsel in the Family Proceedings Court as the same fee will apply to both solicitors and counsel.[2]

Solicitors claim payment from the LSC in the usual way, and if you instruct a solicitor advocate freelancer or from another firm, they act as an agent and you are responsible for their fees. Counsel claim fees from the LSC direct.[3]

The advocacy fee includes all preparation for a hearing, travel to and waiting at court and time spent in advocacy itself. The advocacy fee can only be claimed by the legal representative providing advocacy

---

1 Unified Contract Specification para 10.112.
2 LSC Guidance on the FAS, para 1.8(2).
3 Unified Contract Specification para 10.26.

at a hearing. If a solicitor's representative attends with an advocate, he or she cannot also claim the fee.

Some types of advocacy will continue to be paid under hourly rates:[4]

- Proceedings excluded from the FAS:[5]

    (a) Child Abduction Proceedings;
    (b) Proceedings under the Inheritance (Provision for Family and Dependants) Act 1975;
    (c) Proceedings under the Trusts of Land and Appointment of Trustees Act 1996;
    (d) Separate representation of children in proceedings other than (i) Specified Proceedings (as defined in section 41(6) of the Children Act 1989) or (ii) proceedings which are being heard together with Specified Proceedings;
    (e) Applications for Forced Marriage Protection Orders under the Forced Marriage (Civil Protection) Act 2007;
    (f) Defended proceedings for divorce, judicial separation, dissolution of a civil partnership or for the legal separation of civil partners;
    (g) Nullity proceedings (including proceedings for annulment of a civil partnership);
    (h) Wardship or Inherent Jurisdiction proceedings;
    (i) Applications for Parental Orders under the Human Fertilisation and Embryology Act 2008.

- The following is also excluded;

    – advocacy in relation to final appeals;
    – advocacy provided under a high costs case contract issued by the LSC's Special Cases unit;
    – advocacy by QCs;
    – advocacy before the Court of Appeal or Supreme Court.

The scheme is split into five categories of case:

1 care and supervision proceedings;
2 other public law cases;
3 private law children proceedings;
4 finance cases;
5 domestic abuse cases.

Exceptional cases

13.7   There are no exceptional cases or uplifts payable under the FAS. This is because the payments are based on time periods.

4 Unified Contract Specification para 10.108.
5 Unified Contract Specification para 10.102.

Mixed categories

13.8   Where work covers more than one of the categories above within a single set of proceedings, the advocate can choose which fee to claim:[6]

1. In family cases, the certificate will often either be issued to cover a number of proceedings or be subsequently amended to add or substitute proceedings during the life of the certificate.

2. When the continuing proceedings fall within more than one category, an advocate must, for the purpose of payment under the FAS, choose under which single category they would wish to be paid for all the Advocacy Services performed when making a claim for payment. Usually, an advocate will claim at the category that pays the highest rate. For example, in a residence/contact application that subsequently involves allegations of abuse to a degree that the local authority issues care proceedings, at the point at which a new certificate is issued, an advocate can claim all future work (including issues as to contact) at the higher care proceedings rate.

3. Where an Advocacy Service includes work from two categories but it falls within a single set of proceedings only one fee will be paid eg if a single hearing covers both private law children and financial issues then only one hearing fee will be payable and the advocate can choose which hearing fee to claim.

Hearing fees

13.9   Fees vary according to whether a hearing is interim or final:[7]

Interim and Final Hearings
10.122 A Final Hearing is any hearing which the court has listed for the purpose of making a final determination, either of the whole case or of all issues relating to an Aspect of the case (Domestic Abuse, Children or Finance). Subject to paragraph 7.123, there can only be one Final Hearing per Aspect and a hearing listed only to determine particular facts or issues is not a Final Hearing. A hearing listed with a view to the issues being dealt with under a consent order, or which is otherwise not expected to be effective or contested, is not a Final Hearing. Any hearing which is not a Final Hearing is an Interim Hearing.

6 LSC Guidance on the FAS, para 2.3.
7 Unified Contract Specification paras 10.122–129.

10.123 The following hearings are also deemed to be Final Hearings for the purposes of the FAS only:

(a) In Public Law proceedings, if a case is concluded at an Issues Resolution Hearing and therefore does not proceed further, the Issues Resolution Hearing will be treated as a Final Hearing;

(b) In Private Law Children proceedings, a hearing listed for the purpose of findings of fact in accordance with the Practice Direction dated 14 January 2009 (Residence and Contact Orders: Domestic Violence and Harm).

10.124 If a Final Hearing is listed for a split hearing in a Public Law matter with certain issues being heard and/or determined in advance of other issues, this must be claimed as a Final Hearing, rather than as an Interim Hearing plus a Final Hearing.

10.125 It is possible for more than one Final Hearing fee to be claimed under a single certificate. In particular this can occur where a Final Hearing has taken place but subsequent enforcement proceedings are listed at first instance. Provided the enforcement issues are listed to be finally determined at the further hearing, an additional Final Hearing fee may be justified.

Interim hearing units

13.10   The fee payable depends on the length of the hearing. There are two interim hearing units:

- hearing unit 1: 1 hour or less;
- hearing unit 2: 1 hour but less than or equal to 2.5 hours;
- if a hearing exceeds 2.5 hours, multiples of unit 2 fees will be paid (rounded up).

The applicable hearing time is the time at which the hearing is listed to start (unless the court specifically directs the advocate to attend earlier) until the time the hearing concludes:[8]

10.126 The fee payable under FAS for an Interim Hearing depends on its length. For this purpose the length of hearing is measured from the time that the hearing is listed at court to start (or such earlier time as the court specifically directs the advocate to attend) to the time that the hearing concludes, disregarding any period in which the court is adjourned overnight or for a lunch break. Time spent when a hearing or resumed hearing is delayed because the court is dealing with other business may however be taken into account. In the case of an Interim Hearing taking place by telephone or video link, time only runs from the time the call is made. If for an emergency hearing the court has not listed a time for the hearing or a time for the advocate to

8 Unified Contract Specification para 10.126.

attend and the papers were only issued by the court on the day of the proposed hearing (so that the advocate must wait at court to be heard in the matter), the length of hearing may be measured from the time that the papers were issued.

Hearing unit fees include all preparation for the hearing, travel to court (but see bolt-ons below), waiting and advocacy.

The LSC has provided some additional guidance in relation to interim hearings:[9]

> 5. ... Where for an emergency hearing the court has not listed a time for the hearing and the papers are only issued by the court on the day of the proposed hearing so that the advocate must wait at court to be heard the length of the hearing will be measured from the time that the papers were issued. If the application is issued and the hearing is then not heard until the next day the hearing time for that day will end when the advocate is informed of this and will start again at the time that they are told to attend for the following day.
>
> 6. Where a court directs a party to adjourn for further discussions at court then that time will be included in the calculation of the interim hearing fee
>
> 7. A hearing may take place by any method directed by the court e.g. by either video or telephone conference without attendance at court. If the court directs an alternative method of hearing then the advocate will receive the appropriate fee as if the hearing had taken place at court. However, in these cases the hearing time will start from the time that the telephone call/video conference is first attempted rather than the time that the hearing was listed. Bolt-ons may be claimed for telephone/video hearings if appropriate although due to the nature of these hearings bolt-ons are less likely to be applicable. It is unlikely, for example, that the criteria for the expert bolt-on would be met. As there will be no Advocates Attendance Form detailed notes of the hearing will need to be recorded and the claim justified on the CLAIM 1A or CLAIM 5A.
>
> 8. Where a case is resolved at an Issues Resolution Hearing held under the Public Law Outline (PLO) and no further hearings take place then this hearing will be paid as a final hearing.

Final hearings

13.11   Final hearings are paid under daily rates. A full daily fee is payable, regardless of the length of the hearing on that day.[10]

---

9 LSC Guidance on the FAS, para 3.2.
10 Unified Contract Specification para 10.128.

Finding of fact hearings will be paid for as final hearings. Issues Resolution hearings in public law cases will be paid for as final hearings (if the case concludes at that hearing).[11]

The LSC has provided some additional guidance in relation to final hearings (LSC Guidance on the FAS, para 3.2):

> 10. In care proceedings, the main hearing would be the hearing at which the court determines whether or not a section 31 order is made. If a final hearing is listed for a split hearing with certain issues being heard and/or determined in advance of other issues (for example, findings of fact and/or threshold criteria), this must be claimed as a final hearing rather than an interim hearing plus a final hearing. In ancillary relief proceedings, it is likely to be the hearing at which the court determines the form of relief entitlement and in family injunctions, the on notice hearing which will determine the form and continuation of the without notice injunction order made. The definition includes all preparation or incidental work relating to the hearing including preparation, travel to court and waiting at court as well as the advocacy within the hearing itself.

See also LSC Guidance on the FAS, para 4.2:

> 9. A directions hearing that concludes the case does not make the hearing a 'final hearing'.

> 10. On the making of an order the court may decide to review the position after an interval of some months. That subsequent review is not a continuation of the final hearing but an interim hearing. The court may make further directions, continue or vary the order. None of these circumstances turn that later hearing into either the continuation of the final hearing or a new final hearing.

> 11. It is possible in certain circumstances for more than one final hearing fee to be paid in a case. In particular this can occur where a final hearing has taken place but subsequent enforcement proceedings are issued which are required to be finally determined or where an earlier fact finding hearing has taken place.

Cancelled hearings

13.12   Only counsel may claim a fee for cancelled hearings. Counsel must have done at least 30 minutes' preparation in order to claim a hearing unit 1 fee.[12]

11 Unified Contract Specification para 10.123.
12 Unified Contract Specification para 10.129.

Bolt-ons

13.13 Additional bolt-on fees are available for more complex cases in public and private law children cases. Claims must be verified by the judge, magistrate or legal adviser at the hearing on the Advocates Attendance form (AAF). Bolt-on fees cannot be claimed for cancelled hearings.

Bolt-ons are only available as long as the issue remains live within the proceedings.[13]

No bolt-ons will be available in finance cases and domestic abuse cases, apart from court bundles in finance cases and exceptional travel.

Public law

13.14 In public law cases bolt-ons are claimable where:

- you are acting for a parent or others against whom allegations of serious harm to a child are made by the local authority;
- where the client has difficulty giving instructions/understanding advice;
- expert/s has/have to be cross-examined.

Client – allegations of significant harm

13.15 Paragraph 10.140 of the Specification states:

This Bolt-on Fee is claimable only where your Client is facing allegations that he or she has caused significant harm to a child. It applies only so long as those allegations remain a live issue in the proceedings. For this purpose only the following conditions constitute significant harm:
(a) Death,
(b) Significant head and/or fracture injuries,
(c) Burns or scalds,
(d) Fabricated illness,
(e) Extensive bruising involving more than one part of the body,
(f) Multiple injuries of different kinds,
(g) Other significant ill-treatment (such as suffocation or starvation) likely to endanger life,
(h) Sexual abuse.

Client – lack of understanding etc

13.16 Paragraph 10.142 of the Specification states:

This bolt-on applies to Hearings in Public Law proceedings where:
(a) Your Client has difficulty in giving instructions or understanding advice,

---

13 LSC Guidance on the FAS, para 3.2(29).

(b) This is attributable to a mental disorder (as defined in section 1(2) of the Mental Health Act 1983) or to a significant impairment of intelligence or social functioning, and

(c) The Clients condition is verified by a medical report from either a psychologist or psychiatrist.

Advocates' meetings

13.17   In public law cases, a separate fee is available for advocates attending an advocates' meeting, where such a meeting is directed by the court in accordance with the Public Law Outline. Where in s31 care proceedings, advocates are able to discuss all relevant matters without the need for an advocates' meeting, half the standard fee is payable (without any bolt-ons).[14]

The LSC have provided some additional guidance in relation to advocates' meetings:[15]

15. Although it would usually be expected that two advocates' meetings would take place in accordance with the PLO, provided that the advocates' meeting is held as directed by the court and in accordance with the PLO there is no limit to the number of these fees that may be claimed. No fees for advocates' meetings will be payable in Private Law Children cases.

16. The definition of Advocates' Meeting includes meetings held by video conference, webcam or telephone where this appropriate in the circumstances.

Private law

13.18   In private law children cases, bolt-ons are claimable where:

• you are acting for a parent or others against whom allegations of serious harm to a child are made;[16]

• expert/s has/have to be substantially challenged in court.

In private law finance cases an early resolution fee can be claimed for cases which settle at the first appointment or Financial Dispute Resolution (FDR) Hearing, as long as the advocate materially assisted in the settlement, it is recorded in a consent order and it lasts for six months (as far as you are aware).[17]

Early Resolution Fee
10.147 This Bolt-on Fee is claimable only in Private Law Finance cases which settle at the first appointment or Financial Dispute Resolution

14 Unified Contract Specification para 10.131.
15 LSC Guidance on the FAS, para 3.2.
16 See 10.140 above for the definition.
17 Unified Contract Specification para 10.147.

("FDR") hearing. It may only be claimed by an advocate who is entitled to the Hearing fee for that hearing but only if the following conditions are satisfied:

(a) The Finance Aspect of the case has been fully concluded at the first appointment or FDR hearing;
(b) The advocate attending that hearing materially assisted in the settlement;
(c) The Finance Aspect of the case does not proceed further to a new Level of Service within six months of the settlement, either with you or, so far as you are aware, another Provider;
(d) There has been a genuine settlement to conclude that Aspect of the case, rather than, for example, a reconciliation between the parties or one party dying or disengaging from the case;
(e) The settlement is recorded in a form of a Consent Order approved by the Court, either at the hearing itself or subsequently.

Court bundles

13.19   Additional fees may be claimed for court bundles:[18]

- CBP 1 – over 350 pages;
- CBP 2 – over 700 pages;
- CBP 3 – over 1,400 pages (final hearings only).

> 10.144 There are restrictions on the circumstances and number of times within a set of proceedings that a court bundle payment may be claimed for Interim Hearings. In Public Law proceedings, court bundle payments may be claimed for no more than two Interim Hearings and each of these must be either a Case Management Conference, an Issues Resolution Hearing or otherwise a hearing which is listed for the hearing of contested evidence. A Court Bundle Payment may never be claimed more than once per Hearing.

> 10.145 In Private Law proceedings court bundle payments may only be claimed at one Interim Hearing per case. For this purpose the Children and Finance Aspects of a case will be treated separately.

> 10.146 Court bundle payments may not be claimed in Domestic Abuse proceedings, either for Interim or Final Hearings.

The LSC has provided some additional guidance in relation to court bundles:[19]

> 46. The definition of court bundle for the purposes of the payment only includes the court bundle that is substantially considered by the court. It does not include any additional bundles that are filed

---

18 Unified Contract Specification paras 10.144–10.146.
19 LSC Guidance on the FAS, para 3.2.

in the event that further information may be required, nor does it include the pages of an advocate's brief.

47. An advocate must obtain certification of the relevant number of pages of court bundle on the Advocates Attendance Form in order to claim this payment.

48. An advocate taking on a case part way through must satisfy themselves as to whether the court bundle payment/s have already been or are intended to be claimed by an advocate at an earlier hearing.

Exceptional travel

13.20   Advocates may claim payments for exceptional travel (more than 25 miles each way), as long as it was reasonable for them to be instructed in all the circumstances, rather than someone more local to the court.[20]

All advocates will need to justify the payment either on the CLAIM 1A for solicitors or on the CLAIM 5A for counsel. Counsel should also supply a copy of their brief or instructions with the claim.

Payments for counsel only

13.21   Counsel's fees may be claimed under the FAS:

- for conferences, up to a maximum of two per set of proceedings.[21]
- for opinions, up to a maximum of two per set of proceedings, unless the opinion relates to a proposed appeal against a final order:[22]
  - in private law, counsel may claim two opinions for both the children and finance aspects of a case;
  - no opinion fee may be claimed in domestic abuse proceedings.

The LSC has issued guidance as to what constitutes a single set of proceedings:[23]

> 2.4(1) For particular Advocacy Services only two fees can be claimed per case. In order to determine what is or is not a 'case' for the purposes of determining appropriate claiming, applications to the court constitute a single set of proceedings, irrespective of whether they are

---

20 Unified Contract Specification para 10.149.
21 Unified Contract Specification para 10.136.
22 Unified Contract Specification para 10.133.
23 LSC Guidance on the FAS, para 2.4(1)–(10).

made separately or together, where they are heard together or consecutively or are treated by the court as a single set of proceedings. In private law proceedings each aspect of the case, e.g. children and finance, counts as a separate case for the purposes of claiming opinions and conferences.

Conference fees

13.22 The LSC has provided some additional guidance in relation to conference fees:[24]

21. A conference fee is paid for all work carried out in connection with a conference. This can include conferences by telephone or video link or webcam where this is appropriate in the circumstances. Conference fees may only be claimed by Counsel. No bolt-ons may be claimed for conferences.

22. Up to two conference fees may be claimed in each single set of proceedings. As for opinions in private law proceedings, if there are separate children and finance proceedings these will be considered separately for these purposes. However, no conference fee may be claimed under FAS in Domestic Abuse proceedings.

23. As only two conference fees may be claimed Counsel will need to designate the conferences for which he or she seeks payment under the FAS.

24. No conference fee may be claimed for any conference held on the same day as a Final hearing. Any discussions or negotiations taking place on any day of a final hearing will be covered by the fee for advocacy at that hearing.

25. A conference fee may be claimed for a conference that takes place on the same day as an interim hearing, only if the conference takes place outside of any time period that is taken into account in calculating the fee for the interim hearing. Therefore no conference fee may be claimed for a conference that takes place between the time that the hearing is listed to start and the time that hearing actually starts as this will be claimed as part of the Hearing Unit.

26. Where different Counsel is subsequently instructed and the allowable conference fees have already been claimed, no further claims for conference fees can be made. This is so even in circumstances where the later conference was more substantial. Where one Counsel has replaced another, Counsel must make enquiries as to whether the conference fees payments have been claimed from either the outgoing Counsel or instructing solicitors.

---

24 LSC Guidance on the FAS, para 3.2.

Opinion fees

13.23   The LSC has provided some additional guidance in relation to opinion fees:[25]

> 18. Up to two opinion fees may be claimed in each single set of proceedings. If there are separate children and finance proceedings these will be considered separately for these purposes. No opinion fee may claimed under the FAS in Domestic Abuse proceedings.
>
> 19. In addition to the two opinions claimed per set of proceedings a further opinion may be claimed in relation to any a proposed appeal against a final order.
>
> 20. An opinion may include providing advice or drafting pleadings/affidavits after the issue of proceedings.

Assessment

13.24   The Commission will initially assess all fees due to counsel under the FAS.

Solicitors' profit costs and disbursements will be assessed in the usual way, through assessment either by the LSC or the court. See chapter 10 for more information.

Forms

13.25   Different forms are submitted depending on whether the claim falls under the Family Graduated Fee Scheme (cases started pre 9 May 2011) or the Family Advocacy Scheme (cases started after 9 May 2011).

Counsel claim on form CLSCLAIM5A. There is guidance on how to fill out the form on the LSC's website at: www.legalservices.gov.uk > Community Legal Service (CLS) > Pay rates and schemes > Family fees from 2010.

Solicitors claim on form CLS CLAIM 1A. There is guidance on how to fill out the form on the LSC's website at: www.legalservices. gov.uk > Community Legal Service (CLS) > Pay rates and schemes > Family fees from 2010. You can submit CLSCLAIM1A via the LSC's online facility: www.legalservices.gov.uk/lsconline.asp.

Claims for advocacy under the FAS must be made on an appropriately completed Advocates attendance form (EX506). If such form(s) are not submitted the claim(s) will not be paid.

25 LSC Guidance on the FAS, para 3.2.

Advocacy in criminal cases

by Julia Sherriff

Introduction

14.1   This chapter deals with the conduct of and payment for advocacy in criminal cases.

In criminal proceedings, advocacy can be conducted under:

- Advocacy Assistance;
- Representation Order.

Advocacy may arise at all stages of criminal proceedings, including the investigations stage, where advocacy may arise due to an application for a warrant of further detention or where a client wishes to apply to vary police bail conditions.

In general, we use the term 'advocate' to refer to anyone who has a right of audience to appear in the relevant court or whom the court is willing to hear where the scheme makes no distinction between solicitor and counsel. Where there is a difference according to whether advocacy is conducted by solicitor or by counsel, we will use the terms 'solicitor' and 'counsel' as appropriate.

Who is entitled to conduct advocacy, and the payment arrangements, will depend on the type of hearing and the stage of the case.

All qualified solicitors may represent a client at a hearing in the magistrates' court, as may counsel. However, whether or not counsel may be instructed will depend on the type of hearing and whether it is funded by Advocacy Assistance or a Representation Order.

In general, advocacy at Crown Court hearings and above may only be provided by counsel or a solicitor who has higher rights of audience.

Funding

14.2   In general, advocacy in a criminal case is funded by a Representation Order, which will cover all of the hearings from the first appearance in the magistrates' court up to the final sentencing hearing. A Representation Order will also generally be required for advocacy in appeals.

The main stage at which advocacy is not covered by a Representation Order is the investigations stage. At this stage, funding is provided by Advocacy Assistance. Advocacy Assistance is also available to fund representation by the duty solicitor and representation at prison disciplinary and parole board hearings.

Advocacy Assistance – investigations stage

Clients detained in custody

14.3 A client who is detained in police (or military) custody may require representation at court if there is an application to extend the custody time limit under Police and Criminal Evidence Act 1984 (PACE) s43 or s44, Terrorism Act 2000 Sch 8 para 29 or para 36, or the relevant military legislation.[1]

The funding for such hearings is subject to the 'sufficient benefit' test, however the test is automatically deemed satisfied by the circumstances.[2]

There is no means test[3] and the client is not required to sign any application form.[4] However, you are required to record on the file:

- the client's name and address;
- the unique file number (UFN);
- the date, time and venue of the court appearance; and
- details of the relevant unit of work (as defined by the contract) and how the work falls within the scope of that unit.[5]

These details should be recorded either before the Advocacy Assistance is provided or as soon as practicable after, if the advocacy is required at short notice.[6]

Reasonable preparation and follow-up work will be included within the scope of Advocacy Assistance, as will travel and waiting costs. However there is a costs limit of £1,500.

There are no fixed fees for this type of work so, subject to the costs limit above, work will be claimed at the hourly rates set out in the Payment Annex to the contract. These vary depending on whether the hearing is before a magistrates' court or judicial authority, or before a High Court or senior judge. There are also different rates for own and duty solicitors, and for unsociable hours.

Counsel may only be instructed where the application is before the High Court or a senior judge.[7]

---

1 Standard Crime Contract Specification 2010 (hereafter 'the Specification'), paras B9.145, B9.158.
2 Specification, paras B9.146, B9.160.
3 Specification, paras B9.147, B9.161.
4 Specification, paras B9.148, B9.162.
5 Specification, paras B9.150, B9.163.
6 Specification, paras B9.148, B9.162.
7 Specification, para B9.152.

Bail variations

14.4   A client who is not detained in custody may also require representation at court if there is an application to vary police bail conditions (including 'street bail' conditions).[8]

In this situation there are no qualifying criteria to be met and there is no means test.[9] As above, the client is not required to sign an application form but you must record the same required information on the file.[10]

Advocacy Assistance in this situation includes reasonable preparation, travel, waiting and advocacy at the hearing, and the provision of advice on appeal.

The same costs limit applies, and the rules on claiming are the same. The applicable fees are set out in the Payment Annex to the contract.

You cannot instruct counsel in this case,[11] and you may not claim under this unit of work if you are acting as duty solicitor.[12] However, you can claim under Advocacy Assistance if you represented the client as duty solicitor at the police station and you are subsequently instructed in the bail variation.

Advocacy Assistance – court duty solicitor

14.5   Advocacy Assistance is available to cover the representation of clients by the court duty solicitor at the magistrates' court. In practice it will be claimed together with Advice and Assistance, which covers the provision of advice to such clients outside court. The two forms of assistance will be claimed together in a single claim at the end of the duty day.[13]

Advocacy Assistance under this unit of work may only be provided by a qualified duty solicitor (ie one who has passed both the Police Station Qualification and the Magistrates' Court Qualification and has registered as a duty solicitor with the Legal Services Commission (LSC)).

8   Specification, para B9.171.
9   Specification, para B9.173.
10 Specification, paras B9.174, B9.175.
11 Specification, para B9.177.
12 Specification, para B9.172.
13 Specification, para B10.17.

To qualify for Advocacy Assistance under this scheme, the client's case must come within the scope of the scheme:

- The duty solicitor must:[14]
  - advise any client who requests it who is in custody;
  - make a bail application where a client in custody requires a bail application and such an application has not previously been made by a duty solicitor;
  - advise and represent a client before the court in connection with civil orders deemed to be criminal for legal aid purposes:[15]
    - anti-social behaviour orders;[16]
    - parenting orders;[17]
    - football banning orders;[18]
    - closure orders;[19]
    - sexual offences notification orders;[20]
    - sexual offences prevention orders;[21]
    - foreign travel orders;[22]
    - risk of sexual harm orders;[23]
    - restraining orders.[24]
- The duty solicitor may:[25]
  - advise and represent any client who is in custody on a plea of guilty and wishes the case to be concluded that day;
  - advise and represent any client before the court for failure to pay a fine or other sum or to obey an order of the court, and such failure may lead to the client being at risk of imprisonment;
  - advise and represent a client not in custody in connection with an imprisonable offence;

---

14 Specification, para B10.7.
15 Criminal Defence Service (General) (No 2) Regulations 2001 reg 3(2).
16 Crime and Disorder Act 1998 ss1, 1D, 1G, 1H and 4.
17 Crime and Disorder Act 1998 ss8, 9 and 10; Anti-Social Behaviour Act 2003 ss20, 22, 26 and 28; Powers of Criminal Courts (Sentencing) Act 2000 Sch 1 Part 1A.
18 Football Spectators Act 1989 ss14B, 14D, 14G, 14H, 21B and 21D.
19 Anti-Social Behaviour Act 2003 ss2, 5 and 6.
20 Sexual Offences Act 2003 ss97, 100 and 101.
21 Sexual Offences Act 2003 ss104, 108, 109 and 110.
22 Sexual Offences Act 2003 ss114, 118 and 119.
23 Sexual Offences Act 2003 ss123, 125, 126 and 127.
24 Protection from Harassment Act 1997 s5A.
25 Specification, para B10.8.

- help a client in making an application for a Representation Order, whether the nominated solicitor is the duty solicitor or another solicitor;
- advise and represent a client seeking to vary police-imposed bail conditions pre-charge.
- The duty solicitor must not:
  - represent in committal proceedings;
  - represent at a not guilty trial;[26]
  - advise or represent a client who has had the services of a duty solicitor at a previous hearing in the proceedings (except where they are before the court this time as a result of failure to pay a fine or other sum or comply with an order imposed previously).[27]

The sufficient benefit test applies to representation by the duty solicitor (both under Advocacy Assistance and Advice and Assistance),[28] but there is no means test and clients are not required to complete an application form.[29] However, you are required to record on the file:

- the client's name and address;
- details of the relevant unit of work;
- whether the client is in custody or charged with an imprisonable offence; and
- the date, time and venue of the court appearance.[30]

These details should be recorded either before the Advocacy Assistance is provided or as soon as practicable after, if the advocacy is required at short notice.[31]

The scope of the scheme is limited in terms of the work covered. In addition to the advocacy, you may only claim for reasonable advice and preparation provided during the duty session. This can include advice on the consequences of the outcome and the giving of any notice of appeal or making an application for a case to be stated.[32]

Claiming for duty solicitor advocacy is done as part of a single claim submitted for the duty session. Hourly rates are set out in the Payment Annex and there is a standard hourly rate for both

26 Specification, para B10.9.
27 Specification, para B10.10.
28 Specification, para B10.2.
29 Specification, para B10.4.
30 Specification, para B10.6.
31 Specification, para B10.4.
32 Specification, para B10.16.

attendance and waiting. An enhanced rate applies to sessions on non-business days.

Under the duty solicitor scheme, you cannot claim for travel time other than on a non-business day, unless you are called out having not been on the rota or having been released but then asked to return.

Advocacy under a Representation Order

14.6   All Representation Orders granted for criminal cases in the magistrates' court and the Crown Court will include the provision of advocacy services. This will include representation at all hearings in the case including bail proceedings in the Crown Court or High Court.

Representation Orders in both the magistrates' court and the Crown Court are granted subject to a means test and a merits test. For a full discussion of these tests see chapter 9.

Advocacy under a Representation Order may be carried out either by a solicitor or by counsel, subject to the requirement for higher rights for advocacy in the Crown Court and above.

Magistrates' court

14.7   A Representation Order for a magistrates' court case will generally only cover advocacy provided by a solicitor. Payment for advocacy services provided by a solicitor will be claimed within the magistrates' court standard fee regime.

Advocacy is claimed at the hourly rate prescribed in the Payment Annex to the contract, in the same way as all other types of work provided under the Representation Order.

Travelling and waiting time can only be claimed if neither the court nor your office is in a 'designated area'. The designated areas[33] are:

- Greater Manchester, London, West Midlands and Merseyside Criminal Justice Areas;
- the local authority areas of
  - Brighton and Hove;
  - Bristol;
  - Cardiff;
  - Derby and Erewash;

---

33 Specification, para A1.13.

- Kingston upon Hull;
- Leeds and Bradford;
- Leicester;
- Nottingham;
- Portsmouth;
- Newcastle-upon-Tyne and Sunderland;
- Sheffield;
- Southampton.

Note that you are still required to record the waiting time (but not travel), even if you cannot claim for it.[34]

The total core costs will then be compared against lower and higher fee limits for the particular category of case (determined by outcome) and this will determine whether the lower standard fee, the higher standard fee, or a non-standard fee is payable.

For details of the fee structure under Representation Orders in the magistrates' court, see chapter 11.

Counsel in the magistrates' court

14.8   Although the Representation Order will usually only provide for advocacy by a solicitor, this does not mean that counsel cannot be instructed in the magistrates' court. It simply means that counsel is usually unassigned and cannot claim their costs from the court or the LSC. Therefore you are responsible for agreeing a fee with counsel and paying that fee promptly out of your costs. If you fail to pay within 30 days, counsel can apply to the LSC for payment and that payment will be deducted from your monthly payment.[35]

Unassigned counsel is treated like a solicitor agent. From the point of view of the LSC, their work is treated as your work. Their time should be recorded on your bill as if you had done the work, and counts towards the calculation of the appropriate fee.[36] As for solicitors, counsel's travel and waiting time can only be claimed for cases in 'undesignated areas'.[37]

You must provide counsel with the UFN and a copy of the Representation Order when briefing them.[38]

---

34 Specification, para B10.88.
35 Specification, paras B10.53, B10.54.
36 Specification, para B10.47.
37 Specification, para B10.84.
38 Specification, para B10.42.

Assigned counsel

14.9   In more serious cases, you can apply to the court for counsel (or an independent solicitor advocate) to be assigned. The regulations say that counsel may be assigned in any case where the charge is an indictable offence (that is, an offence capable of being tried on indictment, including either way offences, not just indictable only offences) or where the case is an extradition matter.[39]

Indictable only cases involving adults will be transferred directly to the Crown Court, so in practice counsel can be assigned in adult either way cases, youth cases where the charge would not be summary only were the defendant an adult, and extraditions.

In order to have counsel assigned, you must persuade the court that, because of circumstances which make the case unusually grave or difficult, representation by solicitor and advocate would be desirable.

In extradition proceedings, you can apply for more than one advocate, or for a QC, to be assigned where you can persuade the court that the defendant cannot be adequately represented except by QC or more than one advocate.[40]

In other proceedings, the court does not have the power to assign QC or more than one advocate. However, where counsel has been assigned you can apply to the LSC for prior authority to instruct QC alone.[41]

Where counsel is assigned, they are entitled to be paid directly by the LSC at the rates prescribed in the Payment Annex to the contract, though you should submit their bill with your own – see chapter 11.

Crown Court

14.10   Advocacy in the Crown Court must generally be conducted by counsel or a solicitor with higher rights of audience.

Crown Court Representation Orders automatically allow the instruction of a single junior advocate. Even if counsel was not assigned under the order in the magistrates' court, once the case goes to the Crown Court the order is deemed to include representation by one junior advocate (that is, any advocate other than a QC).[42]

---

39 Criminal Defence Service (General) (No 2) Regulations 2001 reg 12.
40 Criminal Defence Service (General) (No 2) Regulations 2001 reg 12(3).
41 Specification, para A5.28(d).
42 Criminal Defence Service (General) (No 2) Regulations 2001 reg 14(1).

In more serious and complex cases, an application may be made to the court to amend the order to allow for the instruction of QC or more than one advocate. The court can order representation by:

- QC alone;
- two advocates:
  - QC with junior;
  - QC with noting junior;
  - two juniors;
  - junior and noting junior; or
- where three advocates are justified, any of the above plus an additional junior or noting junior.[43]

In order to persuade the court to make an order for senior or more than one advocate, you must demonstrate that the relevant test is met:

- For QC alone:[44]
  - the case involves substantial novel or complex issues of law or fact which could not be adequately presented except by a QC; and
  - either:
    - the prosecution has instructed QC or senior Treasury counsel; or
    - the case for the defence is exceptional compared with the generality of cases involving similar offences.
- For two junior advocates:[45]
  - the case involves substantial novel or complex issues of law or fact which could not be adequately presented by a single advocate; and
  - either:
    - the prosecution have instructed two or more advocates;
    - the case for the defence is exceptional compared with the generality of cases involving similar offences;
    - the number of prosecution witnesses exceeds 80; or
    - the number of pages of prosecution evidence exceeds 1,000.
- For QC plus junior or noting junior:[46]
  - the case involves substantial novel or complex issues of law or fact which could not be adequately presented except by a QC assisted by a junior advocate; and

43 Criminal Defence Service (General) (No 2) Regulations 2001 reg 14(2).
44 Criminal Defence Service (General) (No 2) Regulations 2001 reg 14(3).
45 Criminal Defence Service (General) (No 2) Regulations 2001 reg 14(4).
46 Criminal Defence Service (General) (No 2) Regulations 2001 reg 14(5).

- either:
  - the prosecution has instructed QC or senior Treasury counsel; or
  - the case for the defence is exceptional compared with the generality of cases involving similar offences.
- For three advocates:[47]
  - the case is being prosecuted by the Serious Fraud Office;
  - the court considers three advocates are required; and
  - the conditions for two juniors or QC plus junior are satisfied (as appropriate).

The payment of advocates' fees in the Crown Court is governed by the Advocates Graduated Fee Scheme. This is a similar regime to the Litigator Graduated Fee Scheme that determines payments to solicitors in Crown Court cases. The rules and fees applicable to the Advocates Graduated Fee Scheme are set out in Schedule 1 to the Criminal Defence Service (Funding) Order 2007. This scheme applies to all advocates in the Crown Court, whether they are counsel or solicitor advocates.

Each case will have an instructed advocate, who is the advocate named in the brief and is responsible for claiming fees on behalf of all advocates instructed in the case and then passing payment on.

The scheme provides for a basic fee based on the classification of the offence to which is added uplifts for pages of evidence, length of trial, number of witnesses and additional fees for features such as conferences. There is a higher basic fee for a trial and a lower for a guilty plea case. The basic fee includes payment for attendance at a plea and case management hearing and four other hearings during the case; additional fees can be claimed for other hearings.

The full details are set out in Schedule 1 to the Order.[48]

Appeals

14.11 Although advice on appeals can, in some circumstances, be provided under the Advice and Assistance scheme, advocacy in appeal proceedings can now only be provided under a Representation Order.

Representation in appeal proceedings will require a Representation Order granted by the court in which the appeal is to be heard,

---

47 Criminal Defence Service (General) (No 2) Regulations 2001 reg 14(6).
48 Criminal Defence Service (Funding) Order 2007 Sch 1.

be that the High Court (for appeals by way of case stated), the Crown Court or the Court of Appeal.

It is usual for Representation Orders granted by the Court of Appeal to be granted to an advocate alone.[49]

Advocacy Assistance – prison law

14.12   Advocacy in prison law cases may be provided under the Advocacy Assistance scheme. Representation may be provided in disciplinary cases and in parole board cases.

You may only represent a client at hearings in these matters if the sufficient benefit test is satisfied, and the contract notes specifically that the LSC would not expect to fund a matter which did not raise a significant legal or human rights issue.[50] In addition Advocacy Assistance must not be provided in disciplinary cases where:

- it appears unreasonable to grant in the particular circumstances of the case; or
- (where required) permission to be legally represented has not been granted.[51]

In all cases you should record on the file how the merits test has been and continues to be met.[52]

In addition there is a financial eligibility test for both Advice and Assistance and Advocacy Assistance in prison law cases. The client must complete the relevant forms (CDS1 and CDS2 or CDS3), and must pass the means test. Means are limited by both capital and disposable income, and the eligibility levels can be found on the LSC website at www.legalservices.gov.uk > CDS > Criminal Legal Aid Eligibility in the current keycard. The completed application forms must be retained on your file.[53]

Advocacy under this scheme is paid under a system of standard fees.[54] There are two standard fees for each type of case, and two corresponding standard fee limits. If your costs fall below either limit, you will be paid the respective standard fee. If your costs fall above the higher limit, you will be paid a non-standard fee for which your

49 Criminal Defence Service (General) (No 2) Regulations 2001 reg 15.
50 Specification, para B12.11.
51 Specification, para B12.116.
52 Specification, para B12.7.
53 Specification, para B12.16.
54 Specification, para B12.76.

costs will be assessed by the LSC. See the Payment Annex to the contract for details of the fees and limits.

Under this form of Advocacy Assistance, advocacy may be provided by either a solicitor or counsel. However, counsel is effectively 'unassigned' in that they are not able to claim payment directly from the LSC. Counsel's fees must be agreed and paid by the instructing solicitor from the standard fee.[55]

---

55 Specification, paras B12.55, B12.58.

Managing legal aid work

CHAPTER 15

The legal aid framework

Introduction

15.1   This chapter briefly sets out how the legal aid scheme was developed. It also sets out the legislative framework that underpins legal aid. For information about using legal aid in individual cases, see part A.

The development of exclusivity

15.2   From its inception as a relatively widely available state funded public service in 1948 up to the mid-1990s, the culture of legal aid was that any solicitor who wanted to do so could do legal aid work. Many high street firms offered small amounts of legal aid work, perhaps for divorce or personal injury, alongside their conveyancing and will writing work.

As legal aid expanded, both in terms of scope and budget, in the 1960s and 1970s, specialist legal aid firms, and legal aid departments in larger firms, began to grow up. At the same time, the Law Centres movement was growing and other agencies and voluntary sector groups were expanding the provision of advice services.

By the early 1990s, government policy was changing. Legal aid had moved from being administered by the Law Society to a specialist quasi-governmental body, the Legal Aid Board (LAB). Alongside that, the not-for-profit sector was becoming more significant and taking up a larger share of the overall budget. The LAB wanted to encourage the move to specialisation and introduced a franchise system. The purpose of franchising was to develop a network of specialists accredited as being experts in their type of law, and to ensure that public money was only spent on those who were providing a service of sufficient quality.

However, the LAB did not have the tools to measure legal quality or competency. They did develop the franchise standard, which was a series of criteria concerned with the management and running of a firm, but not with an assessment of the quality of the work done. Firms that applied for a franchise had to demonstrate that they met the standard, and in return were allowed to describe themselves as franchised and charge a slightly higher hourly rate for the work that they did. However, the franchise system was voluntary, and many firms simply did not apply, and in any event it offered little insight into the quality of work done.

Meanwhile, despite periodic attempts to restrict it, expenditure on legal aid was increasing steadily. By the late 1990s, the new Labour government took the view that radical reform was needed and adopted the recommendations of a report commissioned by the previous government and carried out by Sir Peter Middleton.

The result was a complete overhaul of the system. The LAB was abolished and replaced by the Legal Services Commission (LSC), and the entire legislative basis of legal aid was re-written.

The base of the current scheme is the Access to Justice Act 1999. The Act created the LSC, and created two separate funds – the Community Legal Service (CLS) fund for civil work and the Criminal Defence Service (CDS) for crime. Both funds are administered by the LSC and in practice there is one single legal aid budget – there is no ring-fencing of either fund (though many have called for them to be separated, as criminal and family expenditure take an ever larger share).

The Access to Justice Act empowered the LSC to commission and procure legal aid services in such a way as to ensure that they were available to those who need services in almost any way the LSC considered most appropriate. In practice, the LSC have chosen to fund services by exclusive contract.

The franchise standard was replaced by the Specialist Quality Mark (SQM), and made compulsory. Legal aid is funded by contract – without a contract you cannot do legal aid work – and having the SQM or Lexcel is mandatory for being awarded a contract. See chapter 13 for details on the contract award process.

Therefore, since 2000 (for civil) and 2001 (for crime), legal aid work has been the exclusive preserve of organisations the LSC has contracted with to procure services.

For more on the history of legal aid, see Hynes and Robins, *The justice gap*, LAG, 2009.

Regulation of civil work

15.3   Schedule 2 to the Access to Justice Act sets the limits of civil funding; beyond those limits, subject to the power to make directions creating exceptions, work is not funded. Schedule 2 is exclusionary in nature; it sets out what may not be funded, and therefore unless the type of work is named, it will be covered by legal aid. See appendix F.

The Act itself does not contain a great deal of detail about the funding of services. However, it does contain three important provisions which set the shape of civil funding:

- section 8 requires the LSC to prepare a code setting out the criteria for funding cases and the procedures to be followed, and section 9 requires the code to be approved by both Houses of Parliament;

- section 10 authorises the making of regulations setting the terms of grants of funding; and
- section 6 authorises the LSC to fund services by entering into contracts with providers.

Between them the contract, the Code, and the regulations provide the complete framework for civil legal aid.

The Funding Code

15.4   The code prepared under section 8 of the Act is known as the Funding Code. It is in three parts:

- criteria;
- procedures; and
- guidance.

The full text of the code can be found in volume 3 of the LSC Manual.

The criteria define the various levels of funding and specify how all types of civil funding are to be granted, setting out the applicable merits tests.

The procedures define and set out the role of the LSC and of suppliers. For example, A4 states that only suppliers authorised by the LSC by contract or by grant may carry out funded work. They go on to set out the rules and procedures for granting all levels of funding and then define the obligations of clients, suppliers and the LSC. They also make provision for appeals against decisions of the LSC.

The guidance section of the Code is much more extensive than the other parts and consists of a detailed narrative setting out how the LSC treats applications for funding and providing a commentary on and expansion of the rules in the other parts of the Code.

The contracts

15.5   With very limited exceptions, you will not be permitted to do legal aid work without a contract with the LSC. Section 6 of the Act authorises the LSC to enter into contracts, and paragraph A4 of the Funding Code Procedures restricts funding to contracted organisations.

A contract with the LSC consists of three main sections:

- The standard terms govern the relationship between the firm and the LSC and your obligations as an organisation. See chapter 16.

! Change from previous rules !

- The schedule sets out the types of work you are permitted to do, and in the case of Legal Help and Controlled Legal Representation (CLR), the numbers of matters you are allowed to start per year. It will also specify any local requirements in your procurement area or access point, such as presence requirements, and will include any commitments you made as part of your tender for the contract (against the selection criteria, for example). Breach of any provision of your schedule, including any commitment you made in your tender, is a breach of contract subject to sanction in the usual way (see chapter 14).

- The Specification deals with how you should conduct individual cases, and is dealt with in part A of this book.

Other documents which are referred to in the contract, and which you should follow or take account of (though not technically part of the contract) include:

- Equality and Diversity Guidance and Policy;
- Category Definitions 2010;
- Guidance on Category Definitions 2010;
- Standard Monthly Payment (SMP) Reconciliation Protocol;
- Independent Peer Review Process;
- Key Performance Indicator (KPI) Outcome Codes;
- Data Security Requirements.

All of these documents are available on the LSC website: www.legalservices.gov.uk.

The regulations

15.6   A number of important regulations have been made under the Access to Justice Act.

Where the Funding Code deals with whether the client's case is eligible for legal aid, and the contracts with how you should conduct cases and manage your organisation, the regulations deal firstly with the terms on which funding can be granted to clients (looking at the client rather than the case), and secondly with the rates at which you are entitled to be paid.

The key regulations are:

- Community Legal Service (Financial) Regulations 2000 as amended, which deal with a) whether clients are financially eligible to receive legal aid, and b) whether clients will have to reimburse any of the costs of their case via the statutory charge;

- Community Legal Service (Costs) Regulations 2000 and the Community Legal Services (Costs Protection) Regulations 2000 as amended, which deal with the terms of your retainer with the client, and with whether and in what circumstances an order for costs can be made against a legally aided person;
- Community Legal Service (Funding) Order 2007 and Community Legal Service (Funding) Order 2008, which set out the graduated standard fees and payment rates you are entitled to claim – the fees are also reproduced in the Payment Annex to the 2010 Standard Civil Contract.

Regulation of criminal work

15.7   The scope of criminal work is defined by section 12 of the Access to Justice Act 1999. It is an inclusive definition; if work is not listed in section 12 (or in regulation 3(2) of the Criminal Defence Service (General) Regulations 2001, made under section 12(2)(g)), then for the purpose of legal aid it is not criminal work.

Schedule 3 to the Act states that a court may grant a right of representation to an individual involved in criminal proceedings. Section 15 of the Act states than an individual granted such a right may select any representative he or she wishes, subject to regulations which may be made. Regulation 11 of the Criminal Defence Service (General) (No 2) Regulations 2001 says that the right to select a representative is only exercisable in favour of an organisation that is employed by the LSC or has a contract with the LSC. This regulation, coupled with section 13 of the Act empowering the LSC to grant Advice and Assistance in a way it thinks appropriate, means that criminal legal aid is only available from those firms with whom the LSC has a contract (or employees of the Public Defender Service). The effect of regulation 11 is that even those types of work not governed by contract (eg Crown Court work) can only be done by organisations with a contract.

Therefore, criminal work, like civil work, is subject to exclusive contracting. The framework governing the conduct of criminal work is to be found in the contract, and in regulations made under the Access to Justice Act.

The contract

15.8 The contract consists of three parts:

- The standard terms govern the management of the firm and its relationship with the LSC, and is dealt with in chapter 16.
- The schedule sets out the monthly payment the LSC will make and the types of work the organisation can carry out.
- The Specification sets out the rules on conduct of and payment for individual cases, and is dealt with in chapters 9 and 11.

! Change from previous rules !

Other documents which are referred to in the contract, and which you should follow or take account of (though not technically part of the contract) include:

- Equality and Diversity Guidance and Policy;
- Category Definitions 2010;
- Guidance on Category Definitions 2010;
- SMP Reconciliation Protocol;
- Independent Peer Review Process;
- Regional Duty Solicitor Committee Arrangements;
- Data Security Requirements.

All of these documents are available on the LSC website: www.legalservices.gov.uk.

The regulations

15.9 The regulations govern whether a client is eligible for legal aid, whether he or she will be required to contribute to the cost of legal aid, and also deal with work not governed by the contract.

The regulations for criminal work are:

- Criminal Defence Service (General) (No 2) Regulations 2001, which govern:
  - the scope of what is criminal proceedings;
  - financial eligibility for Advice and Assistance;
  - applications for representation and selection of representative(s), both litigators and advocates;
  - rules regarding professional conduct, such as 'topping up', provision of information and notification of high cost cases.
- Criminal Defence Service (Financial Eligibility) Regulations 2006, which govern whether clients are eligible for legal aid in the magistrates' court;

- Criminal Defence Service (Representation Orders and Consequential Amendments) Regulations 2006 and the Criminal Defence Service (Representation Orders: Appeals etc) Regulations 2006, which govern the scope of representation orders and appeals against refusal of representation;
- Criminal Defence Service (Recovery of Defence Costs Orders) Regulations 2001, which govern whether a defendant in the Crown Court may have to refund their legal aid; and
- Criminal Defence Service (Funding) Order 2007, which sets out the payment rules and rates for litigators and advocates in the Crown Court.

CHAPTER 16

Legal aid contracts

Introduction

16.1   This chapter explains the contract documentation, standard terms and obligations imposed by the Standard Contract and the Civil and Crime Specifications. It also covers how to get additional work under an existing contract and how to get a new contract with the Legal Services Commission (LSC).

It also considers some of the other contracts offered by the LSC, such as those for Community Legal Advice Centres.

It is extremely important to become familiar with what your contract allows you to do and prohibits you from doing, since if you overlook something, you could find yourself served with a contract notice. The LSC has a 'two strikes and you're out' policy, so that if you get two contract notices on the same issue, you are very likely to lose your contract altogether.

The Standard Contract 2010/Unified Contract 2007

16.2   The contracts are divided into the following sections:

a   Contract for Signature, Key Information Tables and Annexes;
b   Office Schedule;
c   Standard Terms;
d   Specification, split into:
  •   general rules and category-specific rules (in the Civil Contract);
  •   general rules and specific rules on classes and units of work (in the Crime Contract).

All of the above documents form part of the contract, and you are bound by each and every part of them.

Following the Law Society's successful challenge of the Family tender process,[1] the LSC extended the Unified Contract 2007 for existing Family and Family with Housing contracts, to 30 November 2011.

Although the two contracts are different, for the purposes of this chapter, the structure is very similar. Where there are significant differences, they are noted below.

---

1   Law Society of England and Wales v Legal Services Commission [2010] EWHC 2550 (Admin).

Contract for signature

16.3   As the name suggests, this is the part of the contract that is signed by the organisation and counter-signed by the LSC.

The contract covers the whole organisation (although it specifies the work that can be done at each office through an Office Schedule). This means that a breach at any office would jeopardise the whole contract, whereas in the past it has been possible to withdraw a single office or category of law if it failed to meet the LSC's requirements. The contract for signature also includes any conditions that the LSC has imposed, the office schedules which have been issued, the applicable Quality Standard you must hold (the SQM (Specialist Quality Mark) or Lexcel), any Consortium arrangements which have been authorised, and contact details which the LSC will use to deal with you.

The Crime Contract sets out the types of criminal defence work the organisation is allowed to do, for example, police station and magistrates' court work, Crown Court work, prison law, etc. It also lists your Police Station Duty Schemes.

Office Schedule

16.4   In civil and family, the Office Schedule sets out the details of the work you are allowed to do, including the number of matter starts in each category of work and the monthly controlled work payment.

The schedule will set out the number of new matter starts allowed, by category. It will also show whether you have any 'tolerance' matter starts. These can be used in categories in which you do not hold a contract, except for clinical negligence, family, immigration, actions against the police etc, education, public law, mental health. These are known as 'exclusive categories'.[2]

You will note that, if you have a contract in civil law, you will be authorised to do licensed work in categories other than those in which you hold a contract, with the exception of the 'exclusive' categories. In relation to personal injury, you can only do licensed work, if you have a contract to do so, although you may do controlled work as 'tolerance' work.[3]

Civil Schedules contain the following tables:

• Table 1 gives the start and end dates.

---

2 Standard Contract Specification, para 43.
3 Standard Contract Specification, para 43.

- Table 2 gives the numbers of matter starts you are allowed by category, whether you are allowed to do tolerance work and in which categories you may do licensed work.
- Table 3 sets out the maximum amount of money the LSC will pay you while the schedule is in force and the amount of your monthly payment.
- Table 4 sets out exactly what type of service and where you must provide services, by procurement area and access point, whether the office must be a permanent or part-time presence, the minimum and maximum matter starts you must do, whether you must employ a litigator, whether you are in a consortium, how much of the time a supervisor must be available and whether any outreach work has been authorised.
- Table 5 notes the panel memberships personnel in your organisation must hold for family law.

In the Crime Specification, numbers of cases are not specified and depend on the interests of justice test being met, as defined in the contract (see chapter 9 for more information about conducting criminal cases).

If you do work outside that authorised under your schedule, you will not be paid for it.

Standard Terms 2010

16.5   The Standard Terms apply to civil, family mediation and crime. For Family and Family and Housing contracts, see the Unified Contract Standard Terms www.legalservices.gov.uk > community legal service > civil contracts > The Unified Contract (civil). Key clauses are summarised below:

- Clause 2: You must monitor the email address which you have given to the LSC 'frequently each business day' and communicate with the LSC electronically where stipulated.

- Clause 3: You cannot subcontract, novate or otherwise delegate any of your obligations under the contract without the LSC's prior written consent. However, you can appoint agents to work for you as long as their work is properly supervised.

   If an approved third party, agent, counsel or a subcontractor ceases providing services to you, you are responsible for ensuring that you continue to fulfil the obligations under the contract.

   You must also promptly notify the LSC of any termination or

expiry of any arrangements between you and any of your subcontractors etc. This clause will particularly affect firms which are involved in consortia arrangements to deliver Debt, Housing and Welfare Benefits Contracts.

Note that under clause 3.7, if the fees payable by you exceed £250 per matter or case, you must require agents, counsel or subcontractors in connection with contract work, to keep accurate records of the time they spend on the work you have appointed them to do and of the work done. They must also permit the LSC to audit the records.

- Clause 4: Accounts must be audited or certified within nine months of the year-end. You must notify the LSC within 14 days if your accounts are qualified.

- Clause 5: You must comply with the equality and diversity requirements, and you must have an Equality and Diversity Training Plan.

- Clause 6: Restrictions on marketing your services. You should note particularly that the prohibition on referral fees has been tightened up. It is now absolutely clear that you can neither pay nor receive referral fees nor any other benefit, to any third party (including any Consortium Members or other LSC contractees) for the referral or introduction (directly or indirectly) of any client or potential client.

- Clause 7: You must monitor your performance and compliance with the contract and take corrective action if there are problems. This clause also lists much of the other regulation and legislation you must comply with. It also requires you to have a Business Continuity Plan.

- Clause 8: Requires you to record all information required by the contract promptly and states that material or repeated failure to do so will be deemed to be a fundamental breach.

- Clause 9: Concerns access to your premises and information you must provide. Note that you must inform the LSC of the outcome of third party audits and provide them with a copy of the report within seven days of receipt.

- Clause 10: Sets out standards of work you must meet, including Peer Review. You must achieve at least Threshold Competence (3) at Peer Review in order to hold a contract.

Only personnel approved by the LSC may perform contract

work or be a supervisor. You submit a Supervisor Self-Declaration form[4] and/or an OSS2 (admitted fee earners) or OSS3 Status Enquiry form for each person, except support staff.

- Clause 11: Requires you to meet key performance indicators (KPIs). Failure to meet these is a breach of contract and could result in a contract sanction (see chapter 17 for more information about KPIs).

- Clause 12: Relates to contract documents and precedence.

- Clause 13: The LSC may amend the contract to take account of legislation or the justice system. Minor or technical amendments may be made to individual organisations' contracts. If the LSC wants to make material changes, it has to terminate the contract and issue a new one. You can apply for supplementary matter starts under this clause; but whether you get them will depend on the LSC's budget and whether this would increase your market share in the procurement area to more than 50 per cent. The LSC may need to run a bid round in these circumstances.[5]

- Clause 14: This clause creates a single account for all work done by the organisation which is treated globally. Claims made by you are treated as credits to your account, and any payments made by the LSC as debits.

- Clause 15: Sets out confidentiality arrangements.

- Clause 16: Data protection requirements.

- Clause 17: Freedom of Information Act obligations. The LSC may release information about your organisation either following consultation with you, or not in certain circumstances.

- Clause 18: Warranties that the information provided by you and the LSC is true and accurate.

- Clause 19: Indemnity and giving notices.

- Clause 20: Giving notices under the contract.

- Clause 21: You must notify the LSC as soon as reasonably practicable of any anticipated material constitutional change (within 14 days as a minimum) and any other change that might impact on your ability to do contract work.

---

4 These can be downloaded from the LSC's website at: www.legalservices.gov.uk > Community Legal Service (CLS) > Quality and performance > Quality Mark > Specialist Help. Go to the link on the right-hand side to 'Quality Mark Forms'.

5 See the Standard Contract 2010 Specification, paras 1.32–1.34 for more information.

- Clause 22: Novations.

- Clause 24: Contract sanctions may include; refusal to pay for specified contract work, suspension of payments, or taking on any new matters or cases, exclusion of individuals from being supervisors or performing contract work, suspending or removing your rota allocation (if any) of from holding yourself out as a provider and termination. If you breach the contract, the LSC may serve a Contract Notice under clause 24.2, requiring you not to repeat the breach. If you do so, you risk contract termination.

- Clause 25: You may terminate the contract at any time on three months' notice (subject to clause 13). The LSC can terminate the contract at any time on six months' notice.

- Clause 26: Unless the LSC terminates the contract due to your breach, they will authorise you to finish work on existing cases.

- Clause 27: Reconsidering decisions and reviews of decisions. There is an informal procedure and a formal procedure. Formal reviews may be carried out by the LSC's Legal Director or the Contract Review Body.

Payment Annex

16.6 There is one Payment Annex for crime and one for civil/family. They set out the fixed fees and hourly rates that apply to all work.

Applying for Civil or Family Contracts

16.7 In civil and family, the LSC is moving towards an allocation of funds to geographical areas using a formula devised by its Research Unit, which attempts to estimate the number of potential legal aid clients who might experience legal problems. This is called 'indicative spend'.

The LSC uses the formula as a starting point when considering where to direct available funding.

You should note that although bidding opportunities are expressed in terms of the numbers of matter starts available, where you provide services under a schedule, it will also authorise you to undertake an unlimited number of certificated cases (licensed work).

If you are an existing supplier wanting to add a category, open a new office, or add a substantial number of new matter starts to your existing allocation,[6] or whether you are an organisation wishing to contract with the LSC for the first time, you should contact the LSC regional office that covers your area and make enquiries of the regional contracts and relationships manager. He or she may be able to tell you whether the LSC plans to issue any tenders in your area prior to the next expected date for re-tendering all contracts in 2013. The LSC may use price competition in the next major tendering round. In the meantime, tender opportunities will be advertised on the LSC's tenders page: www.legalservices.gov.uk > Community Legal Service (CLS) > Tenders.

We know that the LSC refines its tender process with every round of tenders it conducts, so it unlikely that the process will be the same in future; but it is worth considering the requirements of the 2010 tenders, as they give an indication of the LSC's preferences.

Tenders

16.8   In the summer of 2010, the LSC issued tenders for all civil and family work. All tenders had to be submitted online through the LSC's tendering portal, https://legalservices.bravosolution.co.uk. This was hosted by a commercial company, Bravo Solution.

In civil and family, the tenders reflected the LSC's policy to commission legal services in larger 'bundles' where possible. So, they specified that in the social welfare law (SWL) categories of debt, housing and welfare benefits must be bid for as a combination (either by a single organisation or as a consortium). In family law, where the LSC considered it would see significant competition, it specified that bidders must offer both public and private family law. Bidders had to complete a pre-qualification questionnaire (PQQ) covering basic information about the organisation and its history of compliance with legal and regulatory requirements.

Criteria for assessing bids

16.9   Tenders for general family services and SWL services had essential criteria and selection criteria.

Essential criteria included; ability and willingness to deliver services (covering the full range of legal help to full representation) in

6 Relatively small numbers of additional matter starts may be authorised by your Relationship Manager.

specified locations. Bidders needed to have someone who met the LSC's supervisor standard in the SQM and meet the supervisor to caseworker ratio (1:6). They needed to have an office within the procurement area.

Organisations with a confirmed peer review result of four or five, or issued with notice to terminate the contract within the last two years were not eligible to bid.

Where the LSC had bids for more work than was available, organisations that met the essential criteria were then assessed against the selection criteria. This meant that it was a competitive bid round, although not in terms of price. The LSC says it preferred applicants that gave them a higher level of confidence in their ability to deliver services from 14 October 2010, based on criteria including: experience of operating services in the geographical area tendered for; particular types of case experience (for example, having taken cases to the Upper Tier Tribunal for Welfare Benefits Contracts); having a lower percentage of caseworkers to recruit to deliver the services tendered for; supervisors being present in the office for a greater percentage of the working week; and personnel who had achieved accreditation to specialist panels (for example, level 3 under the Immigration and Asylum Accreditation Scheme, for Immigration Contracts and accreditation to the Children panel or as a domestic abuse specialist for Family Contracts).

These proved controversial at best and unlawful at worst. There were successful legal challenges, notably the Law Society's, which quashed the Family tender result.

Applying for Crime Contracts

16.10   The LSC tendered all criminal defence work in the summer of 2010. All tenders had to be submitted online through the LSC's tendering portal, https://legalservices.bravosolution.co.uk. New contracts started on 14 July 2010. They were issued as three-year contracts; but there have since been suggestions that the LSC may use its termination powers to implement a new contract on significantly different terms, before 2013.

The crime tender was not competitive. Firms that would satisfy the LSC in relation to the PQQ and Essential Criteria (see above) were awarded contracts.

The LSC intends to implement Best Value Tendering, including price competition at some future date. Tender opportunities will be advertised on the LSC's tenders page: www.legalservices.gov.uk > Criminal defence > Tenders.

The Public Defender Service

16.11   As well as contracting with private practice to deliver criminal defence work, the LSC also employs a small number of salaried lawyers in the Public Defender Service (PDS). This service was set up to benchmark the cost and quality of services provided by private practice and was never intended to be a nationwide scheme.

At the time off writing, there are four PDS offices:

- Cheltenham;
- Darlington;
- Pontypridd; and
- Swansea.

Very high cost case panel

16.12   The LSC's Complex Crime Unit (CCU) manages membership of the very high cost case (VHCC) panel. Only firms that are members of this panel can represent clients in VHCC cases – any case where the trial is expected to last for more than 60 days.

From 14 July 2010, organisations and self-employed advocates wishing to work on cases classified as VHCCs have to obtain the VHCC accreditation. This must be applied for online through the LSC's tendering portal, https://legalservices.bravosolution.co.uk.

At the time of writing there was no closing date for submitting an application.

Community Legal Advice services

16.13   In some areas, the LSC contracts with a single provider to deliver a face-to-face legal advice and representation service concentrating on welfare benefits, debt, employment, housing, education and community care (sometimes referred to as social welfare law (SWL) categories), sometimes with family law services. In urban areas, these are called Community Legal Advice Centres (CLACs), and in rural areas Community Legal Advice Networks (CLANs).

The roll-out of Community Legal Advice services has been slower than the LSC first hoped. However, it is important to be aware of any developments in your area if you deliver SWL services, since where there is a Community Legal Advice service, the LSC will not issue Social Welfare Contracts to other providers. CLACs and CLANs are joint commissioning exercises with local authorities, so not-for-profit sector providers are often aware of early discussions before private practice, since local authorities are usually their key funders. In this respect, as in relation to referrals and sign-posting, it is important for private practice legal aid firms to have good channels of communication with the not-for-profit sector.

Once the decision has been made to go ahead, opportunities are advertised on the LSC's website on the 'tenders' page (see above). Contracts are awarded following an open tendering process listing essential and desirable criteria. The LSC signs a single contract with one organisation, although this can be a joint bid, for example combining not-for-profit and private practice providers through subcontracting arrangements. However, they must have a single legal entity to contract with the LSC.

Other kinds of contract with the LSC

16.14   The LSC has contracts with organisations for other kinds of service, for example:

- immigration advice and representation for people in detention;
- telephone advice, representation and casework for members of the public as part of the Community Legal Advice telephone service in civil and family categories;
- telephone advice to people in police stations (Criminal Defence Service Direct); and
- specialist support to other LSC contractors and organisations holding the Quality Mark at General Help level in various civil categories.

Opportunities are publicised on the LSC's tenders pages: www.legal services.gov.uk > Community Legal Service > Tenders; or www. legalservices.gov.uk > Criminal Defence Service > Tenders, as appropriate.

CHAPTER 17

Quality standards and performance monitoring

continued

Introduction

17.1 This chapter deals with quality standards and performance monitoring under contracts with the Legal Services Commission (LSC), from a management perspective. We will concentrate of the Standard Contract and its Civil and Crime Specifications, as this is the most common type of contract. However, significantly, Family contracts (and Family with Housing) continue under the Unified Contract 2007, following the Law Society's successful challenge to the tender process in 2010. There are also others, for example to provide telephone advice and casework as part of the Community Legal Advice telephone service, specialist support, or Community Legal Advice Centres and Networks. These have similar provisions to mainstream contracts, but have all been modified to suit each particular service.

Whatever kind of contract you have with the LSC, there is no substitute for reading it! The worst-case scenario is that you overlook something fundamental, for example your supervisor may not meet the supervisor standards, the LSC discovers this and your contract is terminated, because there is nothing you can do to remedy the historic breach.

Practice management and quality of advice standards

17.2 The LSC has created a series of quality standards for practice management, known as the Quality Mark (QM). There are several varieties of the standard: Specialist Quality Mark (SQM) (for professional legal advisers), Quality Mark for the Bar (for barristers), and other quality marks for telephone services and family mediation.

The LSC worked with the Institute of Advanced Legal Studies to create a peer review scheme that assesses the quality of legal advice. It is presently working with the Bar Council, the Law Society and other interested parties to develop a quality standard for advocates.

At the time of writing, the current version of the SQM is the second edition dated September 2009. It applied from the start of new contracts in 2010.

Specialist Quality Mark

17.3 Organisations wanting a contract with the LSC must submit an application for SQM accreditation unless they already hold the

Lexcel standard. Forms can be downloaded from the LSC website www.legalservices.gov.uk > Community Legal Service (CLS) > Quality and performance > Quality Mark > Specialist Help.

The LSC will outsource auditing of the SQM to external auditors in the autumn of 2010. The LSC will continue to audit contracts awarded in 2010, but all providers must possess an up to date quality management standard that they have paid for in time to be awarded contracts in April 2013.

The LSC has appointed the SQM Delivery Partnership to deliver auditing services for the SQM. It is a consortium of three established bodies: Quality South East Ltd, Capital Quality Limited and the Centre for Assessment and Recognition. The consortium covers England and Wales and has significant audit experience as it conducts assessment processes for both Lexcel and Investors in People amongst other quality standards.

The LSC has provided information regarding the costs of the audits and says that further information about changes to the SQM auditing process will be available on its website shortly.

Forms to be submitted

17.4   The forms to be submitted are:
- application form QM1;
- Office Manual/Documented Procedures;
- Supervisor Self-Declaration form(s);
- Status Enquiry Forms; OSS1, OSS2, OSS3, SIF1.

There is also a useful Self-Assessment Audit Checklist. By completing it with specific page or paragraph numbers you will be able to identify how closely you meet the SQM's requirements. Note, though, that not all questions on the checklist have a corresponding written procedure, simply requiring a 'yes' answer.

Desktop audit

17.5   This is the first stage of assessment. The documentation submitted will be reviewed against the requirements of the Quality Mark. If the documentation is incomplete or so deficient that it is clear the organisation cannot meet the standard, the application will be refused. The documentation will be returned within 28 days with comments so that the organisation knows the issues it needs to address.

If the organisation passes the desktop audit, and its application for a contract is also successful (see chapter 13 for more information), it will be awarded a provisional quality mark and a contract.

Pre-Quality Mark audit

17.6 Before the QM is confirmed, an on-site audit will be carried out, usually four to six months after the desk top audit, to make sure that the QM requirements are in effective operation.

Opening meeting

17.7 The audit will start with an opening meeting at which the auditor will explain its scope and purpose. It is useful to have a copy of the Self-Assessment Audit Checklist (SAAC) to hand as the auditor is likely to check his or her understanding of procedures and check any queries.

Discussions with the auditor

17.8 If it appears that an auditor is requiring procedures to operate in a certain way, which does not coincide with the organisation's interpretation of QM requirements, (and particularly if it appears that implementing such a system could cause difficulty), it is advisable to ask him or her to refer you to the requirement in the standard. It may be that the organisation has not understood the requirement. On the other hand, as auditors are human too, they can make mistakes. Many QM requirements are so detailed that there is a limited number of ways in which they can be met. Auditors can become so used to seeing something being implemented in a certain way that they fail to recognise that an unusual system may still comply. If you both consider the system against the actual wording of the requirement, and any mandatory definition, you are most likely to reach a consensus.

Audit procedure and outcomes

17.9 In practice LSC audits are likely to focus on supervision, individual competence, file management and file review.
The result will be one of:

- pass;
- pass with acceptable corrective action – usually relating to general quality concerns in non-critical management areas. This is the most common result; or
- fail (recommendation not to award or to terminate the QM). This usually relates to critical quality concerns which cannot be addressed.

There is a representation process which can be invoked if the organisation considers that the audit was not correctly carried out, a critical quality concern should have been disregarded, or any other reasonable grounds. However, since key requirements of the SQM are now incorporated into the contract, breaching them results in a breach of contract, and the LSC may decide to use the contract sanctions process instead of the SQM process.

Quality Mark requirements

17.10   First, the standard itself is set out. It is split into 'Requirements', which are mandatory, and 'Definitions'. The definitions are only mandatory where the word 'must' is used.

Each standard is followed by a guidance section, which is not mandatory. It is important to bear the distinction in mind, as the LSC's staff are so familiar with the Guidance that they can occasionally quote it as though it is the only acceptable way of demonstrating compliance.

See 17.31 below for a compliance aide-memoire, to assist you in maintaining compliance with SQM and contract requirements.

SQM
A: Access to service
Business plan – in detail for one year and outline for two further years. Non-discrimination in the provision of services. Six-monthly review of plan. Providing information to LSC about service provision.
B: Seamless service
Signposting – as a minimum providing CLS/CDS call centre details. Referral – records kept when a client is referred elsewhere on an existing matter.
C: Running the organisation
Staff structure. Key roles and decision-making structure. Financial control. Demonstrate independence – *NB not all SQM holders will be bound by professional rules.*

D: People management

Job descriptions, responsibilities and objectives.
Equal opportunities and non discrimination.
Open recruitment process.
Induction procedure.
Annual performance review and feedback.
Training plans, training and records.
Named Supervisors – *meeting very detailed technical requirements (see note below for more information).*
Supervisory skills and conditions for supervision.
Limits of individual competence.
Legal qualifications or 12 hours' casework per week.

E: Running the service

File management – *file lists, conflict of interest, locating files and tracing documents, key dates, solicitor undertakings, monitoring files for inactivity, identifying all matters for one client, logical and orderly files.*
File reviews for all conducting cases – *including legal and procedural issues – by Supervisor with corrective action taken where required (see note below for more information).*
File review records monitored annually.

F: Meeting clients' needs

Procedures for recording and confirming information and advice at the outset, during and at the end of the case.

Code of Conduct Rule 2 requirements; case plans in complex cases; costs and cost/benefit advice; considering legal aid entitlement.
Confidentiality and privacy.
Use of approved suppliers *(eg counsel, experts, interpreters) – selected on the basis of objective assessment, evaluation, consultation with the client, instructions in prescribed form.*

G: Commitment to quality

Complaints procedure.
Quality management – *responsibility for, review of all quality procedures annually, Quality Manual.*
Client satisfaction feedback – *LSC has a suggested form available in many languages.*
Risk management (optional requirement) – *Risk Manager, identifying operational risks, risk management procedures, annual risk review.*
Quality Manual.

Supervisors – technical legal competence

17.11   Supervisors must demonstrate that they have experience in their category of 1,050 hours over the preceding three years if full-time, or five years if part-time (supervisors who have been on maternity leave or long-term sick in the last three years can demonstrate the five-year requirement even if they work full-time).

In some categories, supervisors must be members of a specialist panel, eg family, mental health; in immigration, supervisors must be accredited to that level under the IAAS, as well as providing evidence of 350 hours' case involvement over the preceding 12 months. Evidence of that experience can be direct casework (which may be easier as that will be time-recorded in any event), or it can include up to 115 hours' supervision, file review, training and research for publication.

The Supervisor Self-Declaration Forms have caused some confusion. Practitioners should remember that boxes (iii)(b), (c), (d) and (e) are optional, not mandatory, as long as the individual can show 350 hours direct personal casework in box (iii)(a).

In categories where there is no panel, supervisors must demonstrate that they have closely defined experience of case types. As for panel members, this must be maintained by at least 350 hours' experience in that category annually.

If you cannot recruit someone who meets the supervisor requirements, you can apply to your account or relationship manager for authority to appoint an external supervisor; but this is entirely at their discretion.[1]

Supervisors – file reviews

17.12   File reviews must cover legal and procedural points. This can cause problems when considering who should review the supervisor's files. If there is another experienced practitioner in the same area of law, they can review each other's files. Where there is not, perhaps because there is no one else who practises in that specialism, the supervisor will have to review his or her own files (as objectively as possible!) for legal issues and someone else will review it for procedural points. The LSC does not expect an organisation to incur the expense of an external supervisor in these circumstances.

1   Standard Contract Specification 2010, para 2.34.

Key issues from recent audits

- Do the management/organisation structure and individual job descriptions agree? *It's amazing how disorganised you can look to an outsider if they don't!*
- If the supervisor has to demonstrate compliance through the portfolio route (as opposed to panel membership), can they do so over the last 12 months? *Consider the numbers of hours required and the range of cases.*
- Were independent file reviews undertaken by an appropriate person? *If you are developing a member of staff as a deputy supervisor and delegating some file reviews to them, make sure this is all properly documented.*
- Are the independent file review records completely up to date – *if there are gaps, eg someone was on maternity leave or on the holiday of a lifetime, are the reasons for them clear?*
- Is corrective action required recorded on the file review forms, with appropriate dates?
- Do they also show what action was taken and by when?
- Did file reviews identify any non compliances with SQM or contract requirements? If the supervisor is lenient, the LSC cannot be confident that the organisation meets its requirements.

Peer review

17.13   Peer review is the measure that the LSC use to assess quality of advice. It has been developed over several years under the auspices of the Institute of Advanced Legal Studies (IALS). Peer reviewers have carried out thousands of assessments since 2000 and refined the process over the years. The LSC published a definitive version of the process in November 2005. It can be downloaded from the LSC's website at: www.legalservices.gov.uk > Community Legal Service (CLS) > Quality and performance > Peer Review.

There are five possible scores: excellence (1), competence plus (2), threshold competence (3), below competence (4) and failure in performance (5). The LSC has defined the level of skill required under the Unified Contract as at least threshold competence. At below competence level, the provider will be given six months to improve, if they do not achieve at least threshold competence at their next assessment, their contract will be terminated. An organisation assessed at failure in performance will have its contract terminated quickly, because of the risk to clients.

The LSC has disseminated good practice guides via its website: www.legalservices.gov.uk > Community Legal Service (CLS) > Quality and performance > Peer Review > Improving your quality.

The peer review process

17.14   All peer reviewers are experienced practitioners, trained by the IALS to carry out peer review using their framework. A sample of their own files has to be assessed at competence plus or above. Peer reviewers are consistency-checked against each other and receive regular training.

There are various reasons why a review might be carried out, eg routine bench-marking, concern about quality, application for the Very High Costs Cases (VHCC) Panel for criminal work; but the reviewer is not told what it is. This ensures that they can approach all peer reviews with an open mind.

Twenty files are requested, of which at least 15 are assessed. They are selected to cover all the different types of work carried out by the organisation within a category of law and are cases closed during the preceding 12 months. Peer reviewers carry out the assessment at an LSC regional office. They do not meet the staff of the organisation being reviewed, which never finds out the identity of its particular reviewer, although they are sent a list of all the reviewers and asked to identify any possible conflict of interest. It usually takes one to two days to do an assessment and write a report.

The reviewers evaluate issues that relate to quality of advice and service. They do not look at how long was spent on the file and they do not carry out a transaction criteria[2] audit. They apply the 'pick up test', which is the basic question – if I, as another fee-earner, picked up this file, could I understand what had been done and why, and what remained to be done?

They assess individual files and then consider the sample as a whole and form a conclusion about its overall quality. In many cases this involves a balancing act as some files may be good, others less so. Organisations scoring competence plus tend to have a higher level of consistency. For example, if there is a change of caseworker part way through the case the peer reviewer would look at the whole case, and

---

2 Transaction criteria will be remembered by many legal aid practitioners from the early days of 'franchising'. They enabled the LSC to assess the extent to which a lawyer had obtained appropriate information and followed steps associated with best practice. They did not allow any assessment to be made of the quality of legal advice. They have been superseded by peer review.

in order to score competence plus or excellence, both caseworkers would need to achieve that level.

They also apply the 'friend and family test', which is simply 'would I refer a friend or family member to this organisation?' If the answer is 'no', the sample will be assessed below threshold competence or worse.

Peer reviewers use checklists of criteria, which they score individually; but the overall score is not simply an average of the scores on individual files. Peer reviewers take account of any trends and patterns identified, including evidence of supervision. Having assessed the 15 files, the reviewer compiles a report identifying; positive findings, major areas of concern (if any), areas for development, suggested areas for improvement and any other comments.

Reports are checked by IALS to ensure that the score reflects the comments the reviewer has made about the files. So, for example they would pick up a contradiction if the sample scored competence plus but the reviewer had identified major areas of concern, and ask the reviewer to look at the report again. IALS does not double-check the assessment. The provider should receive the final report within 28 days.

Tips for passing peer review

17.15   The peer reviewers emphasise that good practice helps to improve peer review scores, for example:

- file review and supervision support;
- ensuring workload is appropriate;
- training;
- providing appropriate advice on legal and procedural issues on every file;
- confirming the client's initial instructions and your advice in writing.

Standard letters and documentation

17.16   Peer reviewers accept that standard letters have their place; but that it is important to take an individual approach to them. This means ensuring that standard letters should not be 'catch-alls' which try to cover all eventualities; but should be specific to a client's circumstances. So, for example, a letter setting out the different possession proceedings in relation to both owner-occupiers and tenants would not impress a peer reviewer, who would expect the client to be given only the information that applied to his or her case.

As in all kinds of file-based assessment, it is vital that the file is complete. Some organisations send leaflets to clients; but do not put a copy of standard information on the file, in order to save paper and printing costs. Peer reviewers advise that if that is the way you work, it is important to include copies of all standard information leaflets with the file sample.

Peer review representations

17.17   Representations can only be made if the assessment is category 4 or 5. The LSC's rationale is that since a category 3 is acceptable for a contract, there is no point in allowing representations when only the organisation's professional pride is at stake.

Possible grounds are that: you dispute the overall peer review rating, the sample does not appear to be sufficiently representative, any other reasonable grounds.

Representations must be made on the appropriate form and reach the LSC within 28 days following receipt of the report and the file sample. The representations will be considered by the original peer reviewer and a senior panel member. They may uphold the original rating, revise the original rating, request a new review, or not reach agreement. Where the latter occurs an external expert who is not a peer reviewer will be asked to help the peer reviewers reach a consensus. At the time of writing, 17 per cent of representations resulted in an improved assessment score.

LSC monitoring

17.18   The LSC is increasingly monitoring firms remotely, using the data firms supply, for example when applying for legal aid or submitting claims for costs. The LSC intends that its providers will also be able to access their own data through a secure web portal known as 'LSC Online'. You can find guides to LSC Online on the LSC website: www.legalservices.gov.uk > LSC Online > Using LSC Online > Complete user guides.

There were serious problems in launching this new software, although the LSC has been gradually addressing these. At the time of writing it was not possible for organisations to access their own Management Information (MI) data. Therefore, it is a good idea to ask your relationship manager to send you this data on a quarterly basis.

Key performance indicators

17.19 Both the civil and crime versions of the Standard and Unified Contracts have mandatory key performance indicators (KPIs).

Family and housing with family were still operating under the Unified Contract, which also has many of the same KPIs as the Standard Contract; but these are indicative rather than mandatory.

Relationship managers monitor KPI reports, which are flagged as 'red', 'amber' or 'green', depending on how many 'out of profile' indicators there are. Your relationship manager may contact you to ask you to explain the reasons that your organisation is 'out of profile'. If it is an issue which the relationship manager thinks should be corrected, then you will be asked to formulate an action plan for doing so. Being 'out of profile' may also trigger an on-site or other type of audit.

You need to monitor performance against the KPIs to avoid the risk of contract sanctions under clause 24. If the LSC considers that you have breached a term of the contract it may issue a contract notice. If breaches are 'persistent' defined as three breaches of the same term in 24 consecutive months; or six breaches in 24 consecutive months, the LSC may apply a contract sanction, which could include suspension of part or the contract, or even contract termination.

Key performance standards – civil

17.20 See chapter 3 for the list of KPIs that need to be monitored at an organisational level. Someone needs to collect the data, review it on a monthly basis and feedback to supervisors and their teams where performance needs to be improved.

Service standards – civil

17.21 These are to be found in section 2 of the Standard Contract Specification.

You may use agents, counsel and third parties where it is in your client's best interests. The Specification allows independent consultants to carry out work under the contract as long as the supervision conditions are met. However, it is important to note that you cannot use an agent to meet the service standards set out below. So, for example, you could not use an agent to meet the supervisor standards.

If you hold a contract for debt, housing and welfare benefits in a consortium, one of its members must meet the relevant standards.

Services: You must provide the services as specified, for example combinations of categories and levels of service, and minimum matter starts.

Supervisors: You must have at least one person who meets the LSC's standard for supervisors and they must carry out their duties in accordance with the contract – which contains the familiar SQM standards for supervision and file review. You must employ one person who meets the supervisor standards for every six full-time caseworkers.

Presence in the procurement area: You must comply with the presence requirements set out in your schedule.

If you are in Wales, you must comply with the Welsh Language Act 1993.

Additional service and monitoring requirements

17.22   There are additional service standards for immigration and mental health. Organisations with contracts to deliver housing possession court duty schemes will also need additional monitoring systems, which are also shown below.

Immigration

17.23   The Specification (paras 8.11–8.18) sets down requirements for case-workers and supervisors to be accredited under the Immigration and Asylum Accreditation Scheme. It also limits the type of work that can be done by reference to the level of accreditation. For example, only a level 2 caseworkers can conduct Controlled Legal Representation (CLR) cases or use devolved powers to grant CLR.

In this category you must use 90 per cent of your asylum matter starts and 70 per cent of the immigration non-asylum matter starts.

You will also need to check you contract schedule to see what percentage of clients must be physically located in the designated immigration procurement area.

Mental health

17.24   In this category, there are particular presence requirements, which are set out in paragraphs 9.4–9.5 of the Specification. The require-ments you have to meet will be recorded in your contract schedule.

If you have a contract to work in a high security hospital, you must also employ an Authorised Litigator; have a caseworker with experience of Restricted Cases; and all advocates before the MHT must be members of the Law Society Mental Health Panel Review Tribunal Accreditation Scheme.

In this category, 70 per cent of clients must be physically located in the procurement area in which you have been granted matter starts. Also, 30 per cent of your matter starts may be used for clients who are not physically located in the procurement area in which you have been granted matter starts.

However, you may not use your matter starts allocated for clients outside high security hospitals for clients who are detained in high security hospitals except in some circumstances (see the Specification, para 9.8).

If you do not employ an authorised litigator to do mental health work outside high security hospitals, you must have suitable referral arrangements.

Housing possession court duty schemes

17.25   If you provide a client with advice at court and, within six months of doing so, subsequently open a new housing matter start in relation to the same case then you cannot claim any payment for providing the service at court. The costs of providing the service will be included in the housing matter start fixed fee (see the Specification, para 10.39).

You will need a monitoring system to monitor these cases and make adjustments where necessary.

Key performance indicators – crime

17.26   Under the Crime Specification, para 2.50, failure to achieve a key performance indicator may result in the application of a sanction under clause 11 of the Standard Contract 2010. A repeated breach may result in contract termination.

Crime KPIs

| 1 | Assessment reduction on claims for magistrates' courts non-standard fees and police station Advice and Assistance exceptional cases. | Maximum of 15% reduction on assessment on all your claims for these fees in any three-month period during the contract term. |

2	Acceptance of calls from Defence Solicitor Call Centre (DSCC) for police station telephone advice and police station attendance when you are allocated supplier on rota duty solicitor scheme.	Minimum of 90% of calls made to you by the DSCC during each of the quarter periods accepted and dealt with appropriately.

Service standards – crime

17.27   Section 2 of the Crime Specification contains the service standards for criminal defence work.

Supervisors: You must have at least one person who meets the LSC's standard for supervisors and they must carry out their duties in accordance with the contract – which contains the familiar Specialist Quality Mark standards for supervision and file review.

In the crime category there is no specified ratio of supervisors to designated fee earners or caseworkers, with the exception of Prison law, where you must have at least one full-time equivalent Supervisor for every six full-time equivalent caseworkers.

You must designate the staff who work under the Crime Contract and the work they can do. Designating staff means naming the people who do work under the Criminal Contract, ensuring they meet the standards required by the contract, Specialist Quality Mark and Duty Solicitor Arrangements and keeping records as shown below.

Fee earners should be 'designated', unless they do less than three hours' contract work a month. Those who regularly undertake fee earning criminal work under the contract: crime supervisors, FILEX supervisors, duty solicitors, accredited and probationary representatives, must be designated.

Under the previous Unified Contract, where an individual undertook work for more than one practice, one could be identified as a 'lead' practice and would be responsible for keeping records and carrying out independent file review and other procedures. Practices that make regular use of freelance agents will need to implement much more rigorous supervision procedures than previously to ensure that all required procedures are carried out.

Clause 3.3(ii) of the Standard Contract allows you to employ agents and subcontractors as long as your 'supervision of them is, in all respects, equal to your supervision of your employed solicitors and legal advisers'.

Paragraph 2.14 of the Specification states: 'Each Supervisor must conduct file reviews for each Designated Fee Earner or Case-worker they supervise.'

The Contract Specification sets out percentages of Crime Contract work which must be performed by designated fee earners:

- advocacy in the magistrates' court, 50 per cent must be done by designated staff;
- police stations Advice and Assistance, 80 per cent must be done by designated staff.

Location: You may only perform contract work from the office(s) specified in your schedule. Offices must be physically accessible for clients from Monday to Friday, and you must have arrangements in place to ensure that during opening hours, clients are able to speak to someone by telephone to arrange appointments and to contact you about emergency matters. If you move your office out of your original postcode area, you must ask the LSC's permission. Even if the LSC consents they may make it a condition that your duty solicitors may not undertake work on additional duty schemes which are accessible only by virtue of your new office address.

Referral and signposting arrangements: You must have appropriate arrangements in operation to refer clients or potential clients to another provider if you do not provide the services that the client requires or for some other reason are unable to take on their case.

If you are in Wales, you must comply with the Welsh Language Act 1993.

CHAPTER 18

Financial and contract management

Introduction

18.1   This chapter deals with issues that affect an organisation's financial and contractual position: reconciliation; payments on account; key performance indicators (KPIs); contract compliance audits; and financial stewardship visits.

Reconciliation of contracts

18.2   When the Unified Contract was brought in, in 2007, it was highly controversial, particularly because of the provisions introducing payment by fixed and graduated fees. The Law Society judicially reviewed the introduction of the contract, and the case went to the Court of Appeal[1] before eventually being settled. The settlement was drawn up into a deed with lengthy provisions, one of which was a reconciliation protocol setting out the approach the Legal Services Commission (LSC) would take from then on in reconciling contracts. See www.legalservices.gov.uk > About Us > Transforming Legal Aid > A Clear Way Forward, or www.lawsociety.org.uk/documents/downloads/dynamic/finaldeedofsettlement020408.pdf for the full text of the agreement. The reconciliation protocol is one of the supporting documents to the 2010 Standard Civil Contract and will continue to be the approach taken by the LSC.

The reconciliation protocol has since been updated, most recently in September 2010, and the updated text can be found at www.legal services.gov.uk > Community Legal Service (or Criminal Defence Service > Civil Contracts (or Crime Contracts) > Agreement with the Law Society > Reconciliation. It can also be found in appendix I of this book.

Most legal aid work, with the exception of civil certificates and Criminal Crown Court cases, is subject to either the Civil or the Criminal Contract.

Each contract has a schedule, which sets out the LSC will pay you each month. At the end of each month, you submit bills for concluded cases on the CMRF (civil) or CDS6/7 (crime) to the LSC. Each bill submitted has a value, but the LSC do not pay you that amount direct.

---

1   See R (on the application of the Law Society) v Legal Services Commission and Dexter Montague and Partners v Legal Services Commission [2007] EWCA Civ 1264.

Instead, the amount claimed is offset against your monthly payments, with the intention that over the period of the contract claims will equal payments.

The monthly payments are set before the schedule starts, usually on the basis of historical average billing levels, and therefore are no more than a prediction of what the LSC expects that you will bill during the life of the contract. Inevitably, therefore, in many cases the prediction will turn out not to have been completely accurate.

You should keep your own figures for the value of your monthly submissions and monitor them against your payments. The LSC will do the same, and periodically will seek to adjust the payments to ensure that your contract remains on course. As a result of the adjustment, your payments may go up or down. The purpose is to ensure that at the end of the contract, claims equal payments, or at least that the difference between them is within an agreed band. This process is known as reconciliation, and where parity has been achieved the contract has been successfully reconciled. Where it hasn't, arrangements will need to be made to resolve the outstanding balance, either by payment of a lump sum or by carrying forward the balance to the next schedule.

The reconciliation protocol sets out the approach the LSC will take. The key is that the target is always reconciliation to 100 per cent (though the deed confirms that crime providers can choose instead to have a one-month 'pull-forward' – ie to reconcile to 92.5 per cent instead of 100 per cent) – that is, for claims to equal payments over the course of the schedule.

It is recognised that in practice it will often work out that 100 per cent is not exactly achieved. Therefore the LSC will look at the position twice a year – April and September – and determine whether the contract is within the acceptable margin of 90 to 110 per cent (calculated over the shorter of the life of the contract or the last 12 months). Where it is, no action will be taken. Where the contract is outside the acceptable margin, the monthly payment will be revised with a view to paying off any balance within six months.

It is important to remember that each month you claim less than your standard monthly payment (SMP) then the closer to the 90 per cent trigger point you will be. You need to try to avoid any cumulative decline in performance that takes you below 90 per cent. Once you go below the trigger point, the reduction happens automatically and the LSC would not warn you about this in advance. The new payment would remain in place for three months to monitor that it would achieve the desired effect. You would have to ensure that claims stayed at or around the level of the previous SMP, otherwise it could trigger a further reduction at the three-month review stage.

Case study

My firm has Criminal and Civil Contracts. The Civil Contract is currently paid at £10,000 per month. After 12 months, we have claimed £102,000. The Criminal Contract is paid at £5,000 per month and after 12 months we have claimed £64,000. Are we in band? Are the LSC likely to change our payments?

Civil: Total claims = £102,000 over the life of the contract. Payments are £120,000, so the balance on the account is £18,000 owed to the LSC. This is a margin of 82 per cent, so outside the acceptable band (ie below 90 per cent). The payment will be amended. The target is 100 per cent. Average monthly claim is £8,500 (102,000/12) and you owe the LSC £18,000, which must be repaid over the next six months. The new payment will be £8,500 – (£18,000/6) = £5,500 per month.

Crime: Total claims = £64,000, and payments are £60,000. 10 per cent of claims = £6,400, so the acceptable band is £60,000 ± £6,400 – between £53,600 and £66,400. Therefore you are within band and the LSC will not automatically amend your contract payment. However, you are entitled to ask the LSC to amend your payments at any time and may want to ask for an increase. The LSC do not have to agree, but if you can demonstrate that you are likely to continue to claim more than you are paid, they should do so.

Payments on account

18.3   You are entitled to be paid your costs on civil certificates at the end of the case following assessment by the LSC or court – see chapter 10 for details.

In recognition of the fact that such cases often last a considerable time and costs can be substantial, there is provision for you to claim payments on account during the life of the case.

The 2010 Standard Civil Contract entitles you to claim a payment on account of profit costs at any time, provided that a) you may not apply for the first until three months have elapsed since the certificate was issued, and b) you may not apply more than twice in any

12-month period. Also, cumulatively, you are not entitled to be paid more than 75 per cent of your profit costs to date (not including any enhancement).[2] You can make a payment on account for disbursements incurred, or about to be incurred, at any time.[3]

Case study

It is 1 May 2011. I have two certificate files. On the first, the certificate was issued on 1 February 2011 and I have spent £1,000. On the second, the certificate was issued on 1 April 2010. I have spent £5,000 in total, and I received a payment on account of £2,000 in January. Am I entitled to any payments on account? If so, how much?

The first certificate was issue exactly three months ago, so you are entitled to a payment on account. The second was issued more than three months ago and you have only made one application in the 12 months leading up to today, so you are entitled to a payment on account.

You should complete a CLSPOA1, one line for each certificate. You should report your total profit costs to date for each claim, and you will be paid £750 on the first case and £1,750 on the second (75 per cent of £5,000, less the £2,000 already paid).

Payments on account may be paid into your office account (Specification, para 6.28).

Payments on account are re-payable at the end of the case. When each case concludes and the bill is assessed, the LSC will pay the value of the bill and then recoup the payments on account, so that the net effect is that you are paid only the outstanding balance. Where you receive costs from the other side in part or in full, you should notify the LSC even where you are making no claim for legal aid costs so that payments on account can be recouped.

Payment on account limits

18.4   Paragraph 6.26 of the Specification entitles the LSC to impose a maximum payment on account limit. This would be set in each individual contract schedule, and could vary from category of law to category of law, and indeed from firm to firm.

---

2 Specification, para 6.24.
3 Specification, para 6.22.

The limit is calculated by comparing the value of debits (payments to you) as against credits (claims received) on your account with the LSC. The maximum amount by which debits are allowed to exceed credits is the maximum payment on account limit, and once the limit is reached the LSC would refuse to make any further payments on account and would require repayment of the excess.

However, although this clause is in the contract, no schedules currently specify a limit and the LSC undertook not to introduce one without further consultation[4] when the Unified Contract was introduced in 2007. The power in the 2010 contract is discretionary, and the LSC have, at the time of writing, given no indication of whether or in what circumstances they intend to introduce the limit.

Key performance indicators

! Change from previous rules !

18.5   The LSC monitors organisations remotely, using the data they supply as a matter of course when applying for funding or claiming at the end of the case.

The Standard Contract also includes key performance indicators (KPIs). Some KPIs apply to all categories of law and some are category-specific. Standard Contract, paras 2.70–2.117 contain the detailed rules that apply to all categories of law, and there are further requirements in the category-specific provisions.

A key change in the Standard Contract 2010 is that failure to meet KPIs can result in contract sanctions.[5] Therefore, it is important for caseworkers to be aware that their performance under the contract can affect the organisation as a whole.

Summary

18.6   A summary of the KPIs is as follows.

---

4 See Q10, Unified Contract Summary of Contract Documents and FAQ, LSC, February 2007.
5 Standard Contract Specification, para 2.70.

Standard Contract: KPIs summary – all categories (except Family and Family with Housing)

Civil controlled work – substantive benefit to clients	% varies by category of law – see below
Civil licensed work – substantive benefit to clients (except where varied by category of law – see below)	50% (min)
Judicial Review – substantive benefit to clients – all categories	40% (min)
Alternative dispute resolution (ADR) proposed or used (Licensed work) – applies from 1 April 2012	10% (min) (exceptions apply, see below)
Controlled work (non-fixed fee) – assessment reduction	10% (max)
Licensed work – assessment reduction	15% (max)
Fixed fee margin	20% (max)
Matter start usage	85% (min)

Actions against the police etc

Legal Help matters – substantive benefit to clients: does not apply to this category	N/A
Licensed work cases that proceed beyond the Investigative Stage cases – substantive benefit to clients	50% (min)
Certificated cases – substantive benefit to clients	30% (min)
Total net damages recovered for clients must exceed costs – applies from 1 April 2012	2:1

Clinical negligence

Legal Help matters – substantive benefit to clients: does not apply to this category	N/A
Licensed work cases that proceed beyond the Investigative Stage cases – substantive benefit to clients	60% (min)
Certificated cases – substantive benefit to clients	30% (min)
Total net damages recovered for clients must exceed costs – applies from 1 April 2012	2:1

Community care

Legal Help matters – substantive benefit to clients CA, CB, CC, CD, CE, CF, CI, CG, CH	40% (min)
Certificated cases – substantive benefit to clients	40% (min)

Consumer and general contract

Licensed work cases that proceed beyond the Investigative Stage cases – substantive benefit to clients (professional negligence)	60% (min)
Certificated cases – substantive benefit to clients (professional negligence)	30% (min)

Debt

Legal Help matters – substantive benefit to clients DC, DD, DA, DB, DE, DF, DG, DH, DJ	50% (min)
Certificated cases – substantive benefit to clients	50% (min)

Education

Legal Help matters – substantive benefit to clients EA, EB, EC, ED, EE, EF, EG, EH, EI, EJ	40% (min)
Certificated cases – substantive benefit to clients	40% (min)

Family[6] Not in force – included for information only

Legal Help matters – substantive benefit to clients (does not apply to public family law) FA, FB, FC, FD, FE, FF, FG, FH, FI, FJ	40% (min)
Certificated cases – substantive benefit to clients (private law children)	40% (min)
Certificated cases – substantive benefit to clients (other than public law and private law children)	50% (min)
ADR proposed or used (licensed work) except public family law, domestic abuse – applies from 1 April 2012	10% (min)

6 Following the quashing of the tender process in 2010, the Standard Contract was not brought in for family work. However we have included this as an indication of what the LSC wishes to monitor and may use to trigger an audit.

Exemption from family mediation justified (confirmed by mediator or LSC) (excludes domestic abuse and child abduction) – applies from 1 April 2012	30% (min)
Level 2 fee claimed (excludes domestic abuse and child abduction) – applies from 1 April 2012	50% (max)
Excludes domestic abuse and child abduction – applies from 1 April 2012 Of level 2 cases, % proceeding under 'other CLS Funding' must not exceed	35%
Excludes domestic abuse and child abduction – applies from 1 April 2012 Of certificated cases, % proceeding to a final hearing or beyond must not exceed	50%

Housing

Legal Help matters – substantive benefit to clients HA, HB, HC, HD, HE, HF, HG, HH, HI, HJ, HK, HL	40% (min)
Certificated housing possession cases – substantive benefit to clients	40% (min)

Immigration

Legal Help matters – substantive benefit to clients IA, IB, IC, ID, IG	15% (min)
CLR – substantive benefit to clients (fast track cases are excluded)	40%

Mental health

Legal Help matters – substantive benefit to clients – does not apply to this category	N/A

Welfare benefits

Legal Help matters – substantive benefit to clients WA, WB, WD, WE, WC, WF	50% (min)
Certificated cases – substantive benefit to clients	40% (min)

Civil and Family Contract work – matters and cases providing substantive benefit to clients

18.7   These KPIs require that a specified percentage of your completed cases have outcome codes that the LSC considers demonstrate a substantive benefit to clients. It is therefore extremely important to make sure that the correct codes are identified at the end of each matter. The best person to do this is the caseworker, as he or she will have the best understanding of what happened.

The LSC has published the codes it considers to show 'substantive benefit' at paragraph 2.107 of the Standard Contract Specification. If there is a suitable positive outcome code, you should always select it rather than one that the LSC regards as negative. So, for example, where justified by the case, you should select 'client advised and enabled to plan and manage their affairs better' rather than 'client ceased to give instructions'. See LSC website > Civil forms > Family Consolidated Matter Report Form > Civil Code Guidance, for more information on coding.

ADR proposed or used

18.8   This KPI is designed to encourage people to settle cases outside the court system.

Controlled work (non-fixed fee) – assessment reduction 10 per cent max

18.9   When your exceptional cases are assessed, the costs claimed must not be reduced by more than 10 per cent.

Licensed work – assessment reduction 15 per cent max

18.10   This sets the same target in relation to licensed work. The LSC says that its monitoring software gives credit for successful appeals.

Fixed fee margin – 20 per cent max

18.11   The LSC is concerned that some organisations will select clients with straightforward cases that do not require much work, in order to retain a high surplus under each fixed fee case. This KPI can only be met if the total cost of cases under fixed fees when calculated in minutes and items is at least 80 per cent of the appropriate fixed fees.

For example, a provider may have 100 matter starts in debt. The fixed fee for debt cases is £200. If they use all their matter starts and have no exceptional cases, they will be paid £20,000. The reported claims made in financial values must be at least £16,000.

Matter start usage – 85 per cent min

18.12 This KPI encourages organisations to use their allocation of matter starts.

Matter start usage – category-specific provisions

18.13 The following only applies if you hold a contract in the relevant area of law: if you undertake public law children work, you must apply for and be granted at least five full certificates per year.[7]

Service standards

! Change from previous rules !

18.14 The contract specifies service standards in a number of categories. You must comply with them if you hold a contract in the relevant category:

1 Immigration – 90 per cent of your asylum matter starts and 70 per cent of your non-asylum matter starts must be delivered to clients who are, at the time the matter is opened, physically located in your procurement area[8] (excluding clients in immigration removal centres, but including clients in other forms of detention[9]).

2 Mental health – 70 per cent of your matter starts must be delivered to clients who are, at the time the matter is opened, physically located in your procurement area.[10]

3 Actions against the police etc, clinical negligence, consumer, education, personal injury, public law – At least 60 per cent of your matter starts must be delivered to clients based in your procurement area.

Cost and contract compliance audits

18.15 Historically, cost auditing of controlled work was a bone of contention between the LSC and practitioners. Pre-2000, files were assessed on a case-by-case basis, so firms quickly got feedback if the rules changed or their standards slipped. This was replaced by a sampling

7 Specification, para 7.157.
8 Specification, para 8.20.
9 Specification, para 8.21.
10 Specification, para 9.7.

approach, where the result of a once-a-year audit on a sample of 20 files could be extrapolated to all claims under the Contract Schedule. Practitioners felt that the LSC staff did not understand the work that had gone into the files they were assessing, and were making mistakes. The problem was that until these were resolved on appeal, firms were being asked to repay considerable amounts of money, which would have jeopardised their survival.

The introduction of fixed fees in civil and family meant that these audits were no longer relevant, as files were paid according to fixed amounts, rather than fees based on the amount of time that had been put into a case. In crime, immigration and mental health, the audits continued on a reduced scale, and most firms protected themselves by simply under-claiming in the first place. This was clearly an unsatisfactory state of affairs. Happily, one of the results of the legal action taken against the LSC by the Law Society[11] was a working group, including the LSC, Law Society and Advice Services Alliance, to look at regulatory and contract requirements from the LSC's perspective and guidance and transparency from the practitioner's perspective. The group was felt to be so useful to all parties that it continues to meet.

At the end of the working group's initial phase, the LSC agreed to:

• create a file auditing section on its website, so that practitioners could see and understand what they were being audited against;
• move to a system of selecting organisations for audit that was based on their performance:

a) those providers who achieve an A1 or B1 rating for their first audit will be exempt from random selection for the next year (see 18.19 below for rating definitions);[12]

b) those providers who achieve an A1 or B1 rating for their second consecutive audit will be exempt from random selection for the following two years;

c) those providers who achieve an A1 or B1 rating for their third consecutive audit will be exempt from random selection for the following three years;

d) providers receiving an A2/B2 or B3 rating will automatically be re-audited within six to nine months;

---

11 See *R (on the application of the Law Society) v Legal Services Commission and Dexter Montague and Partners v Legal Services Commission* [2007] EWCA Civ 1264.

12 CCA Review – Joint Stakeholder Working Groups October 2008, p4, which can be downloaded from www.legalservices.gov.uk > Community Legal Service (CLS) > Civil contracts > Agreement with The Law Society > Review of contract compliance audits.

e) regional offices may identify providers for audit and will make it clear the basis for their selection, eg an unusual reporting profile;

f) the balance of the audit programme will be made up of providers selected on a totally random basis (excluding a–e above).

Although contract compliance audits are still carried out by the LSC, many of the issues are covered in the new financial stewardship visits introduced by the LSC in 2010 (see below for more information).

Contract compliance audit civil criteria

18.16 The criteria for audit of civil files is:

- Scope – the matter must be within scope of the Access to Justice Act 1999 (as amended).
- Financial eligibility – the client must meet the criteria.
- Evidence of means – this must be on the file (unless a permitted exception applies).
- Disbursements – these must be reasonable in amount and reasonably incurred.
- Sufficient benefit – the case must meet the test at the outset and throughout.
- Reporting – the case must have been reported using the correct codings.

Contract compliance audit crime criteria

18.17 These were still in development at the time of writing.

Contract compliance audit sanctions

18.18 Files are either fully or partly 'nil assessed'. If fully nil assessed, this is because the file could not be funded at all. If partly nil assessed, this is because a higher fee was claimed than was appropriate.

If you claimed a full fixed fee for a housing case (£174) instead of a tolerance fee (£138), it would be an over-claim of £36. This would be treated as 21% of a nil assessed file – 36 divided by 174 x 100%.

The LSC agreed to take a graded approach to audit sanctions. At the lowest level of non compliance, no sanctions are applied. After that, sanctions start with recoupment of fees on the actual files assessed and progress to a point where the result of that particular audit is extrapolated and applied to all claims made over the preceding year.

In addition, contract notices may be served. Two contract notices on the same issue can result in contract termination and in an extreme case, the LSC might consider the non compliance to amount to a fundamental breach of contract and terminate the contract quickly.

If the first sample of files has seven or more files nil assessed, a much larger sample will be taken. The result of the extended audit determines whether the result will be extrapolated.

18.19   **Initial sample of 20 files**

Category A1	0–2 files nil assessed	No recoupment
Category A2	2.01–6.99 files nil assessed	Recoupment of cash value Possible Contract Notice Further audit within 6 months
Category A3	7+ files nil assessed	Further files required for extended Audit

18.20   **Second sample – calculated to be representative – number varies**

Category B1	0–10% nil assessed	No recoupment
Category B2	10+%–20% nil assessed	Extrapolation Contract Notice(s) Further audit within 6 months
Category B3	20+% nil assessed	Extrapolation Contract Notice(s) Possible fundamental breach

Extrapolation

18.21   The LSC provides this illustration:[13]

> **Example:**
> 1. Initial sample of 20 files called from period July 2007 – to May 2008.
> 2. All files audited – 9 Files nil assessed.
> 3. Representations received. As a result 7 files nil assessed.

13   CCA Review – Joint Stakeholder Working Groups October 2008, Appendix F.

4. Audit proceeds to extended file sample. A total of 15 files nil assessed of 60 audited, i.e. 25% reduction.
5. Value of claims July 2007 – May 2008 = £146,000.
6. Recoupment = 25% of £146,000, i.e. £36,500

Contract compliance audit – appeal process

18.22 The first stage of the appeal process[14] is an internal review by another member of the LSC's audit team. You must set out the reasons for the appeal in writing and send the file(s) back with it. If this is not successful, you move to independent costs assessment.

These appeals are generally considered on the papers only, although in exceptional circumstances either party can apply to the Assessor for an oral hearing, although these are rarely granted. The Assessor reviews the assessment and may confirm, increase or decrease the amount assessed.

At any point after the submitting an appeal to the Assessor, but not later than 21 days after receipt of the final decision, you (or the LSC) can seek clarification on the costs rules. You do this by applying for a certificate of a point of principle of general importance (POP). Applications can be made to the LSC or direct to an Assessor if one has been appointed. The application must set out the exact wording of the POP sought. However, these are rarely certified. They are listed at www.legalservices.gov.uk > Community Legal Service (CLS) > Guidance on fees and funding > Points of Principle or www.legal services.gov.uk > Criminal Defence Service (CLS) > Guidance on fees and funding > Points of Principle, as appropriate.

The LSC's Legal Director will decide whether the matter should progress to the Costs Appeals Committee. Applications for POPs are considered on the papers only. You will be sent the LSC's Legal Director's and/or the Costs Appeals Committee's decision.

Financial stewardship

Process

18.23 The LSC introduced its financial stewardship process from early 2010. It was designed to counter criticism by the Public Accounts Committee and the National Audit Office.

---

14 The appeal process is set out in the Standard Contract, paras 4.35–4.31 in the Civil Specification and paras 8.13–8.45 in the Crime Specification.

The process involves a relatively new department of the LSC, Provider Assurance. Relationship Managers carry out an initial on-site visit. Provider Assurance carries out data analysis and any further in-depth audits which may be needed. The LSC has stated that this process will be developed, further to discussions with the various bodies which represent providers (eg the Law Society, Advice Services Alliance) and a revised manual was posted on its website in the autumn of 2010 at www.legalservices.gov.uk > Community Legal Service (CLS) > Civil contracts.

The audits are scheduled after a risk assessment based on:

- results of contract compliance audits, which check that forms have been completed correctly, other contract requirements have been observed, eg rules for opening more than one file for a client, evidence of means on the file;
- data validation exercises, eg to check that the allocated number of new matter starts (Legal Help files) have not been exceeded, that work in progress (WIP) claims do not exceed 75 per cent of profit costs, and that certificated cases have been billed promptly.
- referrals from Relationship Managers, where they have concerns.

Scope

18.24   Financial stewardship audits cover the following areas:

- evidence of means;
- case splitting/multiple matters for a client;
- Family level 1 and level 2 fees;
- work in progress and payments on account on certificated files;
- tolerance claims;
- incorrect claiming of duty work and travel (crime);
- attendance at interview, incorrect stage billing and fresh claims (immigration).

Evidence of means

18.25   The Relationship Manager will select at least five Legal Help forms. If even one of them fails, (due to no, or invalid, evidence of means) a further sample will be selected. This is then audited by the organisation itself and two files are checked by the Relationship Manager. If three or more of the aggregated sample fail, the organisation may be invited to agree an extrapolation rate across all similar work. The Standard Contract Specification, para 4.39(b) allows the LSC to extrapolate back 12 months or to the last contract compliance audit.

If agreement is not forthcoming, the organisation may be asked to review a large number of files, which is likely to be very time-consuming. If six files fail, it is likely that Provider Assurance will carry out a Controlled Audit, and the LSC will seek to recover the cost if the result is confirmed.

What you should do

18.26 Make sure you obtain valid evidence of means before advising clients. The key document is the LSC Manual, volume 2, section E. Check that the Relationship Manager has applied it correctly before accepting any determination.

Case splitting/multiple matters for a client

18.27 The Relationship Manager will seek evidence that new matter starts have been opened correctly. The method and consequences are as in evidence of means above.

What you should do

18.28 It is important to be familiar with the Standard Contract Specification, both general and category-specific rules, and be prepared to engage the Relationship Manager in discussion if you think he or she has made a mistake.

Family level 1 and 2 fees

18.29 The Relationship Manager will be checking that level 2 fees have been claimed correctly. The method and consequences are as in evidence of means above.

The Unified Contract Specification, rule 10.55 (pre 9 May 2011), appeared to require a second meeting with the client as evidence of a 'significant family dispute'. Point of Principle of General Importance CLS 54 was certified on 20 December 2010, which confirmed that a second face to face meeting was not essential.

Post 9 May 2011, the requirement for a second meeting was dropped, and instead a requirement for 'substantive negotiations with a third party' was substituted. The LSC's guidance states that there must be proposals and counter proposals to demonstrate this Family Fee Scheme Guidance (para 4.10).

The LSC's guidance to the Family Fee Scheme (para 4.13) states that where there are no assets and a clean break order, it does not meet the criteria for level 2 as is unlikely that any significant dispute could arise leading to family proceedings.

This changed in the Standard Contract. Paragraph 7.58 dropped the requirement for a second meeting, and substituted instead a requirement for 'substantive negotiations with a third party'. There is no definition of this phrase.

The LSC's guidance states that where there is a clean break order, it does not meet the criteria for level 2 as there is no significant dispute.[15]

What you should do

18.30   Become familiar with the family category Specification (section 10 in the Unified Contract), and the general rules. Be prepared to justify claims in terms of their provisions.

Work in progress calculations and payments on account for certificated civil cases

18.31   The concern is that claims may be inflated and the LSC might be unable to recover over-claimed fees if the organisation became insolvent. Relationship Managers will check whether there is a robust system for ensuring that payments on account are correctly calculated by checking ledgers and asking about your systems. You will be graded 'red', 'amber' or 'green', as appropriate.

What you should do

18.32   Ensure your time recording and systems for claiming payments on account and final claims are robust. Be aware that the LSC's data may contain errors and be prepared to show the Relationship Manager where this is the case. Relationship Managers may not understand that WIP calculated at hourly rates may appear high when work is paid under fixed fees. Point out where payments on account were in respect of disbursements rather than profit costs.

Tolerance claims

18.33   The LSC will check to ensure that the correct (lower) fees are claimed.

Audit outcomes

18.34   The LSC has a range of powers, including:

- recovering fees mis-claimed on individual files;
- extrapolating mis-claims across all similar files;

---

15   See appendix E.

- informal warnings;
- Contract Notices (which can result in contract termination if breaches are repeated);
- suspension of payments for failure to co-operate.

Appeals

18.35   If you disagree with your Relationship Manager on a costs point, see the costs appeal process, set out in relation to contract compliance audits, above. If you disagree with your Relationship Manager on a non-costs contract point, the reconsideration and review procedures under clause 32 of the Unified Contract or clause 27 of the Standard Contract would apply.

Legal aid: how did we get here?

by Steve Hynes

Introduction

19.1   Lawyers and advisers want to get on with helping the public rather than worrying about the bureaucracy of the legal aid system. They frequently complain to Legal Action Group (LAG) about the difficulty of providing a service while having to keep an eye on proposed policy changes in the administration of the legal aid system. Over the last few years these changes have come thick and fast, leading to a reduction in providers as each new storm of change breaks over them.

19.2   This chapter provides an overview of the developments in legal aid policy over the last 12 months or so, putting into context the preceding chapters on managing a legal aid practice.

19.3   In keeping with the legal aid system this chapter breaks down into two main sections: criminal and civil. These are followed by a short section that examines the Legal Services Commission (LSC) and the Magee Review which was published last year. This first section deals with developments within the Criminal Defence Service.

19.4   The government has published a consultation paper on legal aid which is discussed in the next chapter and a legal aid bill is expected soon. So more change is on the way.

Criminal legal aid

First came means test, then came no legal aid.

The one part the state cannot refuse to pay for?

19.5   To maintain equality before the law and to comply with the European Convention on Human Rights (ECHR) criminal legal aid is essential. For the government there is little choice but to provide state support for lawyers to defend those accused of a crime; the main point of contention is how much is paid to secure these services. In both criminal and civil legal aid the fees paid for work are set by the LSC after consultations with the legal professions and not-for-profit sector.

19.6   As with civil legal aid, eligibility is one of the key controls on the criminal legal aid budget. Means testing in Crown Court cases was introduced at the beginning of 2010 as a cost cutting measure. This was rolled out across the country, with London being the last region to introduce the means test in June. Owing to the vast majority of criminal legal aid clients having limited income and assets, the sums saved by introducing the means test are relatively small. The LSC claims that £35 million is saved a year from the reintroduction of the means test for magistrates' court work[1] and LAG believes that in

Before 2010 it was free for all. Paid for by gov.

many lawyers could have be employed. A private lawyer for people who have no to pay him.

---

1 www.legalservices.gov.uk/criminal/criminal_legal_aid_eligibility.asp.

the Crown and higher court cases savings will be less than this as far fewer clients will have to make contributions.

[handwritten: If entered into police work first, then magistrates court work — open market for that bids to the to give the least legal aid possible]

Goodbye BVT – gone but not forgotten

19.7   Over the years the notion that a process of market testing the price of legal services was needed has percolated around the legal aid policy world. The Carter Report published in July 2006[2] was the latest manifestation of this. Carter suggested a period of fixed fees as a prelude to the introduction of Best Value Tendering (BVT) for legal aid services. In one of the boldest moves in the recent history of legal aid, the LSC announced its intention to introduce BVT for police station and magistrates' court work in April 2009. The proposal was to pilot the scheme in two areas: Avon and Somerset and Greater Manchester. After this it would be rolled out in three phases to cover the whole country. These plans met with opposition from most practitioners. *[handwritten: The pressure of fresh giddy innocence of governmental change coming in]*

19.8   At a special meeting in London of the Criminal Law Solicitors' Association in May 2009, chair Joy Merriam warned that up to 80 per cent of firms might face closure and that the costs of closing a firm were expensive. She told the audience of solicitors that with redundancy payments, run off insurance and other costs, the bill for winding up her own practice came to £100,000. She pledged they would, 'Fight the introduction of best value tendering and we have the heart and belly to take on that fight'. *[handwritten: wanted from universities piling into new private firms on the market again]*

19.9   The then minister for legal aid, Lord Bach, addressed the hostile audience saying, 'No other field of government expenditure has grown as much as legal aid ... Don't believe any promises from the opposition'. This drew the first of many heckles from the audience, 'We don't believe them and we don't believe you'. Bach argued that they had to identify the priorities for expenditure on legal aid and said, '... in a recession I want to protect social welfare law expenditure'. *[handwritten: those who could work at a loss could survive... standard]*

19.10 Many practitioners had become increasing hostile to BVT once the bidding documentation was published, as the process seemed too complex. There was also bitter resentment that the Bar got a deal on very high cost cases (see 19.20) by using a boycott, while in contrast many solicitors would face a Hobson's Choice of risking a 'suicide bid' to keep police station and magistrates' court work or pull out at a

---

2   Lord Carter's Review of Legal Aid Procurement, *Legal Aid: a market based approach to reform*, July 2006. Available at www.legalaidprocurementreview. gov.uk.

time when the recession was making it difficult to switch into other areas of law.

19.11   On 15 July 2009, the All Party Parliamentary Group on Legal Aid heard evidence from legal aid practitioners near despair at the government's plans for BVT for police station and magistrates' court work. Tony Edwards (TV Edwards LLP, London) told the committee in his view BVT as it was proposed was 'all about price competition and this will drive down quality'. Edwards pointed out that in his firm he has a supervisor to junior staff ratio of 2:1 whereas the proposal under BVT would allow up to 1:4. 'To compete on these terms my firm would have to change this by a factor of eight'. He went on to describe how most practitioners build their businesses on own client work, which in itself is a method of quality control as clients return to or recommend a solicitor only if he or she does a good job. He said as the BVT proposals were currently drafted clients would be only able to choose a solicitor in the police station area in which they are arrested and that, while a market mechanism might control the price of the work, what was proposed could 'destroy the very best firms'. The Conservative shadow legal aid minister, Henry Bellingham MP, spoke at the same meeting. He argued, 'It is vital that BVT has a proper evaluation before rolling it out across the country'.

19.12   Opposition to the BVT proposals was not unanimous. While not prepared to go on the record, some solicitors did tell LAG at the time that they were happy with the proposals, as they believed their firms would bid successfully. It seems to LAG there were sharply different views behind the scenes between the Ministry of Justice (MoJ) and the LSC over BVT.

19.13   Officials at the LSC such as Derek Hill, head of policy, insisted that the primary reason for BVT was not to save money, but to find a market price for police and magistrates' court work. He argued that prices might increase in some areas. The MoJ was under pressure from the Treasury to make £1 billion in savings in the department and felt that the introduction of BVT could contribute towards these. When it became apparent that BVT would not save any cash, once the costs of its introduction were taken into account, and that it could potentially lead to hundreds of firms going to the wall a few months from a general election, a policy u-turn was inevitable. This came on 20 July 2009. The government announced that it was abandoning the plans for BVT across the country. Instead it was going to allow the pilots in Somerset and Avon and Greater Manchester to go ahead and evaluate these before making a decision on a nationwide roll out. However, this plan was also soon scrapped as it proved impossible to

but the cont fees are decided by the gov. With a market price apart. More juniors and items, more law students demanding less money.

run a BVT tendering process while reviewing the fees for Crown and higher court work, which had taken over as the priority to save cash in the legal aid budget.

19.14   The climbdown over BVT was particularly humiliating for the LSC as it had invested so much time and effort in trying to get the scheme off the ground. The main lessons on BVT that can be drawn from the experience of the last government are to plan and evaluate pilots prior to committing to a complete roll out, not to assume it would bring quick budget savings and not to plan it in a general election year.

Plan B   *What is police station work – they want this to be the cheapest.*

19.15   With the failure of BVT the government had to rethink its policy on criminal legal aid. On 20 August 2009[3] the LSC announced a consultation on reducing the fees for Crown and higher courts work as well as a flat fee for all police station work.

19.16   In LAG's view, this consultation led directly to the government abandoning plans for the piloting of BVT as it feared a legal challenge, since firms in the pilot areas would be bidding for police and magistrates' court work without knowing the price of the Crown Court and other higher court work. It is readily accepted that for many firms a cross-subsidy operates between the two areas of work and, without knowing what they would be paid for the more lucrative Crown Court and higher court work, realistic bids could not be prepared. The paper proposed the following:

– up to a 23 per cent cut in advocacy fees in the Crown Court;
– a flat fee for all police station work (ending the different fee structure in different areas);
– an end to the duplication of fees for committals before trial; and
– a cut in the costs of expert reports.

19.17   The fee cuts were announced on 16 December 2009. The main difference from the above proposals was that the government went for a reduction in police station fees only in the areas it described as 'the most expensive and over-subscribed'. Overall, a saving of £23 million was the target. In a move welcomed by LAG, the government also reaffirmed that its priority was to preserve expenditure on social welfare law.

19.18   In December 2009, the LSC opened the tender round for the new Standard Crime Contract, replacing the Unified Criminal Contract *once unified, now standard, how ironic.*

---

3 *Legal aid: funding reforms*, 20 August 2009, Ministry of Justice.

which terminated on 13 July 2010. The new contracts are due to last for three years, with a possibility of an extension of up to two years. Firms were requested to submit bids using a new e-tendering process. 1,788 firms secured new contacts. Only 5 per cent of firms which applied for contracts were unsuccessful.[4] Some well-respected management consultants believe that the new contract round was used by a significant number of new firms to enter the market,[5] supporting the view that the number of firms undertaking criminal legal aid work remains relatively stable.

Advocacy fee cuts

19.19   At £700 million the cost of advocacy before Crown and other higher courts makes up the bulk of expenditure in criminal legal aid. Just under 18 per cent (£125m) of this budget was spent on 397 Very High Cost Cases (VHCCs) in the year 2008/09. VHCCs, which include complex fraud and terrorism cases, make up less than 1 per cent of the higher courts budget and have been the target of a number of government-inspired initiatives to cut their costs in recent years. There have been two stand-offs, in 2004 and 2008, between the Bar and the government over VHCC pay rates. On both occasions the Bar has managed to boycott taking on new cases as a protest against rate cuts and wrung concessions from the government, the most eye-catching being a £17 million overall increase in cash in 2004. In 2008 also a compromise was reached over fee rates.[6]

19.20   The rush to push through reductions to advocates' fees in criminal cases, prior to the general election, would seem to imply that ministers felt they had a score to settle with the Bar. Only five days after a consultation on proposed new rates closed, the government tabled the changes in a statutory instrument, prompting Paul Mendelle QC, the then chair of the Criminal Bar Association, to say that the government had 'done exactly what it planned to do all along'.[7] From 27 April 2010, nine days before the general election, fees in Crown Court cases were cut by 4.5 per cent, with further cuts planned over the next two years to lead to a total cut of 13.5 per cent.

---

4   Catherine Baksi, 'Criminal defence firms fail to secure legal aid contracts beyond July 2010', *Law Society Gazette*, 9 April 2010.
5   Catherine Baksi, 'Criminal law firm start-ups confound cull predictions', *Law Society Gazette*, 13 May 2010.
6   Steve Hynes and Jon Robins, *The Justice Gap: whatever happened to legal aid?*, Legal Action Group, 2009 at p119.
7   May 2010 *Legal Action* 4.

19.21 From 14 July 2010, the threshold at which VHCC fees apply was raised from 40 to 60 days. The government also decided to abandon the VHCC specialist panel system and revert to contracts with individual firms for new cases, which had been established as part of the negotiations over fees two years before. Whilst this was welcomed by the Law Society, practitioners were concerned about the wasted time and resources the panel had cost. 'The tender process was monumental. The LSC must have wasted millions on it. Add to that the sheer waste of time and money for those solicitors who spent days working on applications to go on the panel, and the cost is immense', said Roy Morgan, Chair of the Legal Aid Practitioners Group.[8]

[handwritten margin note: WELCOME TO A CLASS OF LAWYERS]

[handwritten note: EXPAND, MERGE, OR DIE. BIG BOYS DONT NEED TO MERGE. SIZE MATTERS. GOV SAY THE NUMBER THEY WANT - THAT SETS A BASE LIMIT FOR THE CONTRACT BID.]

A cull of firms possible

19.22 Legal aid policy has never been an area of policy to excite much party political debate. Over its history there has often been political consensus around major changes, for example the ideas of quality marks and block contracting for services, which were pioneered under the last Conservative government and were adopted by Labour. One of the Labour government's last initiatives was to float the idea of a radical culling of the number of criminal legal aid firms.

19.23 In a paper published on 22 March 2010[9] the government outlined plans to reduce the number of legal aid firms to around 8–10 in each of the 42 criminal justice areas and compel these firms to do the full range of criminal law work. Up to 75 per cent of firms would be forced to close under the proposals. The MoJ said that the changes would lead to 'significant savings to taxpayers and a more sustainable future for the legal aid budget'. Legal aid minister Lord Bach told LAG at the time, 'It is not an option not to make changes. We cannot raise rates, but firms are saying they are not being paid enough to be viable'. Under the proposals he said many firms would be forced to close or merge as '... only efficient firms will thrive'.

19.24 LAG estimated that up to 1,500 firms could close down or be forced to merge if the government carried through with the plans, which would also mean that the current contracts, due to run to 2013, would have to be terminated early. The current coalition government is looking again at introducing price competitive tendering

---

8 Catherine Baksi, 'The LSC accused of squandering millions on VHCC tender process', *Law Society Gazette*, 3 June 2010.

9 *Restructuring the delivery of criminal defence services*, Ministry of Justice, 22 March 2010.

[handwritten: large firms, more people, and contracts]

(see chapter 20) as it believes, like the previous government, that savings can be made by dealing with fewer, but larger, firms providing services in all areas of criminal law, from the police station to the higher courts.

19.25   A strong lobby exists amongst large criminal firms, which are pushing for the change. They met the new government at an early stage to discuss the proposals outlined in the MoJ paper on restructuring criminal defence services. Franklin Sinclair, a senior partner at one of these firms, Tuckers, believes the market place is not yet ready for BVT, though the sort of consolidation which was proposed in the MoJ paper, he thinks, would lead to cost savings of 10 per cent on the criminal legal aid budget. Sinclair, who is based in Greater Manchester, gives an example of the impact in this region. He argues that the 81 firms which currently serve the area could be reduced to 12. He believes this would be more efficient, for an increased in volume of work would lead to fewer solicitors being needed to cover the courts. He also argues that the police station rotas need to be redesigned so that one solicitor can cover one session. 'All the government needs to worry about is they are purchasing a good quality service and that the police stations and magistrates' courts are covered. We need to get rid of those firms that only do Crown Court and VHCC work and do not do any other crime work', he says. *[handwritten: NO COMPETITION. THINK ABOUT IT.]*

[handwritten margin note: AREAS OF importance]

19.26   As discussed below in the context of family law, reducing the number of legal aid firms is hugely controversial. The fear is that the public loses out as they either have to travel further or miss out altogether on being able to access services in a local area. In the context of competitive tendering for services, LAG has always argued that this leads to consolidation of the market into fewer firms and runs the risk of stifling competition.[10] Such a drastic reduction in the supply base for criminal legal aid would run a similar risk.

19.27   The government is severely limited in its options around criminal legal aid. Cutting back in scope is curtailed by the European Convention on Human Rights (specifically article 5 on the right to liberty and article 6 on the right to a fair trial). A further tightening of the means test could be an option but, as discussed above in relation to the introduction of means testing in the magistrates' courts, the sums saved by such a move would be relatively small. Restricting face-to-face advice in the police station is another option the previous government examined, but this might be precluded by developments

[handwritten: "I WANNA HELP PEOPLE, I WANNA BE A LAWYER! TOUGH LUCK. I WANNA ARGUE THIS SHIT OUT, I WANNA BE STRONGER AND AS WISE AS THEY. TOUGH SHIT ITS]

10 Roger Smith, *Legal Aid Contracting: lessons from North America*, Legal Action Group, 1998. *[handwritten: our courtroom AND WE DECIDE THE LAWYERS WHO COME IN THEM]*

[handwritten: OK - I'LL JUST EMPOWER THE PEOPLE WITH ALL THE LEGAL KNOWLEDGE THEY NEED TO KNOW - & THEY CAN BE CITIGANTS IN PERSON, MCENZIE FRIENDS, OR JUST HAVE THE LAWYER THERE -]

in European Court of Human Rights case-law[11] which favour the physical presence of representation in the police station for suspects.

Civil legal aid

19.28   For much of the last year of the Labour administration the government and the LSC were focused on getting criminal BVT to fly. While the policy reached the runway it never took off and was replaced with a contract round which has left the provider base pretty much intact. In contrast, while the civil bid round seemed far less politically controversial, it is this which will have the greatest long-term impact on both legal aid providers and the general public. *Civil*

19.29   In contrast to criminal legal aid, the number of firms and not-for-profit organisations contracting with the LSC for civil legal aid has decreased at a higher rate over recent years. The introduction of civil fixed fees in October 2007, according to the LSC, led to around 5 per cent of suppliers leaving legal aid.[12] Over the last three years these have been joined by other providers, a recent high profile example being Refugee and Migrant Justice (RMJ), which went into administration owing, in large part, to the difficulties in making fixed fees pay.

19.30   The case of RMJ is noteworthy as it was the largest single legal aid provider of immigration advice. At the time of its closure in July 2010 it held 12,500 active files, which is around a tenth of the total market. The nub of its difficulties was the changeover to the fixed fee system. Not-for-profit organisations had previously been paid in advance for work at an hourly rate. The changeover to fixed fees led to a drop in income and severe cash flow difficulties for the organisation. Over 50 per cent of RMJ's work was on asylum cases. The length of these cases, and the delay in receiving payments for disbursements, were the main reasons RMJ claimed for their cash problems.[13] RMJ launched a high profile campaign to appeal to the new coalition government to bail it out, but the government took the view that the system was working well, 'providing value for money', and that an exception could not be made for RMJ.[14]

11 See *Salduz v Turkey*, ECtHR application no 36391/02, 27 November 2008.
12 Steve Hynes and Jon Robins, *The Justice Gap: whatever happened to legal aid?*, Legal Action Group, 2009 at p57.
13 'Refugee charity faces closure', July 2010 *Legal Action* 5.
14 See the statement made by the Secretary of State for Justice, Kenneth Clarke, in the House of Common on RMJ made on Thursday 17 June 2010: *Hansard Commons Deb* Col 1023.

19.31   Adjustments to eligibility and scope, most often in response to budget crisis, have shaped the current civil legal aid system. Different types of civil legal problems enjoy varying degrees of support from the legal aid budget, and for this reason it is difficult treat the system as a homogeneous one. One of the main policy themes over recent years in civil legal aid has been the government and LSC's attempts to bring together services in the disparate civil legal aid areas of law. This was one of the main aims of the civil bids round which ran in 2010.

Social welfare law

NEW MATTER IS ALLOWING AN EXISTING ORGANISATION TO EXPAND WITH MORE CONTRACTS. — BUT IN FACT THEY ENCOURAGE NEW COMPANIES

19.32   Providers bidding for Social Welfare Law Contracts had to satisfy the LSC that they could provide services in housing, benefits and debt, either alone or as part of a consortium. Housing law providers also had the option of applying for a contract to provide housing and services under a Family Contract (in some non-urban areas this could be private or public law or both). Providers could also apply for stand alone contracts in employment and community care law. *FRESH TO LEGAL AID, IN.*

19.33   Research by the Advice Services Alliance, published by LAG, indicated that there was a 17 per cent reduction in the numbers of matters starts available for social welfare law across all of the procurement areas. The LSC's explanation was that expenditure had been increased temporarily in response to increased demand for advice during the recession in 2009–10, and the tender process would simply restore overall spend to around the previous level. One of the most important findings of the research was that, for the first time, it appears that money for legal help work was transferred away from higher spending areas to lower spending ones, in accordance with the LSC's 'indicative spend' formula based on perceived need for legal aid services.[15] The reduction in new matter starts in these areas contributed to around 30 per cent of applicants for new contracts being turned down. Also, many of the providers who were successful complained that they had not been allocated sufficient matters to make contracts viable.

19.34   The Community Law Partnership (CLP), a solicitors' firm based in Birmingham with a national profile for its work, especially in Gypsy and Traveller law, was not granted any new matter starts. CLP brought a judicial review against the LSC. At an initial hearing on the judicial review, Mr Justice Collins said, 'I am bound to say this is

15 A Griffith, '2010 social welfare law bid round: what is on offer?' April 2010 *Legal Action* 6.

a dreadful decision and on the face of it the approach [taken by the LSC] is totally irrational'. The case hinged on the LSC's insistence on using success at higher tribunal appeals as a selection criterion. CLP had argued that they did not need to take many of these cases because they generally win their clients' cases at the lower tribunal. LAG understands that some legal aid providers in Birmingham had overbid for work and agreed smaller contracts. This freed up cash for the LSC to grant CLP a contract prior to the full hearing of the judicial review. — DIDN'T WANT A PRECEDENT BEING MADE ABOUT PcP

It seems to LAG that providers have fared well where they have CONSTRAINT little competition and the allocation of matter starts was not reduced. MAKING For example, Stoke on Trent Citizens Advice Bureau, which serves such an area, reported to LAG that they got 'virtually everything we asked for'.

19.35   At the time of writing, the LSC had yet to release the numbers and location of providers of social welfare law. LAG fears that, while the attrition level would not be as bad as for family law (discussed below), there would be many good quality providers lost to legal aid clients because of the overall cutback in the numbers of new matter starts compared with the recession adjusted peak and the difficulties of forming viable consortia to bid for contracts. There is also the impact of the recession at work on the supply side as firms either seek to increase or move into legal aid work for the first time to compensate for commercial work lost in the downturn. Islington Law Centre undertook 271 legal help cases last year in employment law and they were allocated only 47 matter starts for employment cases, 'We are devastated by this, but we are hoping to avoid compulsory redundancies', director Ruth Hayes told LAG. According to Hayes, the LSC had already halved the number of matter starts available for employment cases in Islington and it appears those remaining were split between the Law Centre and three other providers, two of whom were new to legal aid work. — why allow New when there is old, already crippled, they can.

firstly, there is a limit. People also, like competing

19.36   Aside from the mainstream contracts for social welfare law, five Community Advice Centres (CLACs) and two Community Legal Advice Networks (CLANs) were established to integrate social welfare law and other civil legal aid services. The Manchester CLAC tender or CLAS (Community Legal Advice Service), as the LSC now calls CLACs and CLANs, was won at the end of August 2010 by the CAB service in Manchester, in partnership with two private practices and an independent advice agency. It is the largest such service. A CLAS has also been established in Wakefield and will commence at the same time as the Manchester service. The CLAC and CLAN initiative was evaluated by the Legal Services Research Centre in 2010. Amongst other findings, the report identified that local authorities often had sharply contrasting reasons for engaging in a joint commissioning process with the LSC.[16]

Mental health and immigration

19.37   Figures released by the LSC show that there was an increase in the number of firms bidding for mental health work. This has meant that much of the work was carved up into smaller contracts. London was the worst affected area as 67 firms were provisionally successful in bidding for contracts and 34 of these firms were new entrants to the market. LAG believes that many of these new bidders are firms which have recruited mental health specialists for the first time because they saw mental health as a potential 'recession proof' growth area, as well as solicitors taking the opportunity of the new bid round to split off from existing firms to form new ones. The LSC said that all the successful firms in each procurement area for mental health were allocated a minimum of 30 cases, topped up with pro-rata allocation between firms of the remaining cases available in each procurement area.

19.38   The LSC reported that only 252 out of over 400 applicants were successful in their bids for Immigration and Asylum Contracts. LAG understands that the LSC received applications for over double the number of new matter starts available. The LSC said 47,744 new matter starts for immigration cases and 48,761 new matter starts for asylum cases were awarded in the tender round. Providers were told whether they had been successful or not at the end of June 2010. Many were disappointed about the number of new matter starts allocated to them. One London firm told LAG that they had been allocated less than half of the immigration cases and only 70 per cent of the asylum cases which they had applied for.

Family law

19.39   The largest part of expenditure on civil legal aid is family law. In 2007, out of 137,963 civil legal aid certificates issued, 115,086 were for family cases.[17] LAG estimates that, out of the 2,613 Civil Contract

16 *Community Legal Advice Centres and Networks: a process of evaluation*, Legal Services Commission, June 2010.

17 Steve Hynes and Jon Robins, *The Justice Gap: whatever happened to legal aid?*, Legal Action Group, 2009 at p78.

holders in 2008/09,[18] close to 2,000 of these will have been family law providers and that around two-thirds of the total budget (about £600m) for civil legal aid is spent on family law cases. The contract bid round ended on 21 April 2010 and providers were advised of the outcome of their bids in August. Resolution, which represents family lawyers, surveyed its members on the impact of the family law bid round. Of the 561 firms which took part in the survey, 40 per cent had been unsuccessful in their bids and 86 per cent of these had appealed against the decision.[19]

19.40   In the family law category, according to the LSC, 1,300 existing offices were awarded contracts and 1,100 were not. The LSC has expressed surprise at this result as, according to chief executive Carolyn Downs, it was not their intention to reduce the numbers of providers, but it was due to the provider representatives' insistence on higher quality criteria which led to so many failing to get contracts.[20] According to the LSC, the overall amount of work available was not reduced, it was instead concentrated into fewer, larger, firms who bid for more work than they previously undertook and scored highly on the quality criteria, thus bumping out the firms which scored lower.

19.41   Carol Storer, director of the Legal Aid Practitioners Group, does not accept that the selection criteria weeded out the weaker firms, 'Many very good firms did not get contracts; some firms specialising in child protection and domestic violence cases with excellent reputations might have to leave the legal aid system if they do not win their appeals'. An example Storer points to is Stamps Family Solicitors based in Hull. The firm provides a free telephone advice line for domestic violence victims, in addition to the usual family law services. According to Oliver Hudson, the firm's chief executive, 'The helpline and counselling service are absolutely vital to local people, particularly the victims of domestic violence, as it offers them immediate legal advice together with compassion and support all at the same time'. With the loss of the contract, Hudson fears victims of domestic violence will be left 'high and dry'. He says, 'Where else can they now go for legal advice about domestic violence at 3 am on a Sunday morning?'.

19.42   The Law Society issued judicial review proceedings against the LSC over the result of the family bid round in September (2010). The

---

18 *LSC Annual Report and Accounts 2008/09.* Available at www.legalservices.gov.uk.

19 www.resolution.org.uk/site_content_files/files/family_legal_aid_contracts_survey.pdf.

20 'LSC chief: tender outcome "unintentional"', *Law Society Gazette,* 5 August 2010.

decision to go to judicial review split solicitors. Resolution did not back the decision, as LAG understands that the organisation's board took the view that the judicial review would only create more uncertainty. The politics of the issue mirrors the split amongst criminal firms, where the larger firms favour undertaking greater volumes of work across all areas of criminal law, against those firms which wish to undertake specialist, and arguably more lucrative, work. Many family law providers tended to specialise in public law work such as child protection, but they lost out if they were in one of the procurement areas in which they had to undertake both public and private law work to secure a contract.

19.43   After a three-day hearing before Lord Justice Moses and Mr Justice Beatson, the family law tender process was found to be illegal (CO/9207/2010, 30 September 2010). This was a significant victory for the Law Society, which argued that the results of the family tender round, if they had been allowed to stand, would have had a devastating impact on access to justice for the public because, potentially, the number of firms undertaking family law would have been cut from 2,400 to 1,300.

19.44   While the Law Society's grounds for judicial review included points on the impact of the reduction in the number of firms on access to justice and the LSC's failure properly to consider its equality duties, the case turned on the panel membership selection criteria. Firms were only advised that they would receive extra marks in the selection process for membership of both the specialist child care and domestic abuse panels when the tender documentation was published in February 2010. The LSC argued that it had no obligation to advise practitioners about the selection criteria before commencing the tender process. However, Moses LJ reasoned that, because the LSC had published a consultation paper on the tender process in 2008, it had therefore chosen to consult and so could not use this as a defence. In his judgment, Moses LJ said that the LSC could '... provide no rational basis for denying a case-worker the opportunity to apply to both panels'. In his view, the effect of the late notice of the criteria was to 'unfairly and arbitrarily reduce the number of family law suppliers'.

19.45   The judgment affects only contracts relating to housing and family, family, children only and child abduction. Contracts concerning immigration, mental health and social welfare law are not affected by the ruling. Firms that were awarded contracts for the first time, or increased contracts in the tender round, lost these as the LSC had to extend the existing contracts to comply with the judgment.

19.46   After the hearing, Liz Fitzpatrick, partner at IBB Solicitors in west London, spoke to *Legal Action* about her relief over the decision. She said that her firm 'has a long-standing commitment and history in undertaking work for vulnerable children' and, while IBB has five children panel members on the staff, it does not have a domestic violence panel member and, therefore, failed to get a contract. 'It has been an anxious time for us and I am so pleased for our staff who stuck with us, but it was what Lord Justice Moses said about the damage this would have done to the provision of services to the vulnerable which is so true.'

19.47   Law Society president Linda Lee said in a statement: 'The failure of the LSC to anticipate, let alone manage, the outcome of the process was the latest and perhaps most alarming of the LSC's apparently haphazard attempts to reshape legal aid. We are extremely disappointed to have been left with no choice but to take legal action against the LSC, which refused to acknowledge the detrimental effect that this outcome would have on families.'

19.48   Sir Bill Callaghan, chairperson of the LSC, said after the hearing: 'We are currently considering the detail of the judgment and its implications, including whether to appeal. We are conscious of the uncertainty facing providers and will publish further information in due course.'

19.49   Carol Storer, Director of the Legal Aid Practitioners Group said after the hearing, 'I'm very pleased that many good providers are back in the system, but the many firms who were allocated larger contracts and have committed themselves to new premises and staff presumably might now take action against the LSC.'

The Legal Services Commission and the Magee Review

19.50   2010 was an annus horribilis for the LSC. The abandonment of criminal BVT can be marked down as its biggest policy failure of the year, but at least with this the LSC can argue that it was overruled by its political masters at the Ministry of Justice. LAG suspects that the simmering tensions between the LSC and the MoJ over control of policy were brought to the fore by the difficulties over implementing criminal BVT, and this led the Secretary of State for Justice and Lord Chancellor, Jack Straw, in October 2009, to call in the former civil servant Sir Ian Magee to undertake a review of the legal aid system and its governance (the 'Magee Review').

19.51   Magee's report was published in March 2010. In it he acknowledged that, as his review had gone on, there was an increasing focus
on what was going wrong with the financial management at the
LSC.[21] The National Audit Office's report on the LSC in October 2009
found that just under £25 million in solicitors' fees had been claimed
incorrectly, and the Public Accounts Committee's report, which was
published in January 2010, was also critical of the LSC's financial
management.[22] Magee found serious weaknesses in the management
and financial systems at the LSC. In all, said Magee, the LSC's forecasting process involves the use of over 200 models and tools, including manual analysis. As a result of this Magee doubted the LSC's
ability to predict expenditure accurately.

19.52   In response to the Magee Review, the government announced
its intention to take direct control of the Legal Services Commission by making it an executive agency of the Ministry of Justice.
Magee had argued that this would lead to 'one policy voice' on legal
aid. Lord Bach, the then legal aid minister, told LAG: 'We will be
bringing legal aid into the ministry as an agency, in the same way
as we have the Courts Service and NOMS [the National Offender
Management Service]'. He acknowledged that: 'We cannot do this
without primary legislation', which would involve the amendment
or repeal and replacement of the Access to Justice Act 1999. The LSC
chief executive, Carolyn Regan, announced her resignation when
the report was published. This was presented as a stepping stone to
the LSC's new status, but LAG speculated at the time that Regan had
been made the scapegoat for failings in the LSC's financial management which, it should be said, must have preceded her appointment
in 2007.

19.53   There was agreement amongst practitioners about the MoJ's
move to take over policy. Robert Heslett, the Law Society's president,
said, 'Lack of clarity on responsibility for policy-making between the
commission and the MoJ has been a significant problem area and
the Law Society is glad that the government has accepted Sir Ian's
recommendation that the LSC should become an executive agency
of the MoJ'. Nicholas Green QC, chairman of the Bar Council, also
welcomed the report, 'As Sir Ian recognises, there has been a lack

21 See *Review of Legal Aid Delivery and Governance*, Ministry of Justice, March
2010 at p4.

22 *The procurement of legal aid in England and Wales by the Legal Services
Commission, ninth report of session 2009–10*, House of Commons Committee
of Public Accounts, February 2010, available at www.publications.parliament.
uk/pa/cm200910/cmselect/cmpubacc/322/322.pdf.

of clarity about who is calling the shots over policy', he said. 'He identifies a number of serious issues which we will need to consider further'.

19.54 In an important finding, which was welcomed by LAG, Magee recognised the cost drivers in legal aid, pointing out that, among other things, new legislation and the creation of new criminal offences lead to increased costs in the legal aid system. In civil legal aid, the report said that new rights created under the Mental Health Act 2007 and the introduction of working families tax credits are examples of measures which increased the demand for social welfare law advice. Magee came down firmly against the option of separating the criminal and civil legal aid funds, which LAG had argued for, but he acknowledged that there could be an argument in favour of separating out social welfare law advice.[23]

19.55 In the consultation paper on the future of legal aid (discussed in the next chapter) the government states that it intends to create a new executive agency under the direct control of the Ministry of Justice to administer legal aid. LAG's main concern is that the government has to ensure that there remains independence in the decision-making process on entitlement to legal aid. We believe this is essential both to uphold human rights principles and for the public to accept that decisions on entitlement to legal aid are fair, as so often the other party in a case is an arm of the government.

23 At page 69.

Facing the future

by Steve Hynes

20.1   A consultation paper on the future of the legal aid system was published by the government late last year. The consultation closed on 14 February 2011. The paper outlines proposals for reductions in fees and in the scope of legal aid in order to make savings of £350m, 23 per cent of present spending. While the overall proposed cuts might be less than was first feared, (it had been rumoured that £500 million would be cut[1]) the bulk of the cuts (£279m) will fall on civil legal aid. A high proportion of current services will be lost, for example 68 per cent of civil legal help services would go.[2] This chapter discusses the legal aid budget, the current state of legal aid provision, as well as the green paper and the future of legal aid services.

A few financial skeletons

20.2   As Labour left office in May last year the overall legal aid budget did appear to be under control. Mainly due to the cutbacks, such as the reintroduction of the means test in the magistrates' court five years ago, spending on criminal legal aid fell in the five years ending in April 2009 by 12 per cent in real terms.[3] There was some growth in expenditure on civil, but overall the budget was contained within a £2.1bn cap. The following table summarises spending on legal aid and the cost of the LSC for the last three years.

	2009–10		2008–09		2007–08	
	£000	cases	£000	cases	£000	cases
Criminal Defence Service (CDS)						
Police station suspects not charged	187,275	853,086	192,460	871,093	164,829	767,360
Lower courts	288,905	643,787	291,216	648,896	289,481	612,340
Higher courts	733,610	293,947	699,447	124,836	692,222	123,913
Total criminal legal aid spend	£1.12 billion*		£1.17 billion		£1.15 billion	

1 'Catherine Baksi, 'Fears mount over "£500m" legal aid cut', *Law Society Gazette*, 22 July 2010.
2 *Legal Aid Scope Changes, Impact Assessment*, Ministry of Justice, p16.
3 *Review of Legal Aid Delivery and Governance*, Ministry of Justice, March 2010, p7.

	2009–10		2008–09		2007–08	
	£000	cases	£000	cases	£000	cases
Community Legal Service (CLS)						
Representation	905,731	159,715	809,990	145,286	541,000	165,800
Legal help	228,412	1.17m	188,262	1.07m	151,000	752,642
Immigration and asylum	95,715	98,643	85,580	94,983	76,000	81,958
Income	209,197		207,372		235,500	
Bad debt	108,449					
Total civil legal aid spend (less income)	£1.34 billion		£876,460		£794,712	
Cost of LSC	120.700		124,400		113,500	
Total	**£2.37 billion**		**£2.17 billion**		**£2.06 billion**	
Release of provision for dormant cases			179,649		350,000	

* after means-tested contributions

20.3   Expenditure on criminal legal aid fell last year by £54m, but expenditure on civil legal aid increased by £121m due to more spending on civil legal help caused by the recession and on child protection cases which was attributed by the Legal Services Commission (LSC) to 'local authorities' reactions to the Baby P case'. Two important adjustments were also made to the accounts.

20.4   A new financial management regime was put in place at the LSC after the criticism levelled at it last year (see previous chapter) and it would appear that the LSC has decided to tidy up some financial skeletons. A provision had been made in previous years for dormant cases – this will no longer be made (see table). Another £108m has been added because the LSC has changed the way in which it calculates the recovery of money outstanding from certificated work (shown in the above table as bad debt). It seems to LAG that, based on previous records of repayment, the LSC was too optimistic about the likelihood of recovering money owed to it by solicitors and others. With these adjustments to the accounts included, the expenditure on the CLS exceeds the amount spent on CDS for the first time. [4]

20.5   Until 2009 the LSC and its predecessor the Legal Aid Board produced accounts prior to parliamentary recess in July, reporting on their expenditure and activities in the preceding financial year. The report and accounts for the financial year 2008/09 took until October 2009 to produce and the latest accounts, for the financial year ending on 31 March 2010, were only published at the end of November 2010.

20.6   The reason for these delays over the last two years has been the qualification of the accounts by the Controller and Auditor General to the House of Commons, Amyas Morse, who heads the Public Accounts Office (PAO). The PAO audits central government to ensure that public money is spent properly and is unhappy about the adequacy of the controls in place to prevent overpayments of legal aid being made.

20.7   In the 2009/10 accounts the PAO has identified an estimated total of £78.6 in overpayments to legal aid providers. This is around 3.2 per cent of the total spend. The figures break down as £43.6m of work over-claimed by practitioners and £32.9 was for claims for legal aid which were not supported by evidence of means from the clients. Morse points out that this is a considerable increase on last year, for which the estimate was £24.7m. The figures are calculated by taking a sample of files for audit and extrapolating the results across the entire budget.

20.8   In civil legal aid the bulk of the errors are found in Immigration and Family legal help cases, £15.7m up from £10.5m last year. In crime, mistakes in police and magistrates' court at £23.4m, up from £3.6m, account for the largest part of the estimated error figure. The report says that many of the errors found in civil were down to practitioners claiming for the wrong fees.

20.9   To tackle the problem the LSC has issued more contract notices for systematic errors in claims or failure to comply with contractual terms, says the report. In the period April to October 2010, 495 contract notices were issued compared with 259 in the period 2009–10. The report argues that, while it is disappointing that the errors have increased from last year, this is 'not surprising' given the pressure the LSC is under to reduce costs. This has led to a reduction of 12.5 per cent in the Commission's staffing from March 2008 to March 2010.

4   LSC Annual Report and Accounts 2009/10, p19.

20.10   What has changed from last year is that the LSC has become more effective at targeting files that it believes are at risk of having been over-claimed. A large number of these have been low value level two family files which practitioners have allegedly claimed in error. It is clear to LAG, though, that the LSC changed its interpretation on what could be claimed. Many firms, as did the LSC, believed that the files could be claimed at level two if they involved complex matters, but the LSC has now ruled that a second meeting with the client needs to take place to qualify for a level two payment.

20.11   Over the last year, the LSC has embarked on a strategy of sending Relationship Managers, who are the main point of contact for legal aid providers, to review files to ensure compliance with the eligibility requirements. LAG believes that using computerised records identifying all the cases files that might not meet the new criteria for family cases go into firms to embark on a process of 'recovering' what are often substantial sums of money on files they believe have been over-claimed for. Many not-for-profit organisations have been similarly caught out by the LSC's strict interpretation on which welfare benefits cases qualify for legal help and have had to pay back money to the LSC. Aside from the fairness of this process, the NAO report makes no allowance for the LSC's changing interpretations on what can be claimed.

20.12   LAG accepts that there is no doubt that proof of means needs to be demonstrated to qualify for legal aid, but the NAO should not make the assumption that the clients who fail to produce evidence of means would not have been entitled to claim legal aid. Legal aid clients often lead chaotic lives which mean that producing papers can be a nightmare. A system based on information already held by the state would lead to a better service and the assurance that every client seen by legal aid providers meets the means test. This already happens in civil licensed work and criminal cases, for which clients' benefits records are cross-checked with their legal aid claim. LAG is suggesting that the LSC or its successor adopt a system of verifying clients benefit payments from records already held by the government.

Retreat from the high street

20.13   The table overleaf shows summarises the number of contracts held by legal aid providers in each area of civil law over the last five years.

	2009–10	2008–09	2007–08	2006–07	2005–06
Family	2434	2677	2692	2756	2887
Housing	501	561	542	571	592
Welfare benefits	428	445	435	459	467
Debt	404	423	405	407	411
Personal injury	386	354	833	914	960
Immigration	223	247	263	313	367
Mental health	210	243	250	273	283
Employment	190	218	200	216	222
Clinical negligence	218	175	262	275	273
Community care	100	113	93	73	76
Actions against the police	57	67	69	72	75
Public law	45	46	49	44	46
Education	38	44	46	51	57
Consumer	33	37	38	39	40
Total non family	2833	2973	3485	3707	3869
Total	**5267**	**5650**	**6177**	**6463**	**6756**

20.14   In most areas of law there has been a steady decline in the number of contracts held by firms and not-for-profit organisations as they continue to leave the legal aid system. The number of legal aid contracts is greater than the number of individual firms and not-for-profit organisations in the system, as some have more than one contract if they operate from locations in different areas of the country. There are now only 2,058 individual civil legal aid solicitor firms in the legal aid system, down 195 on the previous year, and 28 not-for-profit organisations have gone from civil legal aid in the last year leaving 332. There are now 1,697 criminal legal aid firms, 84 fewer than last year.[5] The table below breaks down the numbers of civil

5   LSC Annual Report and Accounts 2009/10, p6 and LSC Annual Report and Accounts 1008/09, p10.

legal aid contracts held by firms, telephone contracts and not-for-profit organisations over the last year.[6]

Contracts held by provider type 2009–10			
	Solicitors	NfP	telephone
Family	2414	16	4
Housing	326	165	10
Welfare benefits	124	297	7
Debt	129	267	8
Personal injury	386		
Immigration	161	62	
Mental health	207	3	
Employment	103	78	9
Clinical negligence	218		
Community care	71	29	
Actions against the police	57		
Public law	45		
Education	29	7	2
Consumer	31	2	
Total non family	1887	910	36
Total	**4301**	**926**	**40**

20.15 Ten years ago there were 4,860 civil legal aid providers and 2,925 criminal legal aid providers. In civil legal aid, family legal aid has always been predominant, with most large towns having at least some family legal aid providers. As the table illustrates though, in other areas of civil law the number of providers is much smaller. This means that coverage outside the larger conurbations has always been at best patchy. The number of criminal legal aid firms has also been declining and there has been a trend towards consolidation, with firms merging or taking over the work of firms which leave the market or close down.

6 LSC Statistical Information 2009–10, p1.

20.16   There has been a gradual retreat from the high street of legal aid services. The LSC has tried in part to offset this by developing more telephone advice services, and opening up the provision of civil legal aid services to not-for-profit agencies under the last government.[7] However, LAG is concerned about the trend towards fewer individual contracts and high street offices because we fear this cuts off many members of the public from access to legal aid. If the government's proposals outlined in its consultation go ahead, an already bad situation will become much worse: it will be not so much a case of retreat from, but carnage on, the high street.

The consultation paper

20.17   On 15 November 2010 the government published the green paper *Proposals for the Reform of Legal Aid in England and Wales*. At the time of writing (April 2011) the government has yet to respond to the 5,000 submissions it received and so its recommendations could change, but as the Ministry of Justice (MoJ) has to find £2 billion of cuts in total[8] it is very likely that a substantial lump will have to come out of the legal aid budget.

20.18   Eligibility cuts are floated in the consultation paper. It suggests that all clients with disposable capital over £1,000 should have to make a contribution of £100 to their legal aid. Little cash would be raised from this and it would act as a disincentive to some people to seek legal advice, as well as being an administrative headache for providers, who would be expected to collect the contributions. Further tightening of the rules on capital disregards is also suggested. For example, a gross capital limit of £200,000 is proposed in cases in which property is being contested.[9] A cut of 10 per cent to expert fee rates is suggested, along with a long-term proposal to introduce a structure of fixed and graduated fees for experts.

20.19   Given the previous government's struggles to implement competitive tendering in criminal work (see last chapter), it is perhaps not surprising that the coalition government has decided to proceed cautiously on this. Another consultation on competitive tendering for criminal contracts was announced in the consultation paper for later

---

7 Hynes and Robins, *The Justice Gap*, Legal Action Group, 2009, p42.
8 *Proposals for the Reform of Legal Aid in England and Wales*, Ministry of Justice, November 2010, p5.
9 *Proposals for the Reform of Legal Aid in England and Wales*, p91.

this year. The paper makes it very clear that competitive tendering for both criminal and eventually civil legal aid 'is the right way forward'.[10] The criminal contracts are due to finish in July 2013 and so the government would have the option of introducing a competitive tendering process for the next round of contracts or at least running some pilots, while extending the bulk of the contracts for two years. It will not be certain what the government intends to do about competitive tendering for criminal legal aid until later in the year, but the consultation paper states that the last government's proposals published in March last year (see previous chapter) 'have a number of attractions' and that the government envisages putting much of the work out to tender, with this happening in some areas this year.[11]

20.20 Officials in both the LSC and Ministry of Justice (MoJ) will be anxious not to repeat the experience of the failed civil bid round of last year, shot down by the Law Society's and the other successful judicial reviews. What seems likely is that in future bid rounds the government will shy away from complex selection criteria, which are open to challenge, and opt for a system that mainly selects on price, with safeguards on quality most likely controlled by the legal professions.

20.21 A further round of cuts to criminal fees is outlined in the consultation document. Proposals include changing the fee structure in Crown Court work to encourage early guilty pleas, as currently practitioners receive a higher fee if a defendant pleads guilty late in the Crown Court (cracked trial), and reducing the fees paid in murder and manslaughter trials to the same level as those paid in cases of rape and other serious sexual offences. The higher fees paid for magistrates' court work in London and Very High Cost Criminal Cases are also amongst the targets for spending cuts.

20.22 An across the board fee cut of 10 per cent is proposed for all civil legal aid cases, including all legal help and certificated cases. Little justification is given in the paper for this proposal. LAG is being told by practitioners that this, combined with the other proposals on cuts to rates paid in civil legal aid cases, will have a detrimental impact on many civil legal providers. The cuts to both criminal and civil fees will, according to the government, cost legal aid providers from £144m to £154m in lost income.[12]

---

10 *Proposals for the Reform of Legal Aid in England and Wales*, p113.
11 *Proposals for the Reform of Legal Aid in England and Wales*, pp114–115.
12 *Impact Assessment Cumulative Legal Aid Reform Proposals*, Ministry of Justice, 2010, p10.

20.23   The largest chunk of the cuts, around £279m, proposed in the green paper fall on scope in civil legal aid cases. Because of the significance of the changes to scope which the government wishes to implement, it has decided that, in contrast to previous cuts to scope,[13] primary legislation will be needed to implement them. LAG understands that the first reading of an Act of Parliament, which will include the many of the changes currently being consulted on, has been scheduled for May this year (see below). Owing to the time it will take for the bill to pass through the parliamentary process, the changes to scope cannot be implemented before October 2012.[14]

20.24   If what the government is proposing on legal aid is approved by parliament this will amount to the most radical reshaping of the civil legal aid system since the introduction of green form (now Legal Help) in 1974. Much of legal aid for family work will go, leaving mainly cases involving domestic violence and care proceedings. A total of £178m will be cut from family law with advice on divorce, money matters to do with relationship break-up, as well as disputes about contact and residence of children, all in the firing line to be removed from scope. Other areas of civil work pencilled in for the chop include welfare benefits, personal injury, employment and much of debt work. A total cut of £101m from the budget will come from non-family civil legal aid.[15] Cases in which clients are at risk of losing their home will remain in scope, though it is unclear how this is defined.

20.25   If these proposed cuts are implemented, according to the government's figures, 550,000 fewer people will receive help with civil legal problems.[16] The civil legal aid system helped just over one million people last year and so this cut represents about 50 per cent of the current civil legal aid services to the public.[17] Sections of the population more likely to suffer disadvantage are hit disproportionately harder by the proposed scope cuts than the general population. For example, 65 per cent of private family law clients are women, 14 per cent above the numbers in the general population; 30 per cent of welfare benefit clients suffer from a disability, compared with 18 per cent in the general population; and 24 per cent of employment clients are from Black and Ethnic Minority Groups compared to 8

13 Hynes and Robins, *The Justice Gap*, Legal Action Group, 2009, p30.
14 *Proposals for the Reform of Legal Aid in England and Wales*, p32.
15 Legal Aid Reform: Scope Changes Impact Assessment, Ministry of Justice, November 2010, p15.
16 LAG contends the real figure is 650,000. See 'The real impact of legal aid advice cuts' March 2011, LAG: www.lag.org.uk/policy.
17 Legal Aid Reform: Scope Changes Impact Assessment, p14.

per cent in the general population. The government's own equalities assessment pulls no punches in acknowledging the disproportionate impact of the cuts on disadvantaged groups.[18]

20.26   A telephone advice line is proposed to replace much of the service people currently get from civil legal aid providers. LAG supports the use of telephone services because they can be useful in dealing with many problems and in signposting people to face-to-face advice if they need it. However, we believe that such services cannot replace legal aid because the results of our recent opinion poll survey indicate that the poorest people are also least likely to use telephone and internet services and are most reliant on local face-to-face legal advice services.[19]

20.27   The bulk of the cuts in non-family civil legal help will fall on the not-for-profit sector. We estimate that out of a total cut of £64m in legal help, over £50m will be cut from local not-for-profit providers such as Citizens Advice Bureaux and Law Centres. These organisations are already experiencing deep cuts from other branches of government. For example, Hammersmith and Fulham London Borough Council recently cut £180,000 from its grant to the Law Centre in the borough.

20.28   In LAG's view the proposed cuts fall disproportionately on the services which help people with the everyday problems of life such as debt and housing. Sixty-eight per cent of the civil legal help scheme which gives initial help and advice on legal problems would go. We believe such deep cuts have not been proposed for any other public services and we will be urging MPs to vote against the legislation unless the draft bill, when it is published later this year, is substantially different from the proposals outlined in the consultation paper.

20.29   The consultation paper explores two possible sources of funds to supplement the legal aid budget. It is suggested that a Supplemental Legal Aid Scheme (SLAS) could be introduced in tandem with reforms to litigation costs, which are also being consulted on.[20] The SLAS would fund some of the cases taken out of scope by recouping a percentage of funds from successful claims for damages. Taking interest earned from money held by solicitors on behalf of clients is also suggested. Similar schemes which collect interest from client deposits have been successfully introduced in countries such as France and the USA. It is difficult to estimate the amounts such

18 Legal Aid Reform: Scope Changes Impact Assessment, p136.
19 *Social Welfare Law: What is fair?* Legal Action Group, November 2010.
20 *Proposals for Reform of Civil Litigation Costs in England and Wales*, Ministry of Justice, November 2010.

a scheme could generate, but the paper quotes the example of the USA, in which $92m was raised in 2009.[21]

Plans for legislation

20.30   We believe that the Ministry of Justice plans to introduce a bill in May this year. The bill will include plans for reforming sentencing policy, legal aid and creating a new executive agency to administer legal aid as recommended by the Magee Report (see previous chapter). The bill might also include provisions for granting voting rights to prisoners since the government has now recognised that it has to do this to comply with a judgment of the European Court of Human Rights.[22]

20.31   There are already rumbles of discontent around a number of provisions likely to be contained in the bill. Michael Howard, the former conservative Home Secretary, writing in the *Times*, while welcoming the sentencing green paper's recommendations on rehabilitation of offenders, was scathing about its proposals on sentencing. In his view, the expansion in prison numbers has helped reduce crime levels since 1993. He believes provisions such as the curtailing of indeterminate sentences, which the paper suggests, is the wrong way to go.[23] His criticisms are the antithesis of a green paper which recognises the failure of prison to prevent reoffending behaviour and seeks to address this by policies which encourage rehabilitation and reduce the use of custodial sentencing.

20.32   Michael Howard, now in the Lords, will be one side of a clear political divide over the sentencing section of the MoJ bill. On the other will be much liberal-leaning opinion, though some would argue that the green paper does not go far enough. Frances Crook, Director of the Howard League for Penal Reform, broadly welcomed the sentencing reform green paper, but said,

> The charity is disappointed that the package is only designed to reduce the prison population by 3,000 men, women and children. As Kenneth Clarke has repeatedly pointed out, the prison population has doubled and there are now 40,000 more people in prison than when he was last in charge of the justice system but the reoffending rate has stayed stubbornly the same.[24]

21 *Proposals for the Reform of Legal Aid in England and Wales*, p130.
22 *Hirst v UK (No 2)* (2004) 38 EHRR 40.
23 Michael Howard, 'More prisoners equals less crime. It's a fact', *Times*, 14 December 2010.
24 Howard League response to Justice Green Paper, The Howard League for Penal Reform.

20.33 Labour, while in government, were in favour of a large expansion of prison places[25] and could use amendments to the bill to divide the coalition government over the legislation. A volatile mixture of opportunism from the Labour opposition, hard line 'prison works' Tories, combined with Eurosceptics, enraged over voting rights for prisoners, could derail the sentencing provisions and detract from the potentially devastating cuts planned for the legal aid system. A failure to pass the proposals on sentencing reform, aside from their reforming merits, would also create a large hole in the MoJ budget plans. The government is likely to try and force through the hybrid bill by arguing that it involves necessary pain to the left and right of the coalition government in order to make the MoJ's budget balance.

20.34 The bill might provide for raising additional cash for legal aid from a SLAS and a client account interest scheme. Whether a SLAS gets off the ground depends on whether the wider reforms proposed on conditional fees are implemented. A client account interest scheme is likely to meet with strong opposition from solicitors as they currently derive some income from this and will probably argue that the amounts at stake are small due to low interest rates and clients insisting on the swift transfer of cash electronically. If the alternative methods of funding can raise sufficient cash to replace services currently funded by the government, we will support these because we see this as a pragmatic solution to the budget crisis. However, we are against the government either holding or managing these funds, since we believe they would be lost eventually to the legal aid budget.

20.35 Despite the difficulties, legal aid continues to play a crucial part in ensuring equality before the law and access to justice for at least two million people a year. LAG hopes that this book will assist practitioners in continuing to provide this worthwhile service. LAG will campaign against the government's current proposals for legal aid, because they would hit the poor and marginalised communities hardest. Through *Legal Action* magazine and the LAG News Blog on our website, we will continue to keep you up to date on developments in legal aid policy, throughout what promises to be a difficult year.

25 'A titan error', editorial, November 2008 *Legal Action* 3.

APPENDICES

McKenzie advisers

The first McKenzie adviser (also known as a McKenzie friend) was an Australian barrister called Ian Hanger. He was instructed in 1970 by Geoffrey Gordon & Co to assist their client, Mr McKenzie, who did not qualify for legal aid. Mr Hangar was not authorised to practise in London, and sat with Mr McKenzie, advising him how to represent himself. The case established rules governing McKenzie advisers to this day.

These rules can be found in the Chancery Guide 2002 (Chapter 15 Miscellaneous Matters), which can be dowloaded from http://www.hmcourts-service.gov.uk/cms/1343.htm.

In the light of the increasing number of litigants in person appearing in Family courts, the President of the Family Division issued a guidance paper in April 2008. This has been updated following the recent decision of Munby J in the case of *Re N (A child) (McKenzie Friend: Rights of Audience)* [2008] EWHC 2042 (Fam). The revised guidance can be downloaded from http://www.judiciary.gov.uk/docs/pfd_guidance_mckenzie_friends_oct_2008.pdf.

New applications checklist – civil

- Have all the forms been signed and dated by the client and the legal representative?
- Are the signatures original and less than two months old?
- Have you submitted the relevant means form?
  - Means 1 (clients not in receipt of passporting benefits);
  - Means 2 (clients on passporting benefits).
- Has the applicant (and partner if appropriate) completed all sections of the means form and signed/dated it?
- Do you need to submit a Form L17?

  If so, has it been stamped/signed by the employer?
- If the client is self-employed submit a Means 1 form together with:
  - Means 1A if sole trader;
  - Means 1B if in partnership;
  - Means 1C if a director.
- If a client is self-employed or in a partnership and does not have accounts covering the last 18 months, the client also needs to complete form L31.
- Has the client provided evidence of the benefits they are receiving?
- Have you included a statement of case and any supporting documents?
- Where appropriate (in Family cases) have you submitted a form CLSAPP7 (mediation)?
- Should devolved powers have been used?

New applications checklist – crime

- Have the forms been signed and dated by the client and the legal representative?
- Are the signatures original?
- Have you included the client's National Insurance number?
- Have you addressed the interests of justice test on the CDS14?
- Has the applicant (and partner if appropriate) completed all sections of the CDS15 form and signed/dated it? This is not needed for Crown Court cases or cases post mode of trial which are going to go to the Crown Court.
- Have you included evidence of means, or if in custody a CDS17? This is not needed for Crown Court cases or cases post mode of trial which are going to go to the Crown Court.
- Has the client provided evidence of the benefits they are receiving? This is not needed for Crown Court cases or cases post mode of trial which are going to go to the Crown Court.
- Have you included any supporting documents? Not always necessary, but if for example you are relying on the client's previous convictions to tip the balance into a potential loss of liberty case, it is useful to include the PNC print-out.

Category definitions 2010

Note: the 2010 Category definitions have been reproduced from the LSC website (www.legalservices.gov.uk) as at September 2010. Please visit the website to check the material is up to date at the point at which you seek to use it.

Introduction

1. These are the Legal Services Commission's Category Definitions 2010 as referred to in the 2010 Standard Civil and Criminal Contracts. Definitions of terms set out in those Contracts also apply to these Category Definitions.
2. In these Category Definitions:
   i) References to 'Legal Help' include Help at Court and, in the Family Category only, Family Help (Lower).
   ii) References to 'proceedings' in a Category cover the provision of Legal Representation (including Controlled Legal Representation) in that Category and, in the Family Category only, Family Help (Higher).
3. Services within the Crime Category are automatically excluded from all Civil Categories, except for any overlap between Categories specified in Guidance. Guidance on these Category Definitions includes examples of overlaps between Civil Categories and examples of services which fall outside all Categories.

Crime

1. Representation in all proceedings defined as criminal proceedings under section 12 of the Access to Justice Act 1999 and regulations made under that section (including regulation 3 CDS (General) (No 2) Regulations 2001).
2. All criminal Advice and Assistance as defined in section 13 of the Act and regulations made under that section (including regulation 4 CDS (General) (No 2) Regulations 2001).
3. All appeals in relation to criminal proceedings including applications for case stated arising out of criminal proceedings.
4. The Crime Category also includes Advice and Assistance and Representation in the following areas (as defined in the 2010 Standard Crime Contract):
   (a) Prison Law;
   (b) Associated CLS Class of Work.
5. The undertaking of civil proceedings is excluded from the Crime Category unless falling within the definitions given above. Proceedings brought under the Environmental Protection Act 1990 for a statutory nuisance where the

client is the complainant are excluded from the Crime Category as are proceedings under the Animal Welfare Act 2006 for the destruction of animals.

Family

1. Legal Help on matters and all proceedings which arise out of family relationships, including proceedings in which the welfare of children is determined.
2. Also included are Legal Help on Matters and all proceedings under any one or more of the following:
   (a) the Matrimonial Causes Act 1973;
   (b) the Inheritance (Provision for Family and Dependants) Act 1975;
   (c) the Adoption Act 1976;
   (d) the Domestic Proceedings and Magistrates' Courts Act 1978;
   (e) Part III of the Matrimonial and Family Proceedings Act 1984;
   (f) Parts I to V of the Children Act 1989;
   (g) Part IV of the Family Law Act 1996;
   (h) The Adoption and Children Act 2002;
   (i) the Civil Partnership Act 2002;
   (j) the inherent jurisdiction of the High Court in relation to children.
3. For the avoidance of doubt, the following matters/proceedings are also included within the category:
   (a) Legal Help in making a will where the client is the parent or guardian of a disabled person who wishes to provide for that person in a will, or of a minor living with the client but not with the other parent, and the client wishes to appoint a guardian for the minor in a will;
   (b) proceedings to enforce any order made within family proceedings;
   (c) proceedings under s20 of the Child Support Act 1991;
   (d) proceedings under the Family Law Act 1986;
   (e) proceedings under the Child Abduction and Custody Act 1985 (but note that devolved powers do not extend to taking such proceedings);
   (f) proceedings under the Protection from Harassment Act 1997 or in assault and trespass where the proceedings are family proceedings and only an injunction and either no or only nominal damages are sought or where an application is made to vary or discharge an order made under section 5, and the proceedings are family proceedings;
   (g) applications to enforce orders made in family/matrimonial proceedings under the Civil Jurisdiction and Judgments Acts 1982 and 1991;
   (h) proceedings under s14 of the Trusts of Land and Appointment of Trustees Act 1996 where the proceedings are family proceedings;
   (i) proceedings under the Maintenance Orders Acts 1950 and 1958;
   (j) proceedings under Part I of the Maintenance Orders (Reciprocal Enforcement) Act 1972 relating to a maintenance order made outside the United Kingdom;
   (k) applications for a parental order under the Human Fertilisation and Embryology Act 1990;
   (l) proceedings under s106 of the Social Security Administration Act 1992;
   (m) proceedings under the Crime and Disorder Act 1998 for:

(i) a Child Safety Order or for a Parenting Order made in proceedings for a Child Safety Order; or

(ii) an Anti-Social Behaviour Order or Sex Offender Order made in relation to a child, and any associated Parenting Order;

(iii) a Parenting Order made on the conviction of a child but only where the parent cannot reasonably be represented by the child's solicitor;

(n) applications to the court to change the name of a child.

Personal Injury

1. Legal Help on matters and all proceedings, other than those falling within the Clinical Negligence Category, in which there is a claim for damages for personal injuries to, or arising out of the death of, the claimant or any other person, including claims to the Criminal Injuries Compensation Authority. However a claim for damages arising out of the disrepair of, eviction from or obligation to allow quiet enjoyment of residential premises is excluded even if it includes damages for personal injury (see Housing Category). Proceedings for assault and trespass are also excluded where substantive damages are not sought (see Family Category).

    Note: 'personal injuries' includes any disease and any impairment of a person's physical or mental condition.

Clinical Negligence

1. Legal Help on matters and all proceedings which include:

    (a) a claim for damages or a complaint to a relevant professional body in respect of an alleged breach of duty of care or trespass to the person committed in the course of the provision of clinical or medical services (including dental or nursing services); or

    (b) a claim for damages in respect of alleged professional negligence in the conduct of such a claim.

Housing

1. Legal Help on matters and all proceedings which concern the possession, status, terms of occupation, repair, improvement, eviction from or quiet enjoyment of, or payment of rent or other charges for premises (including vehicles and sites they occupy) which are occupied as a residence, including the rights of leaseholders under the terms of their lease or under any statutory provision (including enfranchisement). Cases including homelessness, allocation, transfers and the provision of sites for occupation are also included.

2. For the avoidance of doubt, provided the proceedings arise in respect of premises occupied as a residence, the following are included in the category:

    (a) Legal Help in relation to applications under Section 82 of the Environmental Protection Act 1990 for a statutory nuisance;

    (b) proceedings under the Access to Neighbouring Land Act 1992;

    (c) proceedings to recover possession under a mortgage or other charge;

    (d) proceedings under the Housing Act 1985 including those arising out of the right to buy provisions;

    (e) proceedings under the Housing Grants Construction and Regeneration Act 1996;

(f)   proceedings to set aside a legal charge or a transfer of property;
(g)   proceedings in nuisance or trespass;
(h)   proceedings under the Leasehold Reform Act 1967;
(i)   Legal Help and proceedings in relation to Housing Benefit.
3.   Proceedings for an Anti-Social Behaviour Order sought by a local authority against a tenant or a person living with him or her, or by way of an appeal against such an order to the Crown Court, pursuant to sections 1, 1D or 4 of the Crime and Disorder Act 1998, and proceedings under section 1B of that Act.

Immigration

1.   Legal Help on matters and all proceedings concerning immigration, leave to enter or remain in the United Kingdom, removal or deportation from the United Kingdom, asylum, nationality and citizenship.
2.   Proceedings before an Immigration and Asylum Tribunal and any related proceedings before the Upper Tribunal, High Court, Court of Appeal or Supreme Court.

Welfare Benefits

1.   Legal Help in relation to all welfare benefits (including housing benefit, war pensions, state pensions and vaccine damage payments or similar benefits), and in relation to proceedings before any welfare benefit review or appeal body.
2.   Any subsequent or related proceedings before a court.

Employment

1.   Legal Help in relation to a contract of employment or service contract or any matter arising out of an employment relationship, including termination of employment, the enforcement of any statutory rights given to employees or workers, and data protection matters and including Legal Help (but not representation) in proceedings before an Employment Tribunal.
2.   Proceedings before an Employment Appeal Tribunal, proceedings for wrongful dismissal and proceedings before the courts arising out of any of the above.

Mental Health

1.   Legal Help where the primary problem or issue relates to a point of English law concerning mental health, the Mental Health Act 1983 or the Mental Capacity Act 2005, including matters concerning education issues but only where based on mental impairment.
2.   All proceedings before a Mental Health Tribunal (including those arising from criminal proceedings and any related proceedings before the Upper Tribunal, High Court, Court of Appeal or Supreme Court), all other proceedings under the Mental Health Act 1983 or Mental Capacity Act 2005 and any other proceedings where the primary issue is mental health, but excluding any matters falling within the Clinical Negligence or Personal Injury Categories.

Debt

1.   Legal Help in relation to, and all proceedings:
     (a)   for the payment of monies due or the enforcement of orders in such proceedings, including those arising out of the occupation of premises

but excluding any possession proceedings involving a contested counter-claim and any case where possession is sought on grounds additional to those relating to non-payment of monies due or where the occupant has a defence to possession; and

(b) for the recovery of possession of premises for failure to make payments due under a mortgage or other charge; and

(c) arising out of personal insolvency, including bankruptcy, administration, Debt Relief Orders or IVA proceedings whether the client is a creditor or debtor; but excluding representation in proceedings against parties in default of a fine or other order in criminal proceedings in the magistrates' court who are at risk of imprisonment.

Consumer and General Contract

1. Legal Help and all proceedings:
   (a) concerning contracts and their enforcement, including claims for rescission or misrepresentation, for the payment of monies due, or based on discrimination in the provision of goods or services, but excluding cases which in substance fall within the Housing or Employment categories; and
   (b) concerning negligent misstatement or professional negligence other than cases within the Clinical Negligence category (or another civil category).

2. For the avoidance of doubt, the following proceedings are included in the category:
   (a) proceedings under the Tort (Interference with Goods) Act 1977;
   (b) proceedings as interpleader to determine ownership of property except in the case of land; and
   (c) proceedings concerning data protection in a consumer context.

Education

1. Legal Help in relation to matters where the primary problem or issue relates to the provision of or failure to provide education or funding for education, including special educational needs. This would include such issues or problems relating to admissions, exclusions or DDA claims.

2. Any proceedings before a court concerning the above issues. This excludes claims for damages falling within the Personal Injury, though claims for damages arising out of a failure to provide adequate education or assessment for education are included.

Community Care

1. Legal Help and related proceedings concerning the provision of services or facilities in the community, in residential or nursing accommodation and/or hospital arranged by a Social Services or Health Care Authority/Agency to the client or a dependant, but excluding any matters falling within the Welfare Benefits or Clinical Negligence Categories and proceedings before the Mental Health Tribunal.

2. For the avoidance of doubt, Proceedings under section 21 of the National Assistance Act 1948 are included, as are cases brought under the Mental Capacity Act 2005 regarding a person's capacity, their best interests (welfare

and/or medical treatment) and deprivation of liberty issues. MCA cases may be undertaken under the Community Care category in circumstances where they may equally also be within the scope of the Mental Health category.

Actions Against the Police, etc.

1. Legal Help and proceedings concerning:
   (a) Assault, trespass, false imprisonment, wrongful arrest, interference with goods, malicious prosecution, personal injury or death in custody, misfeasance in public office or other abuse of authority or neglect of duty against any body or person, public or private, with power to detain, imprison or prosecute, excluding applications to the Mental Health Tribunal or the Immigration Appellate Authorities. Complaints and claims for damages are included whether or not they also fall within the Personal Injury or any other Category. However, claims for damages for clinical negligence are included only if the clinical negligence forms part of a claim which includes another cause of action against a body or person with power to detain or imprison.
   (b) Personal injury based on an allegation of deliberate abuse of any person whilst in the care of a public authority or other institution.
   (c) Applications to the Home Office under section 133 of the Criminal Justice Act 1988 or the ex gratia scheme for compensation for wrongful conviction.
   (d) Claims to the Criminal Injuries Compensation Authority arising out of a matter falling within the category.
   (e) Claims for damages in respect of alleged professional negligence in the conduct of a matter included in the category.

Public Law

1. Legal Help and related proceedings concerning:
   (a) the civil liberties or human rights of the client or a dependant, including under the Human Rights Act 1998, and matters involving the application of the European Convention on Human Rights (and other human rights instruments ratified by the UK) in English law; and
   (b) public law challenges to the acts, omissions or decisions of public bodies, including challenges by way of judicial review or habeas corpus;
   (c) Proceedings under section 222 Local Government Act 1972.

For the avoidance of doubt, this includes data protection and freedom of information issues, and matters which may also fall within the definition of any other category including crime.

Private family law: new conditions for level 2

Note: the material in this appendix has been reproduced from the LSC website (www.legalservices.gov.uk) as at September 2010. Please visit the website to check the material is up to date at the point at which you seek to use it.

The LSC has removed the requirement for a second meeting (2010 Standard Civil Contract Specification para 7.58[1]):

7.58 Criteria for Family Help (Lower) – meaning of 'significant family dispute'

You may only grant Family Help (Lower) where all relevant Funding Code criteria are satisfied, taking into account any guidance from those criteria in Volume 3 of the LSC Manual (or as published on our website). A grant of Family Help (Lower) is likely to be appropriate in 'Collaborative Law Cases. Family Help (Lower) may not be granted for those Family Disputes:

(a) Which require or involve only taking instructions from and advising the Client, whether or not followed up by written or telephone advice, and do not require or involve substantive negotiations with a third party;

(b) Where the Client's primary concern is with processing a divorce, nullity, judicial separation or dissolution of a civil partnership and any associated property or children disputes do not satisfy the criteria for Family Help;

(c) Where the dispute, if unresolved, would be unlikely to lead to family proceedings;

(d) Where the primary issue is advice about a will;

(e) Where the primary issue relates to a change of name;

(f) Where the Client requires only general advice about the dispute and methods of dispute resolution, such as Family Mediation; or

(g) Where the issue relates to child support only.

Extract from the Funding Code

20.18 Cost Benefit[2]

[Para 1 omitted.]

---

1 Available at www.legalservices.gov.uk. See Standard Civil Contract 2010 and related documents: specification – section 7 (family).
2 Available at www.legalservices.gov.uk. See 'Funding Code Decision Making Guidance – Family (section 20) Sept 07.

2. There are four cost/benefit tests applicable to the Family Category of work. Legal Help has a specific cost benefit test – the 'sufficient benefit' test. Family Help has a cost benefit test by reference to a significant family dispute and a reasonable private paying client and, in addition, the various types of case are subject to different cost benefit tests. The four tests are as follows:

Sufficient Benefit Test
3. There must be sufficient benefit to the client, having regard to the circumstances of the matter, including the personal circumstances of the client, to justify work or further work being carried out.

[Para 4 omitted]

Reasonableness – applicable to other Public Law Children Cases
5. An application for Legal Representation may be refused if it appears unreasonable for funding to be granted, having regard to the importance of the case to the client and all other circumstances.

Cost Benefit Criterion – applicable to Domestic Violence Cases
6. Legal Representation will be refused unless the likely costs are proportionate to the likely benefits of the proceedings having regard to the prospects of obtaining the order sought and all other circumstances.

Private Paying Client – applicable to Private Law Children Cases and Financial Provision and other Proceedings
7. Legal Representation and Family Help will be refused, unless the likely benefits to be gained from the proceedings for the client justify the likely costs, such that a reasonable private paying client would be prepared to take or defend the proceedings in all the circumstances.

The LSC's Family Fee Scheme Guidance[3] (para 4.10) indicates that the LSC considers it is likely to be appropriate for Collaborative Law Cases to be funded under level 2.

From discussions with the LSC Family Policy Team, indications are that the LSC will be rigorous in auditing the element of whether there is a 'dispute' and whether the Funding Code requirements have been met. See extract from the LSC's new guidance below:

Para 4.9
It should be noted that these criteria differ from the criteria applied under the 2007 Unified Contract. There is now no longer any requirement for a second meeting to take place in order for the criteria for Level 2 to be satisfied. However, there must be evidence on the file of substantive negotiations with a third party or their legal representative. Substantive negotiation means that there must have been an exchange of correspondence or records of telephone discussions in which proposals and counter-proposals were put forward to resolve the issues. If, for example, no response is received from the other

---

3 *Private Family Law Representation Scheme (PFLRS) Guidance – Nov 2010* provides guidance on the fee scheme from 15 November 2010. It is available at www. legalservices.gov.uk – see 'training for family fees from 2010'.

party to correspondence sent then this does not meet the criteria to move to Level 2. If one initial letter is sent putting forward proposals to which the respondent replies and agrees then this will not fall within the criteria of Level 2 work.

Para 4.11

Providers should also consider whether the cost benefit criteria in the Funding Code is met in conjunction with the criteria in the Specification. For Level 2 the cost benefit test means that the benefits to be gained from the help provided must justify the likely costs, such that a reasonable private paying client would be prepared to proceed in all the circumstances. If, for example, in a divorce matter there were no assets it is unlikely that Level 2 would be justified to prepare a clean break order. In addition, the criteria in section 7.58 of the Family Specification would not be met in that there is no dispute likely to lead to family proceedings.

Scope of the Community Legal Service

Access to Justice Act 1999, Schedule 2

Community Legal Service: excluded services

The services which may not be funded as part of the Community Legal Service are as follows.

1. Services consisting of the provision of help (beyond the provision of general information about the law and the legal system and the availability of legal services) in relation to –
   (a) allegations of negligently caused injury, death or damage to property, apart from allegations relating to clinical negligence,
   (b) conveyancing,
   (c) boundary disputes,
   (d) the making of wills,
   (e) matters of trust law,
   (f) defamation or malicious falsehood,
   (g) matters of company or partnership law, or
   (h) other matters arising out of the carrying on of a business.
2. Advocacy in any proceedings except –
   (1) proceedings in –
       (a) the Supreme Court,
       (c) the Court of Appeal,
       (d) the High Court,
       (e) any county court,
       (f) the Employment Appeal Tribunal,
       (g) the First-tier Tribunal under any provision of the Mental Health Act 1983 or paragraph 5(2) of the Schedule to the Repatriation of Prisoners Act 1984, or the Mental Health Review Tribunal for Wales,
       (gza) the First-tier Tribunal under –
           (i) Schedule 2 to the Immigration Act 1971,
           (ii) section 40A of the British Nationality Act 1981,
           (iii) Part 5 of the Nationality, Immigration and Asylum Act 2002, or
           (iv) regulation 26 of the Immigration (European Economic Area Regulations 2006),
       (ga) the Upper Tribunal arising out of proceedings within paragraph (g) or (gza),

(ha) the Special Immigration Appeals Commission, or

(i)   the Proscribed Organisations Appeal Commission,

(2) proceedings in the Crown Court –

(a) for the variation or discharge of an order under section 5 of the Protection from Harassment Act 1997,

(b) which relate to an order under section 4 or 10 of the Crime and Disorder Act 1998, or

(c) under section 8 of that Act where the order is made by virtue of subsection (1)(c) of that section,

(3) proceedings in a magistrates' court –

(a) under section 43 or 47 of the National Assistance Act 1948, section 22 of the Maintenance Orders Act 1950, section 4 of the Maintenance Orders Act 1958 or section 106 of the Social Security Administration Act 1992,

(b) under Part I of the Maintenance Orders (Reciprocal Enforcement) Act 1972 relating to a maintenance order made by a court of a country outside the United Kingdom,

(c) in relation to an application for leave of the court to remove a child from a person's custody under section 27 or 28 of the Adoption Act 1976 or in which the making of an order under Part II or section 29 or 55 of that Act is opposed by any party to the proceedings,

(d) for or in relation to an order under Part I of the Domestic Proceedings and Magistrates' Courts Act 1978,

(e) under the Children Act 1989, 1989 c. 41.

(f) under section 30 of the Human Fertilisation and Embryology Act 1990,

(g) under section 20 or 27 of the Child Support Act 1991,

(h) under Part IV of the Family Law Act 1996, 1996 c. 27.

(i) for the variation or discharge of an order under section 5 of the Protection from Harassment Act 1997, or

(j) under section 1, 2, 8 or 11 of the Crime and Disorder Act 1998, and

(4) proceedings before any person to whom a case is referred (in whole or in part) in any proceedings within paragraphs (1) to (3).

Lord Chancellor's Direction

Direction

1. This is a direction by the Lord Chancellor under section 6(1) of the Access to Justice Act 1999 concerning the priorities that the Legal Service Commission should set for funding services as part of the Community Legal Service. It is supplemented by guidance under section 23.

2. In drawing up future annual plans and any revisions to the Funding Code, the Commission shall have regard to the following priorities.

3. The Commission should give top priority to the categories in this paragraph, ensuring that all cases within them that meet appropriate merits criteria can be funded:

(a) special Children Act proceedings (as defined in the Funding Code); and

(b) civil proceedings where the client is at real and immediate risk of loss of life or liberty.

4. After that, the Commission should generally give the following categories higher priority than others:

(a) help with social welfare issues that will enable people to avoid or climb out of social exclusion, including help with housing proceedings (as defined in the Funding Code) and advice relating to debt, employment rights, and entitlement to social security benefits;

(b) domestic violence proceedings;

(c) proceedings concerning the welfare of children (including proceedings under Part IV or V of the Children Act not included above, adoption proceedings, and proceedings concerning residence); and

(d) proceedings against public authorities alleging serious wrong-doing, abuse of position or power or significant breach of human rights.

Guidance

1. My direction under section 6(1) sets out the broad categories of case which should be given priority for funding by the Legal Services Commission as part of the Community Legal Service. Under the new scheme, priorities will be given practical effect through the contracts for different categories of work which the Commission awards (which will reflect regional and local needs) and through the criteria in the Funding Code (which have national application). I have already approved the initial version of the Code and the basis on which contract awards have been made for 2000–01. Before approving the Commission's future Annual Plans and any revisions to the Code, I will look to satisfy myself that these priorities are adequately reflected.

2. Paragraph 3 of the direction defines top priority categories. The Commission should ensure that all cases in these categories that apply for funding receive it, subject to passing the criteria laid down in the Funding Code.

(a) Special Children Act proceedings are public law child protection cases for which legal aid is available now without a means or merits test. In other words, funding is available automatically for cases in this category.

(b) Cases about loss of life or liberty, on the other hand, will involve means and merits tests. These tests will need to be met before funding can be granted. In particular, the Commission will need to satisfy itself that the client faces a genuine threat to his life or of being sent to or held in prison or other detention, and that the proceedings are directly concerned with averting that threat. This will be true of most habeas corpus proceedings for example. Depending in particular on the client's country of origin and the other factual circumstances of the case, so will many (but by no means all) asylum cases.

3. Paragraph 4 of the direction contains other categories of case that deserve a high priority. Unlike paragraph 3, this paragraph is not intended to create a firm rule. It is not my intention that all cases in these categories should receive funding before any case in any other category. All categories contain a range of more and less pressing cases. It is equally important to take account of particular factors like the strength and importance of individual cases, as it

is the category in which they fall. A factor which could arise in any category, and to which I expect the Commission to attach particular importance, is whether a case raises issues of wider public interest.

4. Broadly, there are two ways of giving effect in practice to different priorities for different categories of case. The first is by setting more or less rigorous requirements in the Funding Code for these categories. The second turns on the level of resources allocated to contracts for particular categories of case.

5. At present, the latter approach is only relevant at the Legal Help level (and for representation before immigration and mental health tribunals) where contracts control the amount of work that can be done. This is the principal mechanism by which priority will be given to providing help in the social welfare categories of law. In future years, the Commission should allocate at least the same proportion of the total resources available for Legal Help to the social welfare categories as it has done for 2000–01. I have deliberately expressed this priority at national level in very broad terms. Within it, different regions and localities will have different priorities as between, say, housing, employment and debt. The advice of Regional Legal Services Committees and Community Legal Service Partnerships will ensure that these are reflected in local decisions about contracts. These decisions should, of course, reflect the fact that many asylum cases will have top priority because the client's life will be at risk. Local priorities should not be set that have the effect of reducing a region's allocation of resources in the social welfare category as a whole.

6. For cases that require Legal Representation (or other more substantial levels of service), the Funding Code is the principal mechanism for giving effect to priorities. That is why the Code contains separate criteria for housing cases, claims against public authorities, domestic violence and children cases.

Date: 1st February 2000   *Irvine of Lairg*

Civil costs: what you can claim for

A quick reference guide

This is a summary of the LSC's Costs Assessment Guidance, in respect of the most common queries raised by caseworkers. Paragraph numbers are from the Guidance, which can be found in Part E of the Unified Contract, in the LSC Manual, Volume 2.

Admin work

Opening and setting up files, maintaining time costing records and other time spent in complying with the requirements of the Unified Contract are not chargeable (para 2.1). Letters confirming appointments etc with no legal content are administrative (para 2.19).

Advocacy

Normally (and where claimable), this is time on your feet before a court or tribunal; but note that in the Family Advocacy Scheme advocacy also includes travel to court, waiting time and attendance at advocates' meetings. The Costs Assessment Guidance states that where you do your own advocacy, it is reasonable to claim for preparing a brief to yourself (para 2.39).

Agents

They stand in your shoes and their costs are part of your profit costs. You cannot claim their fees as a disbursement.

Attendance

This is the conventional legal costing term for interviewing someone face-to-face, or speaking to them on the telephone. The presumption is that work will be done as quickly as possible, which can seem strange to some people in the not-for-profit sector who have been trained to let the client take their time.

All claims for attendance must be justified in an attendance note. The longer the time claimed, the more detail is expected.

You may be able to justify more than one caseworker being present; but this would be exceptional, for example, in a complex case, where different aspects of it have been split between different people (para 2.36). In a complex case you may be able to justify the time of two caseworkers in the same category of law where you would be able to justify claiming legal research (see Legal research for more details). You may be able to justify the time of two caseworkers in different categories of law if a difficult or unusual point arises and it would be reasonable. Supervision is overhead and is not chargeable (para 2.37).

Bundles

Fee earners should identify the documents for the master bundle and draft the index to the bundle. Making up or copying of additional bundles is not chargeable. Where the bundles are above average size it is reasonable for fee earners to check that copies have been properly collated and reproduced (para 2.17).

Congestion charge

This is claimable where incurred exclusively in relation to the case but not where your journey to work would have meant you incurred the charge anyway (para 3.19).

Consideration of documents

See Perusal.

Disbursements

Must be reasonably incurred and reasonable in amount (para 3.1). Sign language interpreters' costs can be claimed but must be accounted for separately as they are excluded from the statutory charge (para 3.6).

Distant clients

No extra costs can be claimed that arise because you are in a location that is distant from your client, where it would be reasonable for the client to instruct someone closer (para 2.46) (see also Travel time).

Drafting documents

As a guideline, 6–12 minutes' preparation time would be expected per page of a straightforward document, but more complex documents will take longer (para 2.16). It is reasonable to re-examine the core documents to consider their effect on the case. However, the degree to which this will be justified depends entirely on the complexity of the issues (para 2.9).

Emails

See Letters.

Faxes

These are treated as letters; but you cannot claim for sending a copy by post as well as the fax. See Letters for more detail.

Form completion

Generally not claimable; but there are exceptions (paras 2.58–2.63):
- CW1 where the client is eligible;
- CLR in Immigration cases;
- application forms for CLS Funding certificates (30 minutes is standard but may be exceeded where justifiable);
- applications for amendments to certificates;
- POA claims;
- applications to increase financial limitations on certificates;
- Claim 1 and Claim 2 (12–18 minutes);
- Claim 4 (12 minutes).

Completion of forms on behalf of clients is only claimable where legal assistance is justified, eg sections of the Disability Living Allowance form.

Legal research

Not claimable unless on a novel, developing or unusual point of law or the impact of new legislation to the particular case (para 2.5). However, it may still be reasonable for time for checking on the application of established law or procedural rules to individual circumstances to be claimed, provided the reasons are recorded (para 2.6).

Letters in

You cannot claim for reading routine letters received in any Legal Help matters (para 2.23). You can only charge for reading routine letters received in Family proceedings (para 2.23). You can charge for reading non-routine letters received.

Letters out

These are either 'routine' and claimed at the item rate, because they are standard letters or take up to six minutes to write, or they are preparation rate letters, because they take longer to write than six minutes (para 2.18).

You cannot charge for administrative letters, eg confirming an appointment, with no legal content. You cannot charge for multiple letters sent to the same client or party on the same day, unless there is a good reason that justifies it. You cannot charge for a letter correcting your own mistake (para 2.19).

Office overheads

The following are office overheads and not claimable: costs of postage, stationery, faxes, scanning, typing and the actual cost of telephone calls and most photocopying, but see below for exceptional costs (para 2.1). Supervision is an overhead (para 2.37).

Overnight expenses

These can only be claimed in exceptional circumstances, where it would be unreasonable to travel the distance there and back and carry out whatever was required in one day (para 3.17).

Perusal

This is also known as consideration of documents. An initial brief perusal of all the documents to identify which documents are relevant is reasonable. Later detailed consideration of documents may also be reasonable (para 2.8). As a very rough guide it takes approximately two minutes per A4 page to read the most simple document. Time taken will depend on the quality and layout of the document, eg whether handwritten or typed, single- or double-spaced, large or small font, etc. More complex documents may take a longer (para 2.12).

Photocopying

Photocopying in-house is generally an overhead expense, but if there are 'unusual circumstances', or documents are unusually numerous (as a rule of thumb, 500 pages), you may claim the lowest commercial photocopying rate as a disbursement, even when carried out in-house (para 3.37).

Preparation

Includes drafting of documents, consideration of documents and evidence provided by the client or other parties, and general consideration of strategy, evidence needed and evidence to be put forward and whether to make or accept offers to settle a case, and 'thinking time' (para 2.7).

Reviewing files

You are expected to be familiar with your own files, so you would need to justify any claim for reading a file, eg prior to seeing a client when you had not dealt with the file for some time (para 2.39). You cannot charge for reviewing a file when it is reallocated from one caseworker to another, unless this is due to unforeseeable circumstances, eg the client needs to give urgent instructions and the first caseworker is not available (para 2.41).

Telephone calls

These are either 'routine' and claimed at the item rate, because they take up to six minutes, or they are attendance rate calls, because they take longer than six minutes (para 2.26). You can claim for an unsuccessful call; but if you make repeated calls to the same number, you would have to justify it. You can claim a routine call for leaving a message on an answering machine. If you are put 'on hold', after the first six minutes on the call, you can charge the waiting time at the waiting rate (para 2.27). However, bear in mind that it may be more efficient to write a letter.

Texts

These are treated as telephone calls. See Telephone calls for more detail.

Transferring files between fee earners

See Reviewing files.

Travel time

The general rule is that if the round trip travel time is five hours or more, it is usually more reasonable to instruct an agent than to go yourself. However, in some circumstances it may be reasonable to go (para 2.44):

(a) court applications, other than those that are straightforward;

(b) conference with counsel;

(c) interviewing a witness where the fee earner will wish to test the witnesses credibility for him or herself;

(d) because of the specialised nature of the case, the fee earner's close personal understanding of the matter or the nature of the client,

(e) where there is a lack of suitably qualified agents in the area concerned. The reason for making the journey must be recorded on the file.

Travel time to clients

Usually, the client should come to you; but if the client is housebound, in hospital or detention, it may be reasonable for you to travel to the client (para 2.47).

Travelling expenses (caseworkers')

Caseworkers' travelling expenses can be claimed where the journey was necessary and the most appropriate form of transport used (para 3.10). The

LSC considers that public transport should normally be used; but time saved will be considered as well as travel fares or mileage. Taxis may be justified, eg when transporting heavy bundles. Local travelling expenses to court cannot be claimed (eg within a ten-mile radius) unless public transport is known to be poor. Documentary evidence must support claims over £10 (except mileage) (para 3.16).

Travelling expenses (clients')

You can pay clients' expenses to attend court and claim them back from the LSC as a disbursement (documentary evidence is required as for caseworkers). Prior authority can be sought for a clients' travelling expenses to an expert where the client cannot afford them and a report is essential for the proper conduct of proceedings (para 3.23).

Waiting

You should not normally arrive at court more than 30 minutes before a hearing. If you have to, perhaps due to transport timetables, you should record the reason on file (para 2.53). You cannot claim waiting time during the lunchtime adjournment.

Waiting on the telephone

If you are out 'on hold', after the first six minutes on the call, you can charge the waiting time at the waiting rate (para 2.27).

Criminal costs: what you can claim for

A quick reference guide

This is a summary of the LSC's Costs Assessment Guidance, in respect of the most common queries raised by caseworkers. Paragraph numbers are from the Criminal Bills Assessment Manual, January 2008 edition:

Admin work

Opening and setting up files, maintaining time costing records and other time spent in complying with the requirements of the Unified Contract are not chargeable (para 2.4). Letters confirming appointments etc with no legal content are administrative (para 2.9).

Advocacy

Normally (and where claimable), this is time on your feet before a court, including time while the bench (or jury) has retired (para 2.12).

Agents

They stand in your shoes and their costs are part of your profit costs. You cannot claim their fees as a disbursement.

Attendance

All claims for attendance must be justified in an attendance note. The longer the time claimed, the more detail is expected.

You may be able to justify more than one caseworker being present; but this would be exceptional, for example, in a complex case, where different aspects of it have been split between different people (para 2.10).

Congestion charge

This is claimable where incurred exclusively in relation to the case but not where your journey to work would have meant you incurred the charge anyway (para 4.20).

Consideration of documents

See Perusal.

Disbursements

Must be reasonably incurred and reasonable in amount (para 4.1). See section 4 CBAM for disbursements generally.

Distant clients

No extra costs can be claimed that arise because you are in a location that is distant from your client, where it would be reasonable for the client to instruct someone closer (para 2.46) (see also Travel time).

Drafting documents

As a guideline, 6–12 minutes' preparation time would be expected per page of a straightforward document, but more complex documents will take longer (para 2.8). It is reasonable to re-examine the core documents to consider their effect on the case. However, the degree to which this will be justified depends entirely on the complexity of the issues.

Emails

See Letters.

Faxes

These are treated as letters; but you cannot claim for sending a copy by post as well as the fax. See Letters for more detail.

Legal research

Not claimable unless on a novel, developing or unusual point of law or the impact of new legislation to the particular case (para 2.5). However, it may still be reasonable for time for checking on the application of established law or procedural rules to individual circumstances to be claimed, provided the reasons are recorded (para 2.8).

Letters in

You cannot claim for reading routine letters received (para 2.9). You can charge for non-routine items at the preparation rate.

Letters out

These are either 'routine' and claimed at the item rate, because they are standard letters or take up to six minutes to write, or they are preparation rate letters, because they take longer to write than six minutes (para 2.9).

You cannot charge for administrative letters, eg confirming an appointment, with no legal content. You cannot charge for multiple letters sent on the same day, unless there is a good reason that justifies it. You cannot charge for a letter correcting your own mistake (para 2.4 and 2.9).

Office overheads

The following are office overheads and not claimable: costs of postage, stationery, faxes, scanning, typing and the actual cost of telephone calls and most photocopying, but see below for exceptional costs (para 2.4). Supervision is an overhead.

Overnight expenses

These can only be claimed in exceptional circumstances, where it would be unreasonable to travel the distance there and back and carry out whatever was required in one day (para 4.13).

Perusal

This is also known as consideration of documents. An initial brief perusal of all the documents to identify which documents are relevant is reasonable. Later detailed consideration of documents may also be reasonable (para 2.8). As a very rough guide it takes approximately two minutes per A4 page to read the most simple document. Time taken will depend on the quality and layout of the document eg whether handwritten or typed, single- or double-spaced, large or small font etc. More complex documents may take a longer.

Photocopying
Photocopying in-house is generally an overhead expense but if there 'unusual circumstances' or documents are unusually numerous (as a rule of thumb 500 pages), you may claim the lowest commercial photocopying rate as a disbursement, even when carried out in-house (para 4.12).

Preparation
Includes drafting of documents, consideration of documents and evidence provided by the client or other parties, and general consideration of strategy, evidence needed and evidence to be put forward and whether to make or accept offers to settle a case, and 'thinking time' (para 2.8).

Reviewing files
You are expected to be familiar with your own files, so you would need to justify any claim for reading a file, eg prior to seeing a client when you had not dealt with the file for some time (para 2.8).

Telephone calls
These are either 'routine' and claimed at the item rate, because they take up to six minutes, or they are attendance rate calls, because they take longer than six minutes (para 2.9). You cannot claim for an unsuccessful call, ie where it is not answered and no message is left. You can claim a routine call for leaving a message on an answering machine.

Texts
These are treated as telephone calls. See Telephone calls for more detail.

Transferring files between fee earners
See Reviewing files.

Travel time
The general rule is that if the round trip travel time is more than two hours, it would not be reasonable and you should instruct a local agent or the client should instruct someone more local to them. In exceptional circumstances, this may be extended to four hours, it is usually more reasonable to instruct an agent than to go yourself. The reason for making the journey must be recorded on the file (para 2.15).

Travel time to clients
Usually, the client should come to you; but if the client is housebound, in hospital or detention, it may be reasonable for you to travel to the client (para 2.15).

Travelling expenses (caseworkers)
Caseworkers' travelling expenses can be claimed where the journey was necessary and the most appropriate form of transport used (para 4.13). The LSC considers that public transport should normally be used; but time saved will

be considered as well as travel fares or mileage. Taxis may be justified, eg for an out-of-hours attendance at a police station. Documentary evidence must support claims over £10 (except mileage) (para 3.16).

Travelling expenses (clients)

You can pay clients' expenses to attend court and claim them back from the LSC as a disbursement (documentary evidence is required as for caseworkers). Prior authority can be sought for a clients' travelling expenses to an expert where the client cannot afford them and a report is essential for the proper conduct of proceedings (para 4.6).

Waiting

If at court, you cannot claim waiting time during the lunchtime adjournment (para 2.16).

Standard monthly payment reconciliation process July 2008

[This material has been reproduced from the LSC's website as published there in July 2008. Please go to LSC's website at www.legalservices.gov.uk to check that the material is up to date at the point at which you seek to use it.]

1. Introduction

The Deed of Settlement between the Legal Services Commission (LSC), the Ministry of Justice and The Law Society in April 2008 included a new Protocol for the reconciliation of Standard Monthly Payments (SMP), which was designed to keep SMP changes to a minimum.

The Standard Monthly Payment reconciliation process ('the Process') implements the Protocol set out in the Deed of Settlement. This document provides guidance on how the Process will apply.

2. Who is this document aimed at?

This document is aimed at both LSC Account Managers, and suppliers holding either a Unified Contract (civil), or a Unified Contract (crime). However, this Process is not aimed at Not for Profit suppliers who are already subject to other reconciliation arrangements.

We hope that the introduction of this revised Process will not adversely affect suppliers and we will continue to closely monitor any impacts during the implementation.

The process will commence from July 2008, although the first reviews will take place in September 2008 when the value of July claims are known. Until then the current process will apply.

3. Background information

As part of the negotiations with The Law Society we agreed to revise our approach to the reconciliation of accounts to produce a process that would work better for both suppliers and the LSC. Some of the factors driving the change were:

- The knowledge that the previous reconciliation process, while successful in focusing attention on reconciliation, caused difficulties particularly when forecasting claims meant SMPs were set too high (or low) at the beginning of the contract year, which then required a drastic change later on in the year to balance the position by the year end;

- It was resource intensive for both suppliers and the LSC, with activity heavily reliant on achieving an almost 100% percentage target (of claims versus payments) at the Contract Year end; and

- Reconciliation became over important in meetings and discussions with suppliers, to the detriment of other issues such as how the service was being delivered to clients and quality outcomes.

4. Aim of the Process

The aim of the new Process is to reconcile accounts (claims versus payments) to 100%, but where an account is within the 90–110% band, known throughout this document as the 'In Band Target', then no action will be taken to either increase or reduce the SMP.

This means we will no longer forecast future claims and payments with a view to achieving 100% reconciliation by the end of the contract year. Instead the Process depends on the actual claims a supplier has made over the previous months. From September 2008, Account Managers will review all accounts using the new Process. There will be one of two outcomes from this review, either:

1 The account is **within the In Band Target** and therefore no action will be taken by the Account Manager; or

2 The account is **outside the In Band Target** and therefore reconciliation will take place in accordance with the Process set out in Section 5.

Many of our suppliers will see little or no change to the way their accounts are managed. Our early review indicated that around 60% of our accounts operate within the In Band Target without any intervention to SMP levels. We will make no amendment to SMP levels for such suppliers and we are happy for the accounts to continue to operate in that way.

We will produce monthly reports of all accounts that are outside the In Band Target. Where an account is outside the In Band Target then the Account Manager will take steps to bring the account back within the In Band Target and may contact the supplier to discuss the position.

Should the SMP require amending then the Account Manager will give at least 1 month's written notice of the change to the SMP level. This will mean, for example, that any review undertaken in September will affect the SMP from November. The table below demonstrates the timetable.

July	August	September	October	November
Cases closed				
	Claims submitted – up to 20th			
		Review commences See timetable below*		
			New SMPs loaded into SMS from around 2nd	
				New payment level takes effect

* Majority of submissions processed by around the 5th of each month.
Account Manager review takes place between 10th–20th of each month.
Letters to suppliers to give 1 month's notice of amended to SMP by around 22nd.

5. Reviewing accounts under the Process

Where the Account Manager identifies an account, which is outside the In Band Target, reconciliation will take place in accordance with the Process below. References below to a '10% band' refers to the In Band Target of 90–110%:[1]

a) Consider the balance of claims to payments to date and define the value of the cumulative variance (ie the level of any current underpayment or overpayment).
This restates the current process of reviewing the balance on an account as a starting point to see if we may need to take some action.

b) Where the balance of claims to payments is outside the 10% band the value of the variance to 100% will be brought forward into the monthly SMP amount to be paid over the next 6 months.
See Example One below.

c) Where the balance is within the 10% band then payments will remain at the current level.
We will not be intervening to make changes to any account that is within the In Band Target (ie 90–110%).

---

1   Note that in December 2008, the LSC amended this process so that suppliers that had been underpaid would have their payments increased when claims exceeded payments by 5%.

d) Where LSC amends payments, the SMP for the following 6 months will be a combination of the average claim value of the proceeding 6 months and the variance.

See Example One below.

e) LSC will set a maximum band of plus/minus 50% (calculated on the same basis as the 10% band above) that can be reconciled by changes to SMP alone. If at any time the balance is outside the 50% band then this will trigger an exception review. In these circumstances the variance will be paid or recouped over the following 3 months by ad hoc payments or debits and the SMP reset to the average claim of the preceding 6 months.

We expect this will happen fairly infrequently but wanted to include this as a potential scenario and so that it was clear how we would approach such instances. See Example Three below.

f) In the same way, if following a review, a legal aid provider's account remains outside the 10% range for a period of 3 consecutive months, despite resetting payments under b) above, the variance will be paid or recouped over the following 3 months by ad hoc payments or debits.

We anticipate that the new process set out in b) above will produce the desired result without the need for further intervention but recognise that there will be some occasions where claims are more volatile. See Example Two below.

6. Examples

Example 1:

Account reports, as latest balance is 88%. Cash equivalent is £12,000.
Current SMP = £9,000.
Current 6 month claim rate = £7,500.
The new SMP will therefore be current 6 month claim rate – (balance owed/6).
This would be: £7,500 – (£12,000/6) = £5,500.

We anticipate that a change like this would produce a positive impact on the reconciliation performance within 3 months (ie the level of overpayment will reduce). Where this has not happened however then the Account Manager should undertake a further review to re-set the payments in such a way so that the account is balanced within a further 3 months. Here's an example:

Example 2:

Contract reports as latest balance is 112%. Cash equivalent is £12,000.
Current SMP = £9,000.
Current 6 month claim rate = £11,000.
The new SMP will therefore be current 6 month claim rate + (balance owed/6).
This would be: £11,000 + (£12,000/6) = £13,000.
On the third month of the new SMP the account is reviewed as it is still out of band. The position is:
Contract position 112%. Cash equivalent is £15,000.
The cash balance would therefore be paid to the firm in 3 ad hoc payments over the next 3 months.

The important point in both examples is that there is no projection forward: we are simply looking at the balance on the account at a particular date, and the claim rate over the 6 months to that point if a change is required.

There may be situations where an account is reported as being significantly out of the In Band Target, by this we mean by more than 50%. An example would be a small Crime account that has minimal claims but occasionally submits a large CDS 7 claim. It might look something like this:

Example 3:
Contract reports as latest balance is 155%. Cash equivalent is £6,600.
Current SMP = £0.
Current 6 month claim rate = £75.
The balance here would be cleared by 3 equal ad hoc payments over the next 3 months. Again there is no projection forward: we are simply looking at the balance on the contract at that date and seeking to settle that balance.

7. **Exceptions to the process**
The overarching aim of the Process is to leave a SMP alone while an account is within the In Band Target. This means, for example, that an individual account could be operating at 91% or 109% on a regular basis and we will not approach the supplier to seek an adjustment of the SMP.

While we have tried to keep the Process simple we recognise that it is not possible to produce a Process that works in every case. Inevitably there will be some circumstances where the revised Process will not work and we have highlighted some exceptions to the Process in the scenarios below.

• **New Account** (by which we mean a new Office Schedule has been issued to a supplier or a dormant Office Schedule begins to make claims): We will pay the amount billed by the supplier as an ad hoc payment for months 1–3 and then set an SMP in place for month 4–6. The aim when setting the SMP is that the supplier reaches month 6 with a variance of claims to payments of no more than 10%. At the end of month 6, we use the standard reconciliation process (ie to reconcile an account to 100%) to set a new SMP from month 7, at which point the account will be subject to the full Process.

• **Mergers/acquisitions (Crime only)**: where a merger or acquisition includes the movement of a number of Duty Solicitors, then a supplier can apply to their Account Manager to be removed from this Process. This would allow an increase to the SMP commensurate to the increase in the number of Duty Solicitors, subject to a minimum increase of 20% in the number of Duty Solicitors. Such increase would however only take effect from the date the new Duty Solicitor rota becomes effective and removal from the Process would be for a maximum of 6 months only. The calculation would be by reference to the firm's claim rate over the 6 months prior to receipt of the application, not the SMP at the time of receipt.

• **Novations**: Where contracts are novated and there is no change in the level of service to be delivered, then the new SMP shall be calculated as the sum of the claim rates of the accounts prior to the novation for the 6 months immediately prior to the date of novation.

- **Contract Compliance Audits:** Where any adjustments are made following a CCA and the contract subsequently moves outside of the In Band Target, we would use the standard reconciliation process (ie to reconcile an account to 100%) to bring the account back within the In Band Target going forward.

- **Low-value contracts:** There are around 400 contracts that currently claim less than £2,500 per year and the management of such accounts can take a disproportionate amount of time. We propose, with the agreement of those suppliers, to remove their SMP but instead make ad hoc payments at the 6 monthly reviews.

- **Balance discrepancies:** There may be some accounts where there is a considerable difference between the claims recorded into SMS and those notified to the Account Manager. This might be, for example, where there had been a large number of rejected lines of data. If a supplier indicates that a reduction to their SMP in such circumstances is not sustainable, then the Regional Contract Manager may agree to remove the firm from the Process for a maximum of 3 months. This would however be subject to:

  a) The supplier providing evidence of the discrepancy. So, for example SMS shows claims for October as £4,000 but the supplier can provide a copy of their submission for a much larger amount; and

  b) The agreement of an action plan that would include a full review of claims over the contingency period and a commitment from the supplier that they will work with us to identify and re-submit any missing claims within that 3 month period.

  Once all missing claims had been re-submitted, or at the end of the 3 month period, then the account should be added back into the Process and any remaining variance outside the In Band Target is recovered or paid in accordance with the standard reconciliation process (ie to reconcile an account to 100%).

- **Nil claims:** Suppliers should be submitting claims on a monthly basis. For the avoidance of doubt, a nil claim will still count towards our calculations of an account balance and claim average. If an account does fall outside of the In Band Target as a result of a nil submission then the standard reconciliation process (ie to reconcile to 100%) will be used to bring the account back into line.

NB

- **Exceptional cases/Police Station VAT amendments:** We do not consider that any adjustments that may arise as a result of exceptional cases would be sufficiently large to take a firm out of the In Band Target. Where this does occur however, we would use the standard reconciliation process (ie to reconcile an account to 100%) to adjust the position.

Index

[handwritten top margin: "— Litigants in PERSON — ARE charities like the law centre given legal aid? — No fees at all for them — Legal aid is government charity. As long as there is this — WE CAN TRAIN THE MINDS."]

[handwritten annotations throughout right margin: "Stifle competition, bid competition", "is good", "good for the mind, for the victories against the statehood.", "John seeks out clients who may have a chance at a case for or for ready cash person for the application procedure.", "CROWN COURT. VHCC COURT WORK. PROVIDE IMMIGRATION ADVICE. SELF SUPPORT?", "How do firms make money — since BVT did not quality control. — Only no with my fee does — but the catch is that people need money. Secondly no win no fee is something that the gov can't say.", "PRISON LITIGANT IN PERSON."]

[handwritten annotations next to "Representation Order": "fucked, and prisoners — unless they learn the law too."]

[handwritten annotation next to "Referral fees": "families tho, could still be"]

[handwritten bottom: "new cancel out asylum seekers, babies of troubled families and prisoners from — free legal rights, and you cancel out the people who are paid to help them: - to pay for the grown number of They are cutting the requirement baby people, prisoners and immigrants — if it falls into destitution — then there are prisons for that."]